Our Man in Rome

Our Man in Rome

Henry VIII and his
Italian Ambassador

CATHERINE FLETCHER

THE BODLEY HEAD
LONDON

Published by The Bodley Head 2012

2 4 6 8 10 9 7 5 3 1

First published in Great Britain in 2012 by
The Bodley Head
Random House, 20 Vauxhall Bridge Road,
London SW1V 2SA

www.bodleyhead.co.uk
www.vintage-books.co.uk

Addresses for companies within The Random House Group Limited can be found at:
www.randomhouse.co.uk/offices.htm

The Random House Group Limited Reg. No. 954009

A CIP catalogue record for this book
is available from the British Library

ISBN 9781847921765

The Random House Group Limited supports The Forest Stewardship Council (FSC®), the
leading international forest certification organisation. Our books carrying the FSC label are
printed on FSC® certified paper. FSC is the only forest certification scheme endorsed by
the leading environmental organisations, including Greenpeace. Our paper procurement
policy can be found at www.randomhouse.co.uk/environment

Typeset in Dante MT by Palimpsest Book Production Limited,
Falkirk, Stirlingshire
Printed and bound in Great Britain by
Clays Ltd, St Ives PLC

Contents

For Mark

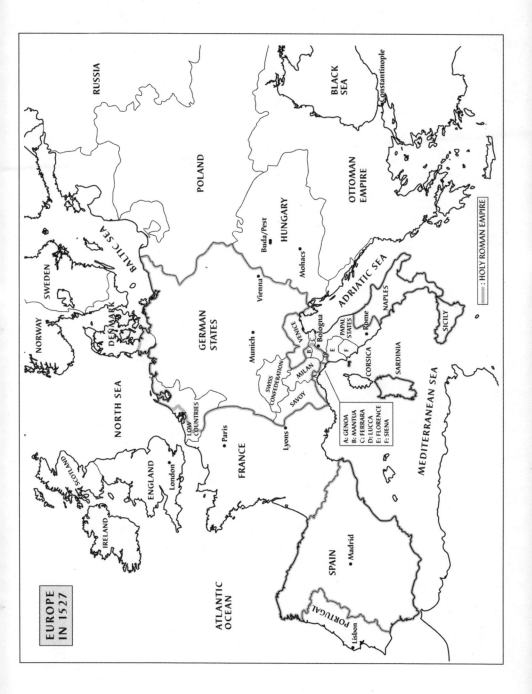

EUROPE IN 1527

Illustrations

Map and family tree

1. Map of Europe in 1527 © 2011 John Bloxam for Upstream Ltd.
2. The Casali family tree.

Illustration section

1. *The Sack of Rome*, unknown Netherlandish artist (*c.* 1527) © Wellcome Library, London.
2. *Henry VIII*, Lucas Horenbout (*c.* 1526–27). The Royal Collection © 2011 Her Majesty Queen Elizabeth II.
3. *Catherine of Aragon*, attr. Lucas Horenbout (*c.* 1525) © National Portrait Gallery, London.
4. *Pope Clement VII*, workshop of Sebastiano del Piombo (*c.* 1531/32) © Kunsthistorisches Museum, Vienna.
5. *Portrait of Ferry Carondelet with his Secretaries*, Sebastiano del Piombo (*c.* 1510-12) © Museo Thyssen-Bornemisza, Madrid.
6. *Anne Boleyn*, unknown artist (late sixteenth century) © National Portrait Gallery, London.
7. The Rocca Pallavicino-Casali, Monticelli d'Ongina. Photo © author.
8. *Charles V with his English Water-hound*, Jakob Seisenegger (1532) © Kunsthistorisches Museum, Vienna.
9. *The Mystical Marriage of St Catherine*, Filippino Lippi (1501), Chiesa di San Domenico, Bologna © 2011: Photo Scala Florence/Luciano Romano/Fondo Edifici di Culto – Min. dell'Interno.
10. *The Procession of Pope Clement VII and the Emperor Charles V after the Coronation at Bologna*, Nicolaus Hogenberg (*c.* 1532) © The British Library Board; shelfmark 144.g.3 (1.).

The Casali family

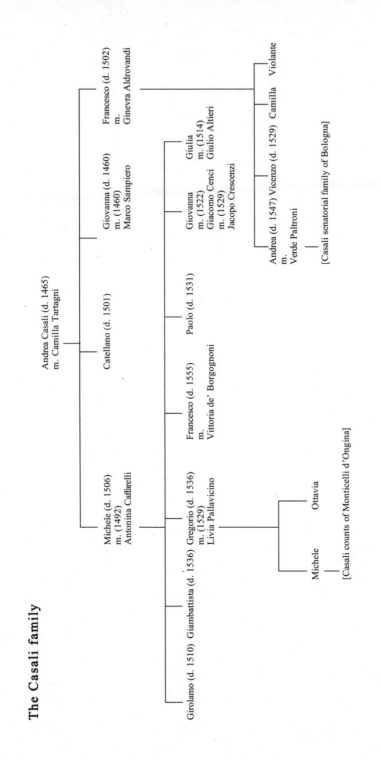

Andrea Casali (d. 1465)
m. Camilla Tartagni

Girolamo (d. 1510) Giambattista (d. 1536) Michele (d. 1506) Catellano (d. 1501) Giovanna (d. 1460) Francesco (d. 1502)
m. (1492) m. (1460) m.
Antonina Caffarelli Marco Sampiero Ginevra Aldrovandi

Gregorio (d. 1536) Francesco (d. 1555) Paolo (d. 1531)
m. (1529) m.
Livia Pallavicino Vittoria de' Borgognoni

Giovanna Giulia
m. (1522) m. (1514)
Giacomo Cenci Giulio Altieri
m. (1529)
Jacopo Crescenzi

Andrea (d. 1547) Vicenzo (d. 1529) Camilla Violante
m.
Verde Paltroni

[Casali senatorial family of Bologna]

Michele Ottavia

[Casali counts of Monticelli d'Ongina]

Preface

The divorce of Henry VIII from Catherine of Aragon is one of those great events of history. You probably know the story. Henry and Catherine have no sons, and Henry comes to believe that this is God's punishment for marrying his brother's widow. Henry falls in love with Anne Boleyn. He decides to have his marriage annulled, but the Pope refuses. Henry declares himself head of the Church of England, breaks with Rome and marries Anne. In fifty words or so, that is the famous tale.

On the other hand, you have probably never heard of Gregorio Casali. Which is strange, because for the six years it took Henry to divorce Catherine, he was our man in Rome, the resident diplomat looking after the king's 'great matter' at the papal court. He was one of the few, in fact, who saw the affair through from start to finish, although before the end of his short life Casali would have reason to curse the 'ingratitude of princes'. For his loyalty to Henry, he said, he had paid a high price.

Casali enjoys a brief mention in Shakespeare and Fletcher's *Henry VIII*, misspelt as 'Gregory de Cassado', though it is surely him. And the fleeting notoriety of a reference in Shakespeare, albeit in a minor work, is not something many Italian noblemen of the period merit. Beyond that, he rarely escapes the footnotes. How is it that someone so close to something so great can be so nearly lost to history?

When I first came across Casali and his role in English diplomacy, I was working for the BBC in Westminster. When I had time on my hands, I used to watch people doing politics. Not, usually, in the House of Commons, but in coffee bars, on the street or waiting to go into the TV studios. My colleagues and I got to know who drank in which bar, and we speculated why. After I'd been around a few years, people occasionally told me stories that they hoped I'd pass on. Everyone knew that the important business rarely happened in official meetings. For some, it happened in the mythical corridors of power, for others in the mystical smoke-filled rooms.

And so, when I read those occasional references to Casali in the standard works of Tudor history, I wondered what he had done from day to day. How did he, and the people around him, do their politics, their diplomacy? Where did they do it, and when? What were the rules of the game? One particular thing intrigued me. Casali was an Italian. How could an Italian be ambassador to the King of England? If, for much of what happened in the world of diplomacy five hundred years ago, I could find at least a superficial parallel in the present, I could not find one for that.

Not quite ten years ago, I decided to try and track down Gregorio Casali, his life and work. Internet searches turned up an attorney-at-law in Massachusetts. I tried libraries: surely, the man who had spent six years of his life handling Henry VIII's divorce from Catherine of Aragon would be the subject, if not of a book, then at least of an article or two. But no. As I said, it is strange that someone apparently so pivotal could be so lost from history.

The obvious explanation for that loss would be that Casali's story isn't worth the telling. But a little bit of investigation convinced me that wasn't true. Gregorio Casali was a man who navigated what the great Renaissance thinker Erasmus called the 'turbulent waves of diplomacy', amid tumultuous times for Europe.[1] His story brings great events of history to life. It is, however, as much an Italian story as an English one. Through Casali's eyes we see England from the outside: from Rome, from Italy, from Europe. There, Henry VIII is not the caricature fat tyrant, nor yet the virtuous Renaissance prince, but a mid-ranking northern monarch, a player on the European stage but far from the star of the show. Reading Casali's letters, we learn much about how the diplomacy of Henry's divorce worked from day to day, and about how to make a fortune (or try to) by throwing your lot in with a foreign power. His tale tells us about family values, and all sorts of things about living in sixteenth-century Europe: how to get from A to B, how to make a present, how to bribe a cardinal, when to go out in disguise, and why it was a good idea to have a secretary who knew the local courtesans. We learn about kidnapping, spying, deciphering coded letters, and other dirty tricks. And about the importance of being magnificent. Our man in Rome was good at that.

Gregorio Casali was born around the year 1500 in Rome – a Rome ruled by the infamous Pope Alexander VI, Rodrigo Borgia. The Borgia papacy would become a byword for corruption, murder and tyranny: everything that, for reformers, was wrong with the Church. And our man in Rome was a child of war. Renaissance Italy might have been home to Leonardo and Michelangelo, but it was a land of terror and conflict too. In 1494, Charles VIII, King of France, had marched his armies into Italy, and the Italian peninsula had become the setting for a European war that would last for decades, between the great rival powers France and the Holy Roman Empire. England allied with one or other of them – usually, but not always, the Empire. The French were long-time enemies. It was hard for the English to make a direct impact in distant Italy, but they could provide a northern distraction for troops that would otherwise be engaged in Italian conflicts, or supply much-needed cash to their allies' coffers.

In 1503, Pope Alexander VI died. His successor Pius III, the compromise candidate, ruled for a bare four weeks, to be followed by Pope Julius II of the Italian della Rovere family. Aptly known as the warrior pope, Julius took up arms to secure the papacy's territorial possessions in central Italy, the swathe of land known as the Papal States, stretching north from Rome, past Perugia and over to Ravenna on the Adriatic coast. In 1506, he and his army marched on Bologna and expelled its ruling clan, the Bentivoglio, re-establishing papal dominion over the city. But as pope after pope conducted himself more like secular prince than Vicar of Christ, and as each papal military campaign demanded more resources from the Christians of Europe, calls for religious reform grew. To subsidise their enterprises, the popes sold 'indulgences', discounting time in Purgatory in return for donations to the Church. One notable case of indulgence-peddling in Germany, during the reign of Pope Leo X de' Medici, prompted particular outrage. In 1517, in protest at such abuse of believers, a young Augustinian monk, Martin Luther, nailed his ninety-five theses to the Wittenberg church door. With an eye to their own wealth, and with few qualms about curtailing Church influence, some German princes were prepared to tolerate Luther and his ideas, though when peasants and townspeople tied the new religion to demands for social reform, their revolts were soon suppressed. These new ideas were known in England too. Many of Henry VIII's counsellors had studied in Europe, but the suggestion that their king, within a few years, might join the Lutheran princes and break with Rome would have been preposterous then. After all, in 1521 Henry had written a book *against* Luther. His defence of the seven sacraments had been presented to the Pope, and in return the king had received the title 'Defender of the Faith', maintained by English monarchs to this day.

As Gregorio Casali made his way into the English diplomatic service in the 1520s, France, ruled by King Francis I, was still at war with the Holy Roman Empire – a conglomerate of the German lands, Austria and, by a quirk of inheritance, Spain too – ruled by the Habsburg dynasty in the person of Charles V (Plate 8). In 1525, Charles's troops had captured Francis at the Battle of Pavia, and Francis had freed himself only by handing over his sons as hostages. But if Charles was heading for victory on the western front, he had problems in the east. The Empire was also at war with the Turks, whose sultan Suleiman the Magnificent had established himself as one of Europe's military giants, conquering Hungary, Rhodes and swathes of north Africa. For opponents of Habsburg power, Suleiman was undoubtedly a useful ally, despite papal injunctions that the Christian princes should stick together.

So, a Protestant challenge in the north; the Catholic princes at war; the French princes imprisoned; the Ottoman Turks under Suleiman, pushing ever further west: this was the world of our man in Rome.

To write Casali's story has been a long and intriguing piece of historical detective work. From the usual sources in London, I began with the story of the divorce. (Technically, Henry was not seeking a divorce but a declaration that his marriage was invalid; however, his contemporaries used the word and I see no reason to avoid it.)[2] But although the London letters – those written by Casali and his colleagues to Henry VIII, Wolsey and others at court – gave me scraps of detail about his life, much was still missing. Next, I went to Bologna, Casali's home town. His family palazzo is long demolished, courtesy of a nineteenth-century road-widening scheme, but in the archives I found detail of his business dealings, and those of his family, and in old chronicles of the city passing references that linked him to important political figures in Rome. I saw his family chapel and his memorial in the Church of San Domenico. One chilly December day I took a trip to the small northern town of Parma, to see if I could find any news of his wife, and found a little. My big stroke of luck, though, came a few stops up the railway line in Piacenza. I had gone there on my way to see the Rocca Pallavicino-Casali, a castle once owned by Gregorio's descendants, in the village of Monticelli d'Ongina near the River Po. I dropped in to the State Archive to ask whether they had any documents relating to Casali. It was a long shot. Nothing was listed in the archive guide. But, the archivist told me, the Casali family still lived in Piacenza. In fact, they had their own private archive: boxes of papers documenting births, marriages and deaths dating back more than five hundred years.

Next stop was Rome and the Vatican. More details, more pieces in the jigsaw. Especially marvellous were the records of Cardinal Accolti's trial for abuse of power, where I found Casali's secretary giving evidence of his master's attempts at bribery. The cardinal's letters (in Florence) were remarkable too. Meanwhile, a researcher at Columbia University had discovered an entirely new set of Casali letters – intercepted by Imperial spies and filed in Vienna. The dispatches of the Mantuan diplomats in Rome added glorious colour to the story of Henry's divorce. And more details kept turning up: Casali's brother appears as a character in a sixteenth-century Venetian best-seller; portrait medals of his uncle survive in the British Museum and the V&A. I began to piece together the details of a short but intensely complex life and a family network that stretched from Constantinople in the east to London in the north. There are still gaps: no portrait of Casali survives, for example, although his code name, Capo Pelato – the bald man – strongly hints at a distinguishing feature.[3]

The historians who come across Gregorio Casali have, usually, taken his letters and scavenged from them the facts of Henry's divorce. He has become a faceless source of dates and detail. But Casali – the real Casali – did not exist for the convenience of Tudor history students. He had his own interests. Sometimes he had an axe to grind. He certainly liked to make a good impression. At Henry's court, and at courts throughout Europe and beyond, appearances counted for a lot. Whenever Gregorio wrote to England, he did so with that in mind. So, can we rely on him? Did he sometimes bend the truth in order to tell people what they wanted to hear? He was prepared to lie and deceive for Henry; did he ever lie to his masters? How far did he flatter, embellish and spin? In Graham Greene's novel *Our Man in Havana*, the hero Wormold, a vacuum-cleaner salesman in need of money, finds an opportunity to pay his daughter's finishing-school fees by taking the job of British agent in Cuba, then faking a series of espionage reports. Was Casali doing the same: stringing the English along for the sake of his daughter's dowry? Some people thought so. Gregorio's fellow agent Richard Croke accused the Casali family of sabotage. Was he right?

We shall see. This, then, is the story of our man in Rome: a man who was not himself great, but who knew the great men of history. And a man who found himself, quite unexpectedly, at the heart of a king's 'great matter'.

I

The King in Love and the Pope Besieged

On Friday 17 May 1527, a secret trial began in Westminster. Cardinal Thomas Wolsey, Henry VIII's chief minister, prince of the Holy Roman Church and papal legate *a latere*, presided over the hearings. At stake was the validity of Henry's marriage to Queen Catherine of Aragon. After eighteen years together, they had only one surviving child, a daughter, Mary. Was the lack of a son God's verdict on a union against divine law? Henry had convinced himself it was so. Might a different queen succeed in producing an heir for England where Catherine had not? Perhaps, and besides, Henry was in love with another woman: Anne Boleyn.[1]

News travelled slowly in sixteenth-century Europe. Even in good circumstances, the journey from Rome to London took an experienced courier two weeks. As Wolsey's proceedings opened, none of the participants knew that for almost a fortnight Pope Clement VII, most of his cardinals and several hundred others – among them Gregorio Casali – had been besieged in the Castel Sant'Angelo in Rome.

Not yet thirty, Casali had been in the English royal service for the past eight years, as messenger, as soldier and now as Henry VIII's ambassador to the Holy See. The son of a Bolognese merchant and a Roman noblewoman, he had done well for himself. Family connections in the curia and a guardian in the College of Cardinals had helped. But with Spanish troops and German *landsknechts* now running amok through Rome, his enjoyment of a lavish ambassadorial lifestyle was temporarily in abeyance.

The Sack had begun on 6 May, when mutinous troops of Charles V,

Holy Roman Emperor, stormed the fog-bound streets. Their pay months in arrears, they went in search of loot. Pope Clement fled from his sumptuous apartments at the Vatican to his fortress at the Castel Sant'Angelo on the banks of the Tiber. The city outside was pillaged, palace after palace ransacked. Its citizens were kidnapped, tortured and murdered. A contemporary painting shows, in the foreground, some of the horrors (Plate 1). Thousands, probably, died, and many more fled. Even nuns and priests were not immune from attack. The tomb of Pope Julius II was opened and his corpse despoiled. Churches were plundered and relics destroyed in a fashion that horrified contemporary observers. The Sack, said more than one, was God's vengeance on a corrupt and failing priesthood.[2] The hundreds inside the castle tried as best they could to defend themselves. They had supplies of ammunition and food to last perhaps a month.

Since 1494, the Italian peninsula had been the theatre for a series of European wars waged between the two great powers of the period, France and the Holy Roman Empire. Italy was divided into a series of small states that vied for great-power backing. The Pope ruled his own Papal States like any other prince. The Marquis of Mantua presided over his principality and the dukes of Urbino and Ferrara theirs; Genoa would soon rebel against French control and become a republic once again, like that other great maritime power, Venice, which ruled much of the Adriatic. In the turmoil that followed the Sack, the city of Florence had broken with the Pope, expelled the Medici family, and declared itself a republic. But Pope Clement – Giulio de' Medici – hoped to restore his exiled clan to the pre-eminence it had once enjoyed in that city. As the Venetian ambassador Gasparo Contarini wrote, Clement had an 'infinite desire' for Florence.[3] That desire coloured his actions. At the time of the Sack, ranged against Charles V were Francis I, King of France, Pope Clement VII, the republics of Venice and Florence, and Francesco II Sforza, Duke of Milan. England had not yet formally taken sides, but Henry and his chief minister Cardinal Thomas Wolsey, the man responsible for England's diplomacy, would in practice defend the papacy.

Castel Sant'Angelo, the fortified mausoleum of the ancient

emperor Hadrian to which Clement and his court had retreated, was surrounded by bastions from which the snipers of the papal garrison took aim at Imperial targets. On its top floors were elegant living quarters, built to afford the popes a modicum of comfort on such occasions; high up on the loggia, the Pope's men were well placed to defend the bridge over the Tiber below. From the top of the castle, where the statue of the warrior archangel Michael now stands, there was a commanding view of the city, although the besieged men of the curia might have reflected that they commanded very little indeed. All they could do was wait, fire back, and hope for relief from the armies of France and its allies in the League of Cognac. The siege was not impossibly tight: some messages went in and out of the castle, though at considerable risk to their bearers. Pietro Cavallucchio, a man we will meet again in this story, made it out, sent by the Pope to Deruta, a hundred miles north, where the League's army was camped. He bore the message that Clement would rather risk his life than come to an arrangement with Charles V's commanders.[4]

Three weeks into the siege, by the beginning of June, it was clear that Rome would not be relieved. The countryside around Deruta had been exhausted the previous summer.[5] Hunger, lack of supplies and bad weather took their toll; the League's army began its retreat. In the city now, food was scarce. Hostages were threatened with death if they did not pay extortionate ransoms. There was more looting; the plague began to spread. Fearing attack, few ventured out to their farms and vineyards, or to feed livestock, storing trouble for the months ahead. Imperial commanders, many of them Italian noblemen serving Charles V in the hope of reward, struggled to control their troops, who threatened mutiny if they were not paid. This was the troubled backdrop to Henry's design for divorce.

It is sometimes hard to pin down the truth of events in the story of Gregorio Casali, but hardest of all in these days of the Sack – days surrounded by myth and imaginings. If we like, we can picture him on the castle ramparts, sniping at the Spanish: he was a military man, that would be plausible. We might imagine him offering urgent counsel to Clement on his next move, or in a quieter moment swapping louche tales with his friend Benedetto Accolti, who had just acquired a cardinal's hat with fulsome promises of cash. It was a far cry from the convivial world of ceremonial entries, dinner parties, minor spying and exchange of gossip that Casali had joined in 1525, when, hoping for a step up the social ladder, he had become Henry VIII's man in Rome.

A handful of details about Casali's activities in these days are more certain. We know that he had already pawned his family silver and jewels to help the French embassy raise funds for Rome's defence. Hoping to make a thousand crowns, he and Nicolas Raince, the French embassy secretary, had managed just six hundred. Ambassadors needed deep pockets, for they often subsidised their masters' adventures for months, if not years. And these were hard times for the Casali. In April, Spanish troops had burnt their country villa, causing damage, so Gregorio's brother Giambattista said, to the tune of sixteen thousand ducats, five times Gregorio's annual stipend from the English.[6] Fortunately for Gregorio, his mother's family, the Caffarelli, rich Roman nobles traditionally allied to the Holy Roman Empire, would endure the Sack better than most.

We hear, too, from an Imperial report that Casali was one of four deputies appointed by the Pope to represent those besieged in the castle: he acted for his fellow patricians; his colleague Alberto Pio da Carpi (an Italian diplomat in the French service) for the ambassadors; Gianmatteo Giberti, Bishop of Verona, represented the prelates; and Giuliano Leno the merchants and artisans.[7] Whether they were chosen by Clement or pressed on him by others in the castle is unclear. But whatever the mechanism, the choice of Casali points both to his good standing among his fellow Romans and also to the influence he wielded as English ambassador. For a diplomat was never simply himself. He personified his prince. When Casali negotiated, he negotiated as a Roman, but he commanded too a certain royal authority. Indeed, his very decision to stay in the siege made a statement about Henry's support for Clement. (It must have been his decision: there was no time for him to receive instructions.) He might well have gone elsewhere. The ambassadors of Venice and Urbino had taken refuge with Isabella d'Este Gonzaga, Marchioness of Mantua, whose son Ferrante commanded

Imperial forces and whose favour the Casali family enjoyed. But Gregorio was smart enough to realise that putting himself at the heart of the papal defence would earn him gratitude from Cardinal Wolsey, and win Henry favour with the Pope.

Almost as soon as the siege began, the diplomacy got under way. The talks centred on money – money badly needed to pay the Imperial mercenaries rioting through Rome. At first, the Imperialists demanded three hundred thousand ducats as the price for ending the siege. Clement made a counter offer, then demurred. News of the Sack had still not reached England. The secret trial of Henry's marriage continued: on 20 May, on the 23rd and the 31st. On 1 June, the news arrived, and proceedings came to an abrupt stop. 'If the Pope's Holiness fortune either to be slain or taken, as God forbid,' wrote Wolsey to Henry the following day, 'it shall not a little hinder Your Grace's affairs.'[8] He was right. Queen Catherine of Aragon could appeal to the Pope against any sentence on the validity of her marriage. She was the aunt of the Holy Roman Emperor, whose troops held Clement prisoner, and Renaissance blood was viscous indeed.

The marriage of Henry VIII and Catherine of Aragon (Plates 2 and 3) was a political one, which is not to say their relationship was less than cordial. It was rare for the princes and princesses of early modern Europe to wed for love. Marriages were the cement for political alliances, a tool of the trade in diplomatic negotiations. This particular match had consolidated Anglo-Spanish ties against a mutual enemy, France. Catherine had been married to Henry's elder brother Arthur, Prince of Wales, in 1501, but Arthur had died less than six months later, and in 1503 she was betrothed to Henry. Marriage to a brother's widow required a dispensation from the Pope, and this was duly obtained, although in the event the pair wed only after Henry's accession to the throne, on 11 June 1509. But if royal marriages were made for political reasons, they were also, sometimes, unmade. Henry's sister Margaret Tudor, Dowager Queen of Scotland, had had her second marriage (to the Earl of Angus) annulled by Clement in March 1527, just weeks before our story begins. Louis XII of France had had his marriage annulled too, in 1498, when, for political reasons, he wanted to make a dynastic alliance with his brother's widow, Anne of Brittany. His legal argument had been quite dubious, but Pope Alexander VI had been on his side, and that was enough. It was not hard to find a technical inadequacy in the betrothal paperwork on which to base an annulment, particularly when everyone involved agreed that the discovery of such an inadequacy was highly desirable. In Henry's case, however, there would be no such easy agreement.

Religious notions of marriage as inviolable, therefore, rarely entered the manoeuvring of Henry's diplomats. It was all about realpolitik. At the papal court, diplomacy was not, very often, a religious matter. The Pope was a curious sort of prince, who on the one hand played a game very similar to his secular counterparts but on the other enjoyed a special status as the Vicar of Christ on Earth. Religious notions would be more important in Catherine of Aragon's opposition to the divorce, though as important was her honour as a queen and the possibility that she might be reduced from that status and her daughter bastardised in favour of the upstart Anne Boleyn and her offspring. Anne as Henry's mistress would be one thing: royal mistresses were an accepted feature of court life. Indeed, Henry had once offered her just that role, only later realising that she might also solve the problem of a legitimate male heir for England. Anne as queen was another matter altogether.[9]

It was a month before Clement and the Imperialists agreed an accord. The deal showed the weakness of Clement's position: the ransom demand had increased from three to four hundred thousand ducats. On 7 June 1527, the siege came to an end and Imperial troops took possession of Castel Sant'Angelo, with Pope and cardinals still inside. As the papal garrison left the castle with colours flying, Gregorio Casali was among its leaders. Even in defeat, they put on a good show. They were escorted out of Rome and headed north towards Perugia. Never one to miss an opportunity for testimony to his merits, Casali brought with him a fistful of thank-you letters to Wolsey extolling his good services: from Clement himself, from cardinals Farnese, Pucci, Gaddi, Campeggio and Benedetto Accolti.[10] The impact of the Sack on contemporary politics was dramatic, and Casali's month in the Castel Sant'Angelo had done him much credit.

In the next two weeks, Gregorio Casali travelled to Florence, Bologna, Ferrara and beyond. Our man in Rome had responsibilities covering most of the Italian peninsula. As an eyewitness to the horrors of the Sack, he would have been able to testify to the chaos in Rome. In Florence he rallied the city against the emperor. In Bologna, his father's home town and the second city of the Papal States, he drew on family connections to raise troops. Gregorio's kin were – as we shall discover – central to the conduct of his diplomacy. In Ferrara he had talks with Duke Alfonso d'Este, once again with the aim of bolstering papal territory. On the evening of 22 June, he arrived in Venice, where he stayed with his brother Giambattista at San Giorgio Maggiore, a Dominican monastery with fine cloisters and a beautiful setting on its own small island next to the long strip of land known as Giudecca, across the water from St Mark's Square. Not long after Gregorio's own promotion to ambassador to Rome in 1525, he had contrived to have the English appoint Giambattista, previously a member of the papal household, ambassador to Venice. On his arrival he addressed the Venetian College in a meeting which the suspicious Imperial ambassador Alonso Sanchez recorded as having lasted over three hours.[11]

In England, the secret divorce trial was secret no more. By 22 June, Queen Catherine knew of her husband's scheme and immediately dispatched a servant to Spain to inform the emperor. For the next six years she would fight her corner, resisting repeated attempts to persuade her to back down, give up, or enter a nunnery. But as yet, Gregorio Casali knew nothing of this. His priority was the war and – immediately – keeping the Venetians sweet. Venice was a vital ally for the papacy against the Holy Roman Empire, not least because, thanks to its merchants, rich from their trade with the East, the city was a valuable source of finance. On papal initiative, the Casali brothers lobbied the Venetians to take on the Marquis of Mantua, Federico II Gonzaga, as their captain-general. Gregorio's diplomatic career often crossed national boundaries. His main loyalty was to England but the Gonzaga rulers of Mantua were useful patrons on the side. So, too, was Clement VII. It was a matter of good sense for a man with family interests to advance to keep his options open. There was always the risk that he might

fall out of favour with one or other capricious prince. When
Gregorio left Venice, in early July, he was given a present of silver
cutlery and silk cloth. Worth two hundred gold crowns, it would
have been a useful supplement to his income.[12] As he travelled
through the north of Italy, there would have been no time for him
to receive new instructions from England, but – like any ambassador in such circumstances – he stuck to England's existing policy
and existing alliances, and got on with the task of reinforcing the
Papal States. His boundless energy for shuttling to and fro across
often hostile territory was one of his great strengths as a diplomat.

On 3 July 1527, Cardinal Wolsey set out for France with extensive
powers to negotiate with King Francis I. He had commissions to
extend England's peace treaty with France, to discuss a French
marriage for Henry's daughter Princess Mary, to conclude a league
for the defence of Italy, and much more besides. Gregorio headed
north to meet him. En route, at Lyons, he held discussions with
the French commander Odet de Foix, Sieur de Lautrec. He reached
Paris on the 23rd, and from there went on to join Wolsey at Amiens.
Wolsey, the second most powerful man in England, was, as a
cardinal, a prince of the Church in his own right. Now in his mid-
fifties, he had charge of Henry's diplomatic service, which he had
considerably professionalised in recent years. Casali, almost thirty
years his junior, cut an impressive figure in Wolsey's diplomatic
corps. One of a small cluster of Italian diplomats in the English
service, he owed his plum job in Rome to the cardinal's patronage,
and it was Wolsey to whom he answered. The king and queen, in
contrast, were for the most part distant figures, and whether Casali
had met Anne Boleyn at all is an open question. During his first
extended stay in England, in 1518–19, she had been at the court of
Queen Claude of France. She had returned to England by the
time of his second long visit, in 1523–4, but whether either Anne
or Gregorio thought the other worthy of their notice is impossible
to say.

His meeting with the cardinal was profitable for Casali. On 29
July, Wolsey wrote to Henry declaring his plan to make Gregorio
commissary of the League's infantry to be sent to Italy. Casali, he
said, was 'animate' with the French king, suggesting that his lively

presence suited the relatively informal environment of Francis'
court; he would offer 'good counsel' to Lautrec and the other
commanders. Besides, 'his being there,' wrote Wolsey, 'shall not a
little confer to other [of] Your Grace's businesses'. Those other
businesses were, no doubt, the divorce. To Gregorio's new role as
commissary of troops were added further diplomatic responsibilities, including talks with the Marquis of Mantua and the Duke of
Ferrara about their entry into the League alongside England,
France, Venice, Milan and the papacy. His commission to Ferrara,
giving him considerable latitude to negotiate on the king's behalf,
would win him that reference in Shakespeare. For good measure,
he acquired French diplomatic credentials too.[13] Casali did like to
collect patrons.

If, to the modern reader, his mixture of military and diplomatic
duties seems a little unusual, it was by no means so in the sixteenth
century. Diplomats were often posted to the front line in order to
provide reliable detail of how a war was progressing. Their reports
were all the more important in complex campaigns like this one,
conducted by means of unstable alliances of princes and city states,
each employing mercenary captains to lead bands of fighting men.
Wolsey's esteem for Casali is evident in the jealousy his appointments prompted in the long-standing English soldier-diplomat
Robert Jerningham, who complained that Gregorio had not waited
for his arrival before paying out fifty-two thousand ducats of the
king's money sent from England. When his diplomatic commission
expired, Jerningham added to his laments that he was now 'the
worse regarded, and accounted not only as [Gregorio's] inferior,
but also as at his commandment under him, rather than as his
fellow to be reputed'.[14] For every courtier who climbed the social
ladder, another slid down. Resentful rivals were a permanent threat.

Yet even as Gregorio Casali was enjoying Wolsey's patronage,
the cardinal had troubles of his own. As he continued discussions
with the French in Amiens, in England Henry was busily working
on a revised strategy for the divorce – without his minister's help.
In the feverish world of court politics, long absence was never
advisable, as Wolsey discovered now. While the cardinal was
meeting King Francis, Henry had effectively sidelined him. The

king planned instead to dispatch to Rome his secretary, William Knight, to obtain the necessary commissions. Knight had a law degree from Ferrara and extensive experience in diplomacy; he had visited Rome before, and was a sensible choice. Yet there was more to it. Knight was to keep the details of his mission secret from Wolsey and from the Italian agents who worked with the cardinal. Henry's letter to Wolsey is telling. 'We have no man resident there [in Rome] to advertise us of the affairs there,' he wrote. This was not simply a reference to Casali's absence from the papal court as he travelled round the Italian peninsula. Henry did not want to trust the Italian agents with such a sensitive matter as his intention to marry Anne Boleyn. In contrast, the king had 'had long proof' of Knight's 'truth and sincerity'. That Casali was a fully accredited ambassador (his credentials had been signed by the king) and was recognised as such at the papal court was of no account.[15]

Alert to the potentially disastrous consequences for his power at court, on hearing of Knight's mission Wolsey intervened with his own plans for securing the documentation. He argued that rather than Knight, an Englishman, it would be preferable to send Italians to Rome, men who were familiar with the papal court. Superficially this was perfectly true. Someone like Gregorio Casali could, and would, pretend to act for another of his multiple patrons, and could play a double game far more easily than any English diplomat – although it was a skill that would come to count against him. For all Knight's Italian education, he could not match that. But Wolsey had another agenda too: to substitute Knight with agents closely tied to himself, and thus reclaim the management of the divorce.

So, on 11 August, Wolsey wrote to Henry promoting the use of his Italian diplomats. Gregorio, along with Girolamo Ghinucci and Giovanni Salviati, would be asked to make approaches to the Pope. Ghinucci, Bishop of Worcester and like Casali an Italian diplomat in English service, was making a brief trip to Rome with letters from the emperor, to whom he was currently posted. Salviati was a papal diplomat known to be friendly to the English. A few weeks later, on 5 September, even as Knight was preparing to depart for Italy, Wolsey wrote again. He conceded tactfully that Knight was 'a wise, trusty, faithful subject, and counsellor, to whom more faith is to be given than to any stranger [foreigner]', but given the circumstances of the Pope's detention it was surely more likely that Ghinucci would be able to gain access to Clement. Wolsey would also send Casali, who 'shall experiment all practices and means possible to come to the Pope's presence' and the papal nuncio Uberto Gambara, recently returned from England. At this stage, though, Casali's involvement in Henry's divorce was limited. It is highly likely that Wolsey confided in him what was going on: when questioned, Casali knew enough to tell the French that Knight's mission was concerned with 'spiritual matters',[16] but for the most part he focused on his usual role in military liaison, leaving Amiens at the end of August to return to the camp of the French commander Lautrec in northern Italy.

In September 1527, notwithstanding Wolsey's advice, William Knight set out to Rome. It was not an auspicious time to travel. The post road to Italy was always difficult and dangerous, but the war made it all the more so. The king's secretary and an experienced diplomat, Knight had been entrusted with the task of broaching Henry's 'great matter', as it was known, with the Pope. He took with him two draft bulls for Clement's agreement. The first would allow Henry to take a second wife while still married to Catherine: a proposal that was rapidly dropped. (This was not quite as extraordinary a suggestion as one might imagine: bigamy has solid Old Testament credentials. Erasmus thought it preferable to divorce, and within less than a decade Martin Luther was implicated in controversy over his support, albeit reluctant, for the secret bigamous marriage of the German prince Philip of Hesse.) The second provided for a dispensation that would, in the event of Henry's marriage to Catherine being declared invalid, allow the king to marry a woman with whom he had contracted 'affinity'. Just as Henry had had to get papal permission to marry Catherine, his brother's widow, so he would need a similar dispensation to marry Anne Boleyn, sister of his former mistress Mary. When, on 10 September, Knight arrived at Compiègne, about fifty miles north of Paris, Wolsey took his chance to intervene in the mission, directing Knight to stay put in Venice until such time as Casali and

Gambara could determine whether there was any possibility of his seeing Clement.[17]

Playing 'fixer' for English special envoys was a central part of Casali's activity as the principal English resident agent in Rome. Organising accommodation, making introductions, advising what to do (and what not to do) in the city was his bread-and-butter work. As Knight (who on Henry's orders had ignored Wolsey's injunction to wait in Venice) arrived in northern Italy, Gregorio turned to his family network, sending letters of introduction for the king's secretary both to his own relations and to his brother's close friend Ercole Gonzaga, Cardinal of Mantua. But he could not work miracles, and when Knight arrived in the Umbrian town of Foligno early in November, he found no way of gaining access to the Pope. Indeed, he was bluntly informed by the papal master of posts that if he went to Rome without a safe-conduct, he would be in 'jeopardy of life and goods'. Given the lawlessness prevailing in Rome, this was a pretty accurate assessment, and Knight would have done well to wait for the safe-conduct he had been promised. But when it did not materialise, he determined to press on without one. New instructions expressing Henry's 'fervent desire and pleasure' in the matter were clear enough to persuade him that delay would be unwelcome. Those Knight met thought his decision to travel to Rome most ill-advised, and marvelled at his lack of a safe-conduct. Knight, in turn, believed he was being spied on by a friar from Calabria, one of the companions with whom he travelled the final sixty miles to Rome from Narni. He made a narrow escape with his guide at Monterotundo, just outside Rome, where the locals were threatening to rob and kill them.[18] Travel was never safe, but the destruction wrought on the Italian countryside by pillaging armies had fomented desperation.

While Knight continued his journey through October and November of 1527, Gregorio made his way first to Florence, where the rebellious citizens hoped for English backing in their opposition to the Medici faction, and thence to the League's camp at Parma, where he arrived on 11 November. In his horseback shuttle diplomacy, he rode between the commanders there, the Duke of Ferrara and the Marquis of Mantua, and represented England in the negotiations to bring the two of them into the League. The Ferrara deal, negotiated by a team including Casali and the Venetian diplomat Gasparo Contarini, demonstrates the complexity of Italian politics in these years. To win over the duke, the allies had to offer him not only territory but also a French bride for one of his sons and the promise of a cardinal's hat for another. He kept them waiting more than two weeks before agreeing to their proposal.[19] And these are the sort of terms in which Italian contemporaries would have thought about Henry VIII's divorce. It was a matter for diplomatic horse-trading, open to negotiation. King, queen, Pope and emperor could surely cut a deal.

Knight's mission to Rome was as much a disaster as Wolsey had hinted it might be: the cardinal would have been entitled to say 'I told you so'. When he eventually made it to the city, Knight rapidly discovered that even the most generous bribery would not secure him a papal audience. He had to keep his presence secret, for although he stayed with a Roman, a number of Spaniards were lodged in the same house. His negotiations with Clement, such as they were, were conducted by means of messages passed to and fro by the chamberlain of a Venetian cardinal. When his presence in the city came to the attention of the Imperial commander, Knight was advised by the Pope to leave town, but assured that the documents he required would be forwarded to him shortly.[20] It was an empty promise.

In the north, in Parma, where the League's commanders had their base, Gregorio encountered his cousin Andrea Casali, ambassador for the ruling council of Bologna, like Gregorio in town to negotiate for his masters' interests.[21] Diplomacy was fast becoming the Casali family business, and everyone got his cut. Gregorio had his post in Rome, and his elder brother Giambattista was in Venice. Their younger brothers Paolo and Francesco were, respectively, on a trading trip to Constantinople and in the Venetian military service. Their cousins Andrea and Vicenzo were in Bologna. Andrea had his cousin's English connection to thank for his promotion to the Quaranta – the Forty – Bologna's city authority. Back in 1522, while still a junior agent responsible for little more than finding Henry the best Italian horses, hawks and hounds, Gregorio had lobbied

Henry and Wolsey, who in turn had lobbied the Pope on Andrea's behalf. Soon enough, Andrea Casali too would be drawn into the quest for Henry's divorce. It was part of Gregorio's attraction as a diplomat that when the English employed him, they gained not the services of one man alone, but a family firm half a dozen strong.

By December 1527, the continuing imprisonment of the Pope was proving too great an embarrassment for the Holy Roman Empire, and Clement was allowed to escape. On 7 December, he fled to Orvieto, about eighty miles north of Rome. There, he and his cardinals dug in. For the next six months this tiny hilltop town would be the seat of the papal court in exile. One by one, the ambassadors of the European princes returned, to find the Pope impoverished but not broken, determined to maintain his authority and restore his power. For Henry VIII, Clement's predicament might work both ways. Anger at Charles V, and gratitude for English succour, might convince him to act in Henry's favour. On the other hand, fear of Charles and his army would play into Catherine's hands. This, then, was the state of the king's great matter as Gregorio Casali took up the diplomacy of the divorce.

Even as he did so, he was accused of indiscretion. The jealous Robert Jerningham wrote on 21 December to Wolsey that not only did the French commander Lautrec know all about Henry's plans, but that he had had the news from Cardinal Cibo. Only one person could have leaked it to Cibo: Casali, who was often in his company (no surprise, for the cardinal was papal legate to Casali's home town of Bologna). Three days later, Jerningham had more tales to tell. He wrote again to Wolsey that 'the secretness and importance of the King's affairs, and your Grace's', committed to Knight and Casali, 'have not been so covertly and privily kept, but that unto some it is very well known'. Jerningham's letter is more likely the product of resentment at his colleague's growing influence than an indicator of serious misconduct on Casali's part. In the world of diplomacy, information was currency and in order to receive, one had to divulge. Niccolò Machiavelli, who had been a diplomatic agent himself, had explained that the ambassador should solicit reports from his home city for just this purpose: 'because men who

see that they can get something are eager to tell what they know'.
Such trading was a delicate business: there was always the risk that
one would lose out in the exchange. But Cibo was a relative of the
Pope and an influential figure, and might have been expected to
give Casali a good return on his gossip. Moreover, Jerningham also
conceded that Casali was not to blame for the leak of the news to
the emperor. Charles had had it from a servant of the queen who
had made it out of England to Spain. It was a manoeuvre that, in
a startling piece of incompetence, no one in England had managed
to prevent.[22] Jerningham might have been unhappy at Casali's rise,
but even he could not blame his colleague for failures back at
Henry's court in England.

2

How to Bribe a Cardinal (Part One)

Even before the outcome of Knight's mission was clear, Wolsey was anticipating failure. In a letter of 5 December 1527, he placed the affair of Henry's divorce firmly in Gregorio's charge. Settled in Orvieto, Casali was endeavouring to ensure he presented a suitably majestic impression as representative of the King of England. Piled on top of a volcanic outcrop, rising 325 metres above sea level, this medieval town was surrounded by huge fortified walls and crowned by a spectacular cathedral clad in black and white marble. Its famous frescoes of the Last Judgement – wraith-like figures rising from their tombs, portents of a vengeful God – might have given pause for thought to the hundreds fleeing post-Sack Rome. The only way into the city was a steep path winding up near-vertical cliffs, and mules were the only means of transport. Despite some forward planning, Orvieto was barely prepared for the arrival of the papal curia. Goods of all sorts were scarce, and prices soared. Without connections a bed was hard to come by, and Casali's skills as fixer were sorely tested. Even the Pope's circumstances were severely reduced. His palace was 'decayed', its chambers 'naked and unhanged' and its personnel 'riff raff'. The furniture of his bedchamber was not worth twenty nobles, bed and all. So observed Casali's colleagues. (Twenty nobles was about half Casali's weekly stipend: a poor show for the once-magnificent Medici.) Quite apart from the run-down surroundings, there were more pressing difficulties for ambassadors. It was hard to get messages in and out of the town. The diplomatic corps were forced to share each other's couriers, which increased the likelihood of tampering with dispatches.[1] There were professional code-crackers in Venice who, for a fee, would break the rather inadequate ciphers commonly used in diplomatic correspondence.

Presiding over this dilapidated excuse for a court was Pope Clement VII (Plate 4). He had been born in Florence in 1478 and christened Giulio. His mother's first name was Fioretta, but her surname, possibly Gorini, is uncertain, a telling indicator of her low social status. Today, the site of Pope Clement's humble birth is marked by a plaque in the incongruous setting of a popular gym, the Palestra Ricciardi. He owed his standing in Florentine society to his father, Giuliano de' Medici, brother of the city's *primus inter pares* and effective ruler, Lorenzo the Magnificent. Giuliano was assassinated shortly after his son's birth, and the child was brought up by his uncle Lorenzo. In 1513, Giulio's cousin Giovanni de' Medici became Pope Leo X, and when the family decided that Giulio should be made an archbishop, his parents' secret marriage was conveniently discovered and his birth declared legitimate in the sort of canon-law manoeuvring of which Henry VIII might well have dreamt. Shortly afterwards Giulio was made a cardinal. Pope Leo was shameless about, and notorious for, appointing to the papal curia a cluster of Medici loyalists. On his appointment he elevated not only his cousin, but a nephew, Innocenzo Cibo, son of Leo's sister Maddelena, and two long-time Florentine allies: Lorenzo Pucci and Bernardo Dovizi da Bibbiena. His brother-in-law, Jacopo Salviati, became an important figure at the curia. In 1517, Leo packed the College of Cardinals with a staggering thirty-one new appointments. (Since the end of the Great Schism in the previous century and the re-establishment of a single papacy in Rome, the record for a single creation had been twelve.) He thus assured himself of a compliant consistory, men who owed him for their appointments, and who would respect his papal authority. Among the new faces were four further relatives (Jacopo's son Giovanni Salviati, Franciotto Orsini, Luigi de' Rossi and Niccolò Ridolfi) and two more Florentines: Niccolò Pandolfini and Ferdinando Ponzetti. Those who wanted to point the finger at papal nepotism would have to use both hands.[2]

That said, these were times in which the line between acceptable family advancement and provocative nepotism was almost invisibly fine. When Wolsey wrote to Casali, with his first detailed instructions concerning Henry's divorce, he left his ambassador in no doubt that success would bring him not only honour and praise, but also substantial reward for his entire family: a recognition that he was engaging the whole Casali consortium. The cardinal had evidently convinced Henry that Casali would be a useful asset to the campaign for the divorce, and wrote to Gregorio that 'the King's Majesty has the fullest confidence in your faith, industry, dexterity and prudence'. (This was Wolsey's specification for a reliable diplomat: two and a half years earlier, he had praised Giambattista Casali's 'diligence, industry, dexterity and prudence'.)[3]

Thus began Gregorio's formal role in Henry VIII's great matter. Wolsey did not yet know of Clement's liberation and, assuming that the Pope remained imprisoned, he ordered Casali to go to him in disguise, concealing the true nature of his mission. He should raise the spectre that England might descend into civil war should there be no male heir to inherit Henry's throne, and he should emphasise Henry's support for the papacy in these difficult times. If Clement were now free, Casali should point to the inadvisability of trusting the emperor's promises. There was much more besides.

Wolsey played on the fact that Casali occasionally acted for other princes besides the English (as with his French accreditation to Ferrara). He was instructed to change his appearance and 'as if you were someone else's agent, or as if you had a commission from the Duke of Ferrara to settle some controversy between him and the Pope, or in some other more secure way – gain access to the Pope's presence and to an interview far away from any witnesses'. Ambassadors often cultivated national styles in their dress, and accessories like the heavy gold chains known as collars of Esses often included symbols of allegiance such as the Tudor rose or portcullis. To feign service to the Duke of Ferrara, Casali would have to abandon such symbols and adopt some favoured local style instead. In theory, the ability to pull off such subterfuges should have been an advantage of keeping Italian agents in Italy. But success could be elusive. When, in early 1526, England had been preparing to switch sides in the Franco-Imperial war, Gregorio had been spotted by an Imperial ambassador as he stole, disguised, into the French ambassador's residence for secret night-time negotiations.[4]

Some time in late December 1527, Casali and William Knight were finally admitted to the Pope's presence. By now they had received Wolsey's new instructions. Their meeting with Clement was decidedly unsatisfactory, however, for in a typical diplomatic gambit, the Pope played for time. Charles V, Holy Roman Emperor and nephew to Catherine of Aragon, had the upper hand on the Italian peninsula, and Clement had no desire to antagonise him. So his strategy was simple: to delay. The war was not yet over, and in a few months the situation may have changed. In the meantime, Henry's adventure could wait. By day, Casali discussed the war with Clement, and at night – to avoid arousing Spanish suspicions – he and Knight crept in to press their case for divorce. They played their best military cards. Clement hoped the French army would advance from the north to support him, but the English ambassadors refused to put pressure on the French, pretending that Casali could not leave Orvieto to meet Lautrec until Clement agreed to grant the commission Henry desired. Henry's alliance with – and supposed sway over – the French was a card played repeatedly in the course of the negotiations. The king, however, had a tendency to exaggerate his influence with King Francis.[5]

Of the gaggle of Florentine advisers who surrounded Clement, the most significant for Henry's divorce was Cardinal Lorenzo Pucci. He regularly joined in the ambassadors' meetings with Clement, and winning him over would clearly be important. That meant money: a reward here, a backhander there. Just as with nepotism, at the sixteenth-century curia there was no clear distinction between legitimate reward for services rendered and corruption. (This was not something unique to Rome: in the other courts of early-modern Europe too, gift-giving eased all manner of transactions.) It was thought perfectly reasonable for a prince to offer lucrative benefices to a cardinal or other churchman who helped him pursue some matter of national interest. Periodic attempts were made to clean up the system, but no serious reform, in these years at least, could be made to stick.[6]

When one bribed a cardinal (so to speak, for the word 'bribe' was only just acquiring its modern definition), etiquette imposed a number of rules. Gifts should be accompanied by words of friendship, and by protestations that this was merely a matter of princely liberality. Gregorio, wrote Wolsey, should first solicit Pucci's 'friendship and favour'. If the response was positive, then and only then should he proceed to the next step. The delicate phrasing, the intricate play of offer and counter-offer, was all but impenetrable to outsiders. Hence the importance of men like Casali, brought up in elite social circles and familiar from childhood with the workings of the system. Late in December, having established Cardinal Pucci's sympathetic demeanour (or so they thought), Casali and Knight proceeded to offer him two thousand gold crowns.[7]

The actual worth of such a sum at that time is difficult to establish. Inflation was a mighty problem: so much so that in 1529, the Bolognese authorities coined a special 'shortage lira' to compensate. But some comparisons are possible. Continental crowns, ducats and scudi were worth between four and five English shillings, depending on the exchange rate (thus there were four or five crowns to the pound; ducats were usually valued a little more highly). The stipend Casali received from England for his diplomatic work equated to a little over three thousand crowns a year. Girolamo Ghinucci had an income of more than four thousand crowns (before tax) from his bishopric of Worcester, in addition to his ambassadorial stipend. In 1521, cardinals' annual incomes ranged from two thousand to fifty thousand gold ducats; Henry VIII's own annual day-to-day expenditure was at the top end of that spectrum. Sir Francis Bryan, a prominent courtier and diplomat, had an income in 1527 of £400, or about 1,750 crowns. But within a few months of travel through war-torn Italy, one English courier ran up expenses of nine hundred gold pieces in fees and bribes, and at that rate, even the ten thousand ducats dispatched to Casali to cover diplomatic expenses would not last long.[8]

The English believed, to start with, that Pucci would take their money, but it soon became clear that their bribery was not working. Pucci might have played up his friendliness, but he also played along with Clement's strategy of delay, making so many cuts to the commission demanded by Henry as to render it virtually worthless. Furthermore, the dispensation allowing Henry to marry Anne was made conditional on his marriage to Catherine being declared void.

That was the trouble with liberality: it might hint politely that something was expected in return, but there were no guarantees. *Caveat emptor* was the rule: the buyer beware. Gifts were not wages; Casali and Knight might proffer a reward, but they could not demand a service in return.

When Knight finally obtained the commission, it crucially did not exclude the possibility of an appeal by Catherine to Rome. His embassy therefore was deemed a failure. On New Year's Day, he left to make his way to England, and Casali headed north to meet the French commander Lautrec in Bologna. Delayed by rain and fearing flooding, Knight had a miserable winter journey home.[9]

News of the Pope's escape from Castel Sant'Angelo had now reached England. On 27 December, Wolsey dispatched further instructions to the ambassadors. Commissions were no longer enough. Now, it was proposed, a cardinal-legate, endowed with delegated papal power, might be sent from Rome to try the case. What prompted Wolsey's sudden desire for a legate is not clear. Perhaps it was pressure from Catherine of Aragon's supporters, perhaps a wish to avoid any suggestion that Wolsey, acting alone or with another English judge, might be accused of bias and the decision overturned. The king's divorce had to be legally unassailable. The favoured option as legate was Cardinal Lorenzo Campeggio, with Cardinal Alessandro Farnese as second choice. Henry and Wolsey knew Campeggio well. From July 1518 to August 1519 he had been papal legate in England, so winning over the monarch and his minister that they presented him with the imposing English Palace (now the Palazzo Giraud-Torlonia) near the Vatican in Rome. In 1524 he became cardinal-protector of England, the man responsible for English affairs in the College of Cardinals. And Casali also knew him. As a young man, he had accompanied the cardinal on that voyage to England as a member of his entourage, and Campeggio had later lobbied the English on his behalf. Gregorio had likewise impressed the English – so much so that at the conclusion of their stay, Henry had given him a knighthood, two hundred gold crowns a year for life and a heavy gold collar of Esses worth over £100. Gold chains were typical gifts to departing envoys, but the knighthood and the pension were far from standard issue. The king's signed bill cited the 'manifold virtues and commendable merits of our dear and well-beloved Sir Gregory de Casalis, being born of the nobles of Rome'. If 'born of the nobles' was a slight exaggeration – it was true only on his mother's side – it could be forgiven. He was far from the only scion of a Bolognese merchant family to invent a distinguished ancestry for himself. Back home, Gregorio made the most of his new knightly status. Though his English colleagues tended to call him 'Sir Gregory' or drop the title altogether, using 'Master Gregory' instead, in Italy he was styled 'Il Cavaliere Casali', the Cavalier or Knight Casali.[10] It was a good fit with his early role in the English service, when, as a young man, he had travelled the peninsula snapping up fine steeds and hunting hawks for his leisure-loving monarch. Perhaps it was an interest in such sporting pursuits that first brought him to the king's attention.

As Wolsey dispatched his revised instructions, there was good news for the Casali family. Giambattista Casali was appointed Bishop of Belluno, near Venice. His selection was a sign of papal favour for the Casali, and perhaps too of papal gratitude to Henry. The benefice should have provided a useful income for Giambattista, enabling him to keep up the style expected of an ambassador, something his English stipend alone did not. There was, however, a problem. Giambattista had been promised the benefice on 10 September, while Clement was still imprisoned, but by that time Giovanni Barozzi, a Venetian, had turned up and taken possession of it himself. Claims of dirty tricks flew back and forth: Giambattista was accused of deceiving the Pope into believing that Barozzi was dead. The whole business was politically awkward, for there was an ongoing dispute between the papacy and Venice over the right to appoint to bishoprics in the Veneto. Barozzi had the backing of the Venetian authorities, and would prove a determined challenger. Even before Clement's official pronouncement, Giambattista had already devoted considerable energy to asserting his rights before the Venetian authorities. In September he had lobbied the College (the large assembly of city patricians) to give him the benefices granted by papal brief. In October, the powerful Council of Ten – the executive power in the republic – had voted in favour of granting him possession of the Abbey of the Holy Trinity in Verona. But that was merely a ploy in the papal–Venetian squabble over appointments, for in the meantime the Pope had granted the Verona abbacy to someone else. Giambattista was left in limbo. His only option was to start a long legal process.[11]

Bearing Cardinal Wolsey's request for a legate, the English courier made the journey to Orvieto remarkably quickly, given the time of year and the risks of the road. Gregorio Casali, now returned from a brief meeting with the French commanders, had received his new instructions, dated 27 December, by 12 January. On that and the following day he had unproductive meetings with the Pope.[12] Clement's stated preference was that Wolsey try the case himself. The Pope had hinted, wrote Casali, that if Wolsey found for Henry, and Catherine then appealed to Rome, Clement would confirm Wolsey's sentence. But he had refused to put anything in writing. However, he did finally agree to send a legate, and was happy for Casali to select one. Campeggio, from Casali's point of view, was undoubtedly the most suitable candidate, but the prospective legate was fully occupied managing papal affairs in Rome, where he must have been conscious of the Imperial pressure bearing down on the Pope and its implications for Henry.

As the discussions continued, stalling and progressing by turns, Casali returned to his usual duties as resident diplomat: monitoring the news, reporting on military progress and encouraging the Pope to stand firm against the emperor. By way of his fellow ambassadors, he lobbied the other princes of Italy and Europe to do the same. On 27 January 1528, Henry and Francis jointly declared war on Charles V. Now that Knight had gone, Casali was the sole representative of the English interest at the papal court. Even when stuck at home with a cold, he met with other members of the diplomatic corps in his apartments, but his illness, late in February, was serious enough to prevent his seeing the Pope.[13]

When Knight reached England, probably sometime in early February, the inadequacy of the first commission and dispensation for the divorce soon became apparent. A new embassy was quickly dispatched to Orvieto. Once again, Casali would be required to play host, easing the way for the new arrivals and advising them on court protocol. He maintained a scrupulous discretion about his personal opinions of the parade of English envoys he was expected to accommodate. We are left to speculate what he thought of his various colleagues, but for the most part they were impressed by him. The new ambassadors sent to Rome in February 1528, Edward Fox and Stephen Gardiner, were Cambridge-educated clerics in Wolsey's service, and relative newcomers to the world of diplomacy. Fox was the cardinal's secretary. Later they would both become bishops, but for now they were still several rungs down the ecclesiastical ladder. Gardiner and Fox were tasked with obtaining a new, 'decretal' commission, which (unlike the previous one) would exclude any possibility of Catherine's appealing to Rome. Theirs was an urgent mission, but circumstances conspired to delay it. The pair were almost shipwrecked crossing the Channel. They had to leave their horses at Calais – not to mention all their spare clothes – and ride post to Italy, changing mounts every few leagues. The physical conditions of their journey did not improve, but given that they were crossing the Alps in mid-winter that is not entirely surprising.[14]

The journey of Gardiner and Fox illustrates some of the practical problems facing diplomats in these years of horseback travel. Unless they rode into the night hours, their voyage would take considerably longer than the professional courier's two weeks. That said, the post route was well-established, equipped along the way with curiously-named inns: travellers might stay at 'the sign of the key', 'the sign of the cat', 'the angel' or 'the peacock'. Having crossed the Channel, those coming from England would make their way south to Paris via Amiens. After Paris, the next major stopping point was Lyons, from where the route headed east, then across the Alps via Susa to Turin. From Turin to Piacenza they might take a direct route or a northern detour to Milan; alternatively they could head for Genoa and do part of the journey by sea, picking up the main route at Florence. Those who opted to travel by land went from Piacenza through Parma, Reggio nell'Emilia, Modena, Bologna, Florence and Siena, perhaps to Orvieto and on to Viterbo and Rome. The elderly or infirm struggled; weather caused delays; war necessitated diversions. Testament to Gregorio Casali's ability as a horseman is the fact that once, in 1525, he travelled from London to Brescia (a town about sixty miles east of Milan) in nine days. That – even to contemporaries – was impressive.[15] But on the whole, diplomacy moved slowly. If new instructions were needed, the turnaround was about a month. In a situation where time was of the essence, like the Sack of Rome, diplomats had to make their own decisions. That made the relationship of trust between ambassador and prince all the more important.

The difficulties of travel, though, could be offset by the opportunities afforded by the post route for meetings. As ambassadors passed through major cities like Paris, Milan, Genoa and Florence, they would often do some diplomacy on the road. Gardiner and Fox stopped off near Paris and saw John Tayler, English ambassador to France, King Francis and the French queen mother, Louise of Savoy. Further south, at Nevers (about halfway to Lyons), they met Giovanni Stafileo, Bishop of Šibenik, briefly a useful ally in Henry's great matter.[16]

On 16 March, Gardiner and Fox arrived in the ancient city of Lucca, fifty miles west of Florence. Lucca enjoyed its independent status thanks to a charter from Emperor Charles IV in 1370, and was traditionally allied to the Holy Roman Empire. Its traders in prized textiles had long-standing ties to England; for example, members of one Lucchese merchant family, the Gigli, had been diplomats for the English crown, Silvestro Gigli serving as Henry VIII's ambassador in Rome from 1512 until his death in 1521.[17] Had the visiting ambassadors entered the church of San Michele in Foro, its frivolous facade of pink, white and grey marble inlaid with intricate patterns, gargoyles and a frieze of beasts and birds belying its austere interior, they might have seen his funeral monument.

The citizens of Lucca greeted Gardiner and Fox with hugely lavish presents, including twenty great pikes, confectionery and wines. The fish were carried aloft in basins of silver by four men. In the strict social hierarchy of food that prevailed in sixteenth-century Europe, large fish like pike were regarded as suitable gifts for people of high standing. Vegetables were peasant food. Wildfowl was another favoured diplomatic gift, but it was Lent, and churchmen like Gardiner and Fox might have been fasting. The gift was adorned with the arms of Henry, Catherine and Charles V, in homage to Lucca's Imperial allegiance. In light of their mission, the ambassadors would have been forgiven for wincing. But they make no mention of discomfort in their report. Rather, they remind us that as ambassadors, they travelled not as private persons but as personifications of their king's majesty. When they wrote that 'the citizens of this city [. . .] presented us with a marvellous goodly and costly present in a solemn manner and fashion, not as our personages, but as Your Grace's honour, did require', they acknowledged that in terms of their own social status this gift was beyond them. But it became appropriate because as ambassadors they were at once individuals and royal representatives.[18]

Gardiner and Fox continued on their way, past tiny hilltop villages, the towers of their fortresses and churches appearing high on the horizon as if poised to tumble downhill; through narrow passes; from hostelry to hostelry. Beyond the problems of weather and terrain, there were often other troubles for the early-modern diplomat en route – not least spies. Just as Knight's presence in Rome had been discovered, so was the reason for Gardiner and Fox's embassy. In their case, the leak came from Lyons, and made its way to Venice, where the authorities were informed that persons 'in a position to know' said they were going to secure the dissolution of Henry's marriage. Even though the pair travelled without the showy train that typically accompanied diplomats on less urgent business, the structures of the post route were such that secrecy was virtually impossible. Local captains checked the identity of travellers before allowing them post horses.[19] Only a very good disguise (and a more effective one than Gregorio's had been in Venice) could have helped to keep travel discreet.

On 21 March 1528, Stephen Gardiner and Edward Fox reached Orvieto. They arrived with nothing but the clothes they stood up in, soaked to the skin after crossing a river on horseback. One of their entourage, Richard Herde, caught a fever and died shortly afterwards. Such were the perils of travel in those days. He was, they wrote, 'a young man, being himself singularly well learned in physic, in the Greek and Latin tongues, as any we know'. But mourning aside, there was work to do. Formally, the English mission was to congratulate the Pope on his liberation, but the pretence did not last long. Within forty-eight hours of their arrival, the Mantuan ambassador Francesco Gonzaga was reporting that 'without any doubt' Gardiner and Fox were there to seek the dissolution of Henry's marriage – and that Henry was procuring that dissolution with 'every instance'.[20]

The ambassadors had one central objective. They had to convince Clement that he should issue a decretal commission to confirm in advance the sentence given by the legates – now almost certain to be Wolsey and Campeggio – at the trial in England of Henry's marriage. On their arrival, Gardiner and Fox consulted Casali on how to 'use and order ourselves at our access unto the pope's presence', taking advantage of his knowledge of the tricky etiquette of curia ceremony. He probably helped with translation, too. Neither English envoy, according to the Mantuan ambassador, could speak Italian, so they had to rely on Latin. But even Latin may not have been easy, for its pronunciation was influenced by the local tongue and differed from place to place. When Casali and another English diplomat, Sir John Russell, had met the Ferrarese envoy Matteo Casella in 1527, they had spoken a mixture of English, French and a 'kind of Italian'. Casali wrote to Russell in French.[21] In fact, there is a question mark over quite how fluent Casali was in English, for he never wrote in the language, had lived in an Italian household in London, and could probably have managed with French at the court of Henry VIII.

To avoid attending immediately on the Pope and give themselves time for a briefing, Gardiner and Fox used the genuine, but convenient, excuse of lack of suitable clothing. They had 'no garments nor apparel other than the coats we did ride in', which were 'much worn and defaced by reason of the foul weather'. They were 'compelled to tarry all that day and the next within the house, while our garments were at the making'. Their description of the shortages in Orvieto is a telling reminder of the depths to which the papal court had sunk. The need to transport everything on 'asses and mules' meant that food could not be brought into the town in any great quantity. Cloth that could be bought for twenty shillings in England was in Orvieto six times that price, and scarce to boot. 'Had we not made provision for our gowns at Lucca,' they wrote, 'we must of necessity have gone in Spanish cloaks, such as we could have borrowed of the Pope's servants, wherein peradventure should have been found some difficulty, forsomuch as few men here, so far as we can perceive, have more garments than one.'[22]

In more normal times, ambassadors were expected to dress the part. Some years earlier, the agent charged with delivering Wolsey his cardinal's hat had been waylaid after the cardinal heard rumours of his inadequate outfitting so that he could be 'newly furnished in all manner of apparel, with all kind of costly silks, which seemed decent for such a high ambassador'. At the papal court, while clerics like Gardiner and Fox had to conform to strict prescriptions concerning their outfits, down to the colour and quality of cloth – usually in reds or blacks – lay diplomats like Casali dressed to impress, in cloth of gold or silver, velvet, satin or silk. 'Better a cheerful red than a sorrowful black,' according to Paris de' Grassi, papal master of ceremonies. Heavy gold chains completed their ensembles, and the inclusion of devices like the Tudor rose signalled their allegiance, as did national fashions (hence the English reluctance to appear in Spanish cloaks). Thus clad, diplomats embodied the magnificence of their prince's person.[23] In better days their clothes, at least for formal occasions, would have matched those of the ambassador, Ferry Carondelet, portrayed by Sebastiano del Piombo in a black velvet gown trimmed with lynx and pink satin sleeves (Plate 5), or of Jean de Dinteville, on the left of Holbein's double portrait of *The Ambassadors*, likewise favouring pink satin (for his doublet) and a lynx-lined gown.

Casali gave over his own lodgings to Gardiner and Fox, 'to his great incommodity and our necessary comfort', they wrote. 'He hath and doth keep here an honourable post, and hath great access of gentlemen unto him to his marvellous cost and charge, and much for the king's honour.' The 'cost and charge' of his diplomatic role was an ongoing problem for Casali, stipend notwithstanding. He had to pay for his household, perhaps fifteen-strong, of secretaries, valets and maids; to buy paper and ink, to tip, to bribe. Fortunately he had income from landholdings and property in Bologna and Rome, and the wealth of his mother's family made him a creditworthy individual. Ten thousand ducats had been forwarded to him from England to fund the divorce campaign, although without his account books it is impossible to say precisely how quickly this was spent. It would not have covered many bribes at the Pucci rate, though that was probably exceptional. What is certain, however, is that the scarcities created by war had driven up prices. Casali would later lament that he had squandered his entire inheritance in the pursuit of English diplomacy – and for little reward. In the meantime, however, his conspicuous consumption made a good impression. He was, wrote Gardiner and Fox to the king, in 'such credit and reputation as we think none other is conversant about the Pope's Holiness, having at all times free access unto his person and secret conferences with the same'. Surely that would ease the way for the divorce.[24]

The negotiations of Gardiner and Fox's embassy were intensive and not particularly friendly. Among those who watched their doings was the Mantuan ambassador Francesco Gonzaga, a sharp observer of curia affairs. He noted the secrecy with which discussions were conducted, the two ambassadors closeted away with Casali and the Pope for hours at a time. They had been directed to work with other curia members too: the learned Cardinal Pietro Accolti, the Cardinal-Protector of England Lorenzo Campeggio (responsible for safeguarding English interests at the curia), and Cardinal Antonio Maria Ciocchi del Monte. In addition, Wolsey had written to the Bishop of Verona, Gianmatteo Giberti, who had retired to his diocese to focus on pastoral affairs, asking him to return to court to assist them. Within a week, however, Gonzaga was commenting that there were 'many difficulties' to settle before the issue would be resolved. And a few days later he observed that if the English were to have any chance of getting their way, they were going to have to offer a lot of money. Gardiner, Fox and Casali evidently agreed, for they went back to Cardinal Pucci and made a second attempt to bribe him. But their discussions were clearly difficult, and it was reported that the cardinal had 'refused to accept the two thousand crowns offered by Mr Secretary [Knight] and Mr Gregory; which his highness thought verily he had accepted and taken'. Gregorio tried to persuade him to accept the money, but 'I could in nowise cause the said cardinal to take one penny by no means.' Tipping the cardinal's secretary thirty crowns, he retained the rest, 'to be offered him again'. It was always worth cultivating an acquaintance with the junior staff: you never knew when they might be able to help, and as the men responsible for copying letters and briefings they were enormously useful as spies. Aware of this, Étienne Dolet, French embassy secretary to Venice in these years, had advised ambassadors to select as amanuenses only men who were 'thoroughly loyal and uncommunicative'.[25]

As the negotiations stalled, Casali took advantage of his slightly ambiguous status in the English diplomatic service – accredited as an ambassador but enjoying independent standing as a favoured man about the papal court too – to float ideas that the English were reluctant to advance officially. Sometimes he did so with the sanction of his colleagues: at other times he may have been freelancing. It was not always easy to tell, and that was the point. Now he proposed in a private conversation with Clement that the Pope might provide the coveted decretal commission secretly. It could be retained by the English (he implied) as security for Clement's confirmation of the legates' sentence, a kind of insurance policy against papal default.[26]

Yet although the secret decretal commission would – in the end – be granted, that would take more time. Gardiner and Fox's embassy concluded, on 13 April 1528, with the grant only of a general commission for Wolsey and Campeggio. There was no guarantee that any sentence they gave would not be overturned on appeal. They also got an alternative commission for Wolsey and William Warham, Archbishop of Canterbury (Campeggio's availability had not yet been confirmed), and a dispensation allowing Henry to marry Anne. Fox returned to England hoping that this would all prove satisfactory. It was a forlorn hope. As he left, the Mantuan ambassador gave an acute assessment of the problems. 'I know,' wrote Gonzaga, 'because the Pope told me, that His Holiness is greatly troubled by this request of the English king to dissolve his marriage; there are many difficulties on both sides, and His Holiness told me that he knows if he comes to any resolution he will make a perpetual enemy of either the Emperor or the King; however I understand that he will drag things out as far as he can.'[27] And although Fox was welcomed back warmly, once Wolsey got his hands on the paperwork, he knew it would not do. Nothing less than a decretal commission would satisfy Henry. Gardiner and Casali, left in Italy, had to begin again.

3

A Short Tale of Kidnapping

Though starting again must have been frustrating for Gregorio Casali and Stephen Gardiner, now the remaining English ambassadors at the papal court, in an odd way things were looking up. The reason had little to do with diplomatic manoeuvring and much to do with the fortunes of war, which were now more favourable to the English than they had been for some time. On both north and south fronts, the anti-Imperial allies were enjoying significant victories, and hopes were high. The Imperial city of Naples was under siege; in Puglia, the towns of Trani and Manfredonia had fallen. The Genoese admiral Andrea Doria had led his fleet to victory against the Spanish. Gregorio's brother Francesco, now commanding a hundred light horse for the Venetians, was a regular source of news from the front line. His first-hand reports on troop numbers (there were five hundred infantry at Trani, he wrote in the early autumn of 1528) were invaluable in a world where reliable information was hard to come by.[1]

Although Gregorio's role was now heavily focused on Henry's matrimonial troubles, when he had been appointed ambassador back in 1525 it had been because of his military expertise. He had begun his diplomatic career while England had been allied with the Holy Roman Empire against France. In the late summer and autumn of 1523, he had been involved in raising troops, and at the end of June 1524, Cardinal Wolsey wrote to the English ambassador Richard Pace, then in France dealing with military issues, that Gregorio was being sent to join him. Casali was, wrote Wolsey, 'well expert in the manner of the wars of those countries, having also many friends, who if need were, would and might at time

convenient serve the King's Grace'. He did not say whether he
referred to his knowledge of the terrain, or of the best ways to
raise troops locally, or indeed of the rapidly developing innovations
in military technique during this period. Initially Casali was a captain
of cavalry: in August 1524 he was reported to have raised five
hundred light horsemen in Bologna, who would be under his
command, and six months later another account described him as
the 'captain of 300 horse'. Whether he personally led these troops
into battle is not clear: he may have been more of an agent or
broker. His 1524 mission, however, had a hidden agenda. Pace was
pro-Imperialist, and Wolsey was worried that his reports were biased
in favour of the Duke of Bourbon, an Imperial commander. Casali
could provide a second opinion. In September 1524, the cardinal
entrusted him with the task of obtaining 'perfect knowledge'
of the progress of Bourbon's troops. On the basis of his assessment,
the English would decide whether or not to advance into France.
It is testament to Casali's skills in warfare that he was thought
competent to make such judgements. He was clearly considered
quite an asset to the English as they intervened in the European
war.[2]

Now, in 1528, divorce practicalities and military management
mingled in Gregorio's work. The more Clement sensed that the
French army was a counterweight to the emperor, the more he
might be persuaded to stand up to Charles. The more Gregorio
and his fellow ambassadors for the League could do to hinder
Imperial efforts, the more Clement would feel under pressure to
please Henry. Although by this time there was little prospect of
outright French victory, it was still possible to hope that they might
inflict enough damage on the Imperial side to make peace on better
terms, to Henry's advantage. Casali kept up a constant liaison with
the representatives of France, Venice, Ferrara and Mantua. If
Campeggio's projected mission to England went ahead against a
backdrop of Imperial losses, so much the better. And the Imperial
diplomats found themselves on the back foot. The ambassador from
Naples declared in a furious row with the Pope that his agreement
to try Henry's marriage in England would sow 'infinite scandal and
disorder' and that the divorce would be 'the ruin of the world'.[3]

Fox had evidently given a good report of Casali's dealings in Rome, for on 10 May Wolsey wrote asking him to use his influence with the Pope. Returning to the idea floated by Casali back in April, the cardinal agreed to negotiate on the basis that the existence of the decretal commission would remain secret. He wished it only, he wrote, 'as a pledge of the Pope's paternal regard towards the King and to himself'. Such a demonstration of Clement's faith in Wolsey would, the cardinal explained, increase his authority with the king. Matters were now urgent, for in April the question of Henry's marriage had been delegated to three cardinals for consideration, and rumour had it that the trio, motivated by a desire 'not to displease the Emperor', were unfavourable to Henry.[4] That did not augur well for Thomas Wolsey.

The cardinal's own position was increasingly dependent on progress with the divorce, and he emphasised the personal urgency of the matter to the envoys. Stephen Gardiner received additional instructions in a letter from his former colleague Fox, passing on Wolsey's directions. Fox told Gardiner that Wolsey, 'as of himself' – that is, on his own behalf rather than the king's – would like Gardiner 'to solicit and move the Pope's Holiness and to experiment with the same all kinds of persuasions you possibly by your wisdom or rhetoric can devise and excogitate, to grant the Commission Decretal in most secret fashion and manner'. The scheme for a secret commission now became key to English strategy. If, after 'three or four congresses', Gardiner saw 'no likelihood' that it would be granted but was rather 'in full despair', he should 'relent and cease your suit', and 'return home with diligence, leaving that suit to be prosecuted by Mr Gregorie, and other the king's agents and friends there'. Having tried everything they could to convince the Pope, if they still did not succeed, they should 'cease of further suit therein; and that ye and Mr Gregorie, with all craft, ways, and means possible, attempt the obtaining the said decretal'.[5] Was that an instruction to bribe or blackmail some papal official into handing it over? It is hard to read it otherwise.

As the manoeuvring for the secret commission continued, Wolsey became increasingly agitated at the delay in Campeggio's departure. It was now over four months since Clement had signalled

agreement to send a legate. On 23 May, the cardinal wrote to
Gregorio that he was 'greatly distressed'. All but accusing his ambassador of lying, he added that 'either you do not write the truth,
or you and I are equally deceived, for I cannot but believe that if
you had used ordinary diligence, this matter would have been
expedited long ago'. If Gregorio wanted to prove his fidelity to the
king, he should make every effort to ready Campeggio for departure. If he failed, no one would believe his claims of influence with
the Pope.[6]

Now that the balance of power in Italy had shifted, the papal
court's six-month exile in Orvieto could come to an end. On 1 June
1528, Clement moved his entourage the thirty miles south to Viterbo,
traditional summer retreat of the popes. Viterbo's beautiful location
in the Lazio hills meant it escaped the worst heat of the season,
and it must have been a relief for Clement's courtiers to find themselves in a larger city, better adapted to accommodate them in its
elegant townhouses. The Pope even had a garden, where he could
enjoy conversation and perhaps music too with his ambassadors, as
was the custom when in more peaceful times he entertained at the
Vatican's Belvedere. Like Orvieto, Viterbo had impressive natural
defences. Sitting high above the plain, with views for miles around,
this was a fortress where the papacy could safely wait out riot and
rebellion in Rome. In 1450, Pope Nicholas V had had a palace built
in Viterbo, remodelled a decade or so later by Pius II. The natural
hot springs, bubbling near boiling point in the fields around the
town, were an added attraction. From the piazza outside
the cathedral, one can still walk up a stone staircase, cross a bridge
and arrive on a loggia with a spectacular vista over the countryside.
From there, we might imagine Clement surveying the lands
around, to his left the medieval conclave hall, behind him the
delicate gothic interlaced stonework, dating from the thirteenth
century when Pope Alexander IV had decamped here to escape
political instability in Rome.[7]

At the centre of the palace loggia was a fountain bearing the
coats of arms of Pope Sixtus IV and his grand-nephew Cardinal
Raffaele Riario. Those arms had a particular significance for
Gregorio, because when his father had died in 1506, Cardinal Riario

had become guardian to the Casali children. Gregorio's younger brother Francesco had even entered the cardinal's household. As papal chamberlain, Riario was one of the most important cardinals, and had been a friend of Gregorio's uncle Catellano. In 1478, the artist Lysippus produced portrait medals featuring both men: one version was cast with their respective portraits on either side, testament to their youthful friendship. When the papal court visited Bologna in November 1506, the cardinal lodged in the Casali palazzo there. It was a significant connection for the young Casali brothers as they made their way in Roman society.[8]

In an effort to keep up the pressure on Clement, Casali turned his mind to military strategy. He took a hawkish stance in favour of French intervention in Italy, writing regularly both to the Grand Master of France, Anne de Montmorency (effectively King Francis I's chief minister), and to French agents. He argued bluntly that the French needed better diplomats. One of the French ambassadors in Orvieto, he observed in a tone bordering on the arrogant, was 'incapable', quite the wrong man to negotiate at the papal court.[9] Gregorio was nothing if not confident in his judgements. It is not always clear in his discussions with the French whether he was acting independently or on English instructions. But there was no doubt that French military success would help Henry's great matter along. And Gregorio had his own reasons to stay on good terms with Montmorency. Just as he used his English diplomatic role to promote his friends and family, so he used his connections in France, lobbying for jobs for his brother Francesco and other friends and acquaintances. That concern for personal and familial advancement was ever-present.

As English ambassador at the papal court, Gregorio worked closely with Nicolas Raince, his nearest counterpart in the French embassy. Although Raince was the embassy secretary, rather than ambassador, in practice he had a similar role to Casali, handling day-to-day business at the papal court and looking after visiting special envoys. Back at the time of the Sack, the pair had raised troops together, and a year on, in May 1528, they embarked on a scheme to intercept an Imperial messenger, one Sigismondo di Ferrara. The unfortunate Sigismondo was travelling back and forth between the two principal fronts of the Italian war, Lombardy and Naples, and Casali was tipped off that he would shortly be arriving with commissions to facilitate a papal accord with the Imperialists – something England and France were keen to avoid, or at least delay. Gregorio suggested, first to the Venetian ambassador Gasparo Contarini, then to Raince, that they might find a way to detain Sigismondo. Tit-for-tat hostage-taking was a feature of wartime diplomacy. Sir Thomas Wyatt, travelling in Italy with the English envoy Sir John Russell, had been captured by Imperial troops the year before: some reprisal was only to be expected. An abortive attempt to seize Sigismondo in the territory of the Duke of Urbino left no option but to capture him within the Papal States. That was politically risky, because the Pope had given the messenger a safe-conduct. Casali dispatched 'good orders and sufficient good men', but problems ensued.[10]

Ludovico Orsini, the Count of Pitigliano, was Raince's candidate to imprison the hostage until such time as he could be handed over to the League's commanders. The countryside around Rome comprised a series of baronial fiefdoms belonging to families like the Orsini – which made them important players in times of war. Many of their lords led mercenary bands of troops for one or other foreign power, and the Orsini tended to ally with France. But not this time. The count proved a disastrous choice. First he tried to seize Sigismondo himself. Then he alerted papal troops to the operation. For four days and nights, Sigismondo and his captors were pursued around the Lazio countryside by a hundred and fifty papal cavalry, over wooded hills and through shady valleys, until they finally reached the fortress of Bracciano, some thirty miles south of Viterbo.

There the castle keep surrounded forbidding prisons, and Orsini's distant cousin Napoleone, Abbot of Farfa, proved more receptive to holding prisoners than the count had been. Napoleone was a law unto himself, a sort of aristocratic bandit or delinquent *condottiere*. Entangled in one of the most vicious family feuds of the period, he was eventually murdered by his half-brother. In short, he was a useful ally for an ambassador engaged in shady business, and the Casali family cultivated a relationship with him. The Sigismondo fiasco was recounted by Casali in a furious letter copied to the French agent Ambrosio da Fiorenza, perhaps with some exaggeration for effect (a *hundred and fifty* cavalry? *four* days and nights?), although his anger with Raince is understandable. The contents of Sigismondo's intercepted dispatches proved highly valuable, revealing details of divisions and distrust between various important figures in the Imperial camp, as well as an assessment of their financial situation. Men with military experience were valued as diplomats (especially in times of war) precisely for their ability to organise this sort of enterprise. They would not do so publicly: it would have been bad form for the English and French embassies to be found so openly disregarding the safe-conduct that Sigismondo had received from the Pope. When challenged, both Casali and Raince feigned ignorance. Faced with their denials of involvement, the Pope could do nothing more than give them what the Mantuan ambassador described as 'a good ticking-off'. Thanks to the lobbying of Casali's Venetian colleague Contarini, copies of Sigismondo's dispatches also ended up in Venice. Casali was reluctant to hand them over: nothing, he said, stayed secret in Venice. Perhaps after his experience with the Count of Pitigliano he was feeling a little jaundiced about trusting supposed allies.[11]

The time constraints mean that this operation was probably not explicitly licensed by the English, and given the risk of upsetting Clement, it is possible that Wolsey would have demurred. But Casali had the latitude to make his own decisions on such occasions. When communication took a month, some degree of autonomy was vital. Casali's contemporary, the famous historian of Italy Francesco Guicciardini, acknowledged: 'It is impossible to give ambassadors instructions so detailed as to cover every circumstance; rather discretion must teach them to accommodate themselves to the end generally being pursued.' The maintenance of a relationship of trust was consequently all-important. But how this should work was a matter of debate, and the contemporary theorists did not all agree. Another well-known Renaissance writer, Giovanni Pontano, former chief minister of Naples and a man with considerable diplomatic experience, had considered in a treatise on obedience whether a diplomat could act autonomously if circumstances suddenly changed. He came to no statement of principle, simply concluding that because rulers' attitudes on this point differed widely, being an ambassador was a difficult task. It was a sentiment with which our man in Rome would indubitably come to agree.[12]

In Casali's case, these general problems were compounded by an element of uncertainty about his status. On the one hand he was a fully accredited ambassador. On the other he was a man whose own king regarded him as being in a category distinct from the Englishmen he employed. That uncertainty was reflected in the letters of his colleagues. Gasparo Contarini, writing rather disingenuously to Venice that he 'did not know who was responsible' for the Sigismondo affair, limited himself to reporting the Pope's claim that the 'French ambassador and the Cavalier Casali' were to blame, which is notable for the citation of Casali as an individual, with no reference to his status as English ambassador. The Mantuan ambassador, Francesco Gonzaga, did likewise, referring to 'the Cavalier Casali and Nicolas, the French secretary' in his letter. That said, in another letter Gonzaga referred to 'these Frenchmen, or the English ambassador' as the likely culprits; however, the variation merely emphasises the ambiguity of Casali's position. That ambiguity would, as the months went on, become increasingly problematic.[13]

Though impressive interceptions of enemy letters were possible now and again, as Cardinal Wolsey became more anxious about progress with the divorce, a missing letter of their own threw the English diplomats into disarray. On 7 June, the ambassadors in France, John Clerk and John Tayler, wrote to Wolsey noting that they had dispatched a courier to Calais with urgent letters sent by Casali and Stephen Gardiner from Rome. Given the vulnerability of their correspondence, it was always important to check on the arrival of earlier letters. But Gardiner's letter had failed to reach England with Casali's. On discovering that the packet had gone astray, a nervous Wolsey, desperately hoping that it might contain if not the longed-for decretal commission then at least some good news, instigated an immediate inquiry, fearing that 'by some undue means those letters be intercepted or otherwise miscarried'. It did not help matters when, back in London, the Master of Posts, Brian

Tuke, discovered that the courier, arriving in Calais to find the city
gates closed, had tossed the parcel over the city walls hoping it
would thereby make its way to its destination. Worse, Clerk had
also apparently sent on letters via Pietro Spina, an agent of Antonio
Vivaldi, a Florentine banker regularly involved in diplomatic
financing. Vivaldi, said Wolsey, was 'totally dedicated to the
Emperor'.[14]

Clerk wrote a heartfelt defence of his actions. 'Was I so foolish,'
he demanded of Wolsey, 'that I could not consider that Master
Stephen's letters in this great matter should be missed? Was I of
so little wit, that I could steal no more craftily? Alas, Sir, have I lost
with you both my wit, my faith, and all my credence?' His sympa-
thies were with Queen Catherine, and perhaps he had worries for
his standing in the English service. But he stood up for himself as
best he could. Even though Spina was Vivaldi's agent, he said, in
matters of trade and exchange political lines were frequently
crossed, even in a time of war. Spina, in fact, was no Imperialist,
'but rather clean affectionated to the contrary'. In such a great
matter, he concluded, the king should be sending his own couriers
to and from Rome weekly. That would avoid the problems.[15]

Clerk's colleague Brian Tuke had no difficulty finding someone
to blame: Casali, he said, was undoubtedly at fault. 'All this business,' he wrote to Wolsey, 'shall be found to proceed of Sir Gregory's
lightness, which I trust in almighty God the king's highness and
your good grace will sooner suspect than either the fidelity of my
lord of Bath [Clerk] or of me.' Just as Jerningham had wanted
someone to blame for leaking the news of Henry's plans, and had
picked his colleague, so Tuke hoped to deflect criticism. In these
days, 'light' could mean unthinking or frivolous, but it could also
imply shifty or fickle. It was an accusation that would plague Casali
in the years to come. Aggrieved opponents were a danger to any
courtier, but all the more so when political tensions rose. And it
may be that, for all the advantages his knowledge of the curia
brought to the English, it would always be hard for Gregorio to
escape his foreignness. On the other hand, perhaps he had indeed
been careless, or perhaps the difficulty of getting couriers out of
Italy was not fully appreciated in England. Whatever the reason,

with Wolsey already accusing Gregorio of lacking the influence he claimed, this was a hazardous time for our man in Rome. Although in the end the confusion was resolved, and apologies made, the sorry tale shows up the suspicions surrounding the loyalty of Henry's agents at this most difficult of times.[16]

However, there was sometimes good reason to be wary of diplomats' dealings. As Clerk was busy justifying himself to Wolsey, Stephen Gardiner was returning from a mission to Venice, 'very dissatisfied' with its outcome. During Clement's imprisonment, the Venetians had occupied the papal towns of Ravenna and Cervia, on the pretext of protecting them from Imperial attack. Clement now wanted the towns back, and the English saw an opportunity to curry favour with the Pope by putting pressure on the Signoria to return them. In June 1528, Stephen Gardiner received orders to go to Venice to lobby directly for the return of Ravenna and Cervia. But Venice had no intention of co-operating. The two towns had strategic advantages, and to relinquish them would significantly alter the balance of power in the region. From the Venetian point of view, the income from the towns (Cervia was an important centre of salt production) would go some way towards meeting Venice's wartime costs, which were heavy indeed. Gardiner's mission met with blunt refusal.[17]

In the run-up to Gardiner's departure, the Venetian ambassador in Viterbo had lobbied the English hard for a change of tack. Gasparo Contarini had been elected ambassador to Rome on 1 January. A member of a leading Venetian patrician family, he had been educated at the University of Padua and was an experienced diplomat, whose service had previously taken him to the court of the Holy Roman Emperor, to England and to Spain. He would later become a cardinal, playing an important role in church reform as the Roman Catholic Church responded to Protestantism. But in 1528–9 he was Venetian ambassador to the papal court: not the easiest of tasks, especially given domestic dissension about whether his mission should go ahead at all.[18]

Contarini described meeting Gardiner as the latter was about to leave and attempting to dissuade him from the mission. He went on: 'I also spoke with the Cavalier Casali, explaining to him how unhelpful it was for the common enterprise at this time to molest Your Serenity [Venice], on whose shoulders the whole burden of the war now rests. He promised me to do dextrously the same work with Doctor Stephen that I have done.' Could this be true? Would Casali really be prepared to try to persuade his colleague to disregard orders? It is hard to discern the truth behind this letter. We could take Contarini at face value, and assume that Casali went on to press Gardiner on the matter. Alternatively, we might imagine that this was Casali stringing Contarini along, telling him what he wanted to hear but with no intention of acting on what he said. Contarini might be exaggerating a throwaway comment for effect, to create a good impression of his own diplomacy. He might even be making the whole thing up. On the other hand, Casali may have genuinely disagreed with English strategy. He was probably right to be sceptical about the suggestion that convincing the Venetians to return Ravenna and Cervia would persuade Clement in Henry's direction. Clement would later tell Giambattista Casali that such lobbying was nothing more than he expected from his allies in the League, and he was certainly not going to do any special favours to England or France in return for their support.[19]

But whatever his view of English interests, Gregorio and his family did have motives to retain Venetian favour. Back in October 1527, the Venetian Council of Ten, 'having been acquainted with Gregorio's good offices re Ravenna and Cervia', had voted to give Francesco Casali an extra fifty light horse to command, doubling his charge to one hundred.[20] Perhaps a little 'lightness' on Gregorio's part was expected in exchange. And the English were not delivering much for the family. While other Italians in Henry's service received lucrative church offices, no benefice was forthcoming for Giambattista. To extract income from the bishopric of Belluno he had to hope that the Venetians would back down and recognise his claim to it. In the circumstances, there was good reason for Gregorio Casali to befriend Contarini.

Manoeuvring with the Venetians aside, there was still work to be done on the divorce paperwork before Cardinal Campeggio could depart on his mission for England. For one thing, Campeggio held the papal governorship of Rome, and a year on from the Sack, the city was still struggling to recover. Much of the destruction had yet to be made good, and Campeggio presided over a precarious situation. Before he could leave for England, he had to be relieved of those duties, which was duly done on 8 June.[21] But the more important thing was the decretal commission, guaranteeing the Legates' verdict, and Casali went to Rome for a last attempt to get it.

By now, Gregorio Casali had probably received Wolsey's castigating letter of 23 May, making it clear that his reputation in England rested on obtaining the commission. Consequently he became all the more determined – determined enough to deceive Campeggio, his patron of ten years before, and to play a double game with Pope and cardinal. He told Clement that Campeggio was happy to take with him to England the decretal commission, and that Campeggio not only approved of Casali procuring the commission, but was positively in favour of his doing so. He then told Campeggio that he and his fellow ambassadors had written to England with the news that the Pope had agreed to grant the decretal commission if Campeggio agreed to take it, thereby putting Campeggio in the position of having to oppose Henry openly if he refused. Moreover, Casali convinced the Pope to confirm in writing that the commission would not be revoked. His double-dealing impressed Wolsey so much that he added the comment 'prudenter factum' – prudently done – in the margin of Casali's letter.[22]

The cardinal's comment was high praise, for prudence was the diplomatic virtue of the day. A French embassy secretary in Venice, Étienne Dolet, Giambattista's contemporary there, thought that under pressure of time it was reasonable for the ambassador to make snap decisions. Provided the diplomat was 'a man of prudence and acumen' there should be no problem. A fifteenth-century Venetian diplomat, Ermolao Barbaro, likewise declared that 'prudence' was the yardstick to be applied in unexpected situations. It might be surprising to the contemporary reader that such explicit deceit should be described as 'prudent', but in fact the Renaissance virtue of prudence allowed for a considerable degree of deception. It was a 'prudent lord' in Machiavelli's The Prince who was permitted to break his word when keeping faith would be 'to his disadvantage'. Lucio Paolo Rosello, in a book on Cosimo I de' Medici published

in 1552, wrote of the difference between a prudent man and a flat-
terer. The latter 'of his own accord, and not because he is pushed
by necessity, approaches others in a deceptive manner and with
false blandishments, but the former is compelled by necessity . . .
and accommodates himself to the times, now concealing, now
revealing, as circumstance allow'. So did Casali now.[23]

And for all that his reliability when it came to sending letters,
or his loyalty over the Ravenna and Cervia affair, might be open
to question, when it came to Campeggio, Casali was prepared to
risk his relationship with a patron of ten years' standing in the
English interest. For a man ever conscious of the need for powerful
friends, that was not something to do lightly.

But one potential friend, at least, was content. Anne Boleyn
wrote to Wolsey, 'I reckon my self much bound to your grace for
all that hath taken pain in the king's matter; it shall be my daily
study to imagine all the ways that I can devise to do them service
and pleasure.'[24] Casali had good cause to hope that his efforts with
Campeggio would bring him favour from the queen-to-be.

4

Cardinal Campeggio has Gout

Casali now found himself with a practical problem on his hands. Cardinal Campeggio had gout. Although he was only in his mid-fifties, the curial lifestyle was not conducive to good health and he was not the sort of person to be put on a post horse and pointed north. Apart from the fact that he might not survive the journey, it would be quite beneath his dignity. A suspicious man might have been inclined to think that this was 'diplomatic gout', an excuse for further delay in Henry's divorce. But given that risk factors for gout include excess consumption of meat, seafood and alcohol, all popular constituents of the episcopal diet, the evidence weighs in favour of the diagnosis.

Casali might well have worried that the mission to England would leave Campeggio in a less than charitable mood. But his family was always on the lookout for new opportunities. If Campeggio was now a less promising patron, there were other options. We left Gregorio's younger brother Paolo in 1527 on a trading mission to Constantinople. In June the following year, he returned. No one recorded what exactly he had been doing in the eastern Mediterranean, other than *'molte facende'*, an unspecific phrase meaning 'many dealings', but with the implication that these may have been a little dubious. Paolo had gone to trade jewels for horses in the company of the lavishly named Vicenzo Rosello, also known as Vicenzo Rosetto and Vicenzo Gioielero (Vincent the Jeweller). He took with him a pair of dogs, obtained by his brother Giambattista through the good offices of the Marquis of Mantua, prince of one of Italy's small northern statelets, as a present for Sultan Suleiman the Magnificent.[1]

In Constantinople, Paolo probably stayed in the old quarter of Galata, north of the Golden Horn, long home to the Genoese colony in the city. Since the Ottoman conquest of Constantinople in 1453, foreigners had been constrained to live in this district, and its steep, narrow streets hosted merchants of numerous nations. One of the people he likely met was Lodovico Gritti, a jewel merchant who lived between the districts of Galata and Pera, for whom he was later described as having 'great affection'. The illegitimate son of Venice's elected ruler, the Doge, Gritti was Constantinople's leading Christian resident and a close friend of the sultan's chief minister, Ibrahim Pasha. Across the river from Galata was the magnificent Topkapi Palace, residence of the sultan and his government. If Paolo had been admitted here to present his gift, he would have progressed through a series of courtyards to the newly rebuilt Chamber of Petitions, a colonnaded pavilion at the entrance to the inner palace apartments. It was a fabulous setting for diplomatic receptions, its outer walls clad in marble, its inner walls covered with jewelled mosaics, its silver fireplace studded with rubies, emeralds and pearls, and extravagant gold-embroidered cushions lying around its walls. Gifts to the sultan were traditionally displayed before a large window in the kiosk's facade: perhaps Paolo's hunting dogs were too.[2]

During his stay in Constantinople, Paolo made an important contact: Hieronym Laski, envoy of John Szapolyai, a Transylvanian nobleman who claimed the throne of Hungary. The realm of Hungary then extended well beyond its present borders to encompass much of what is now Slovakia, Croatia and part of Romania. Szapolyai, however, had competition to rule these lands – from the Habsburg King Ferdinand, younger brother of Charles V. The previous king, Louis II, Ferdinand's brother-in-law, had been killed by Sultan Suleiman's troops at the Battle of Mohács in August 1526, and in the aftermath the country's surviving nobility had divided over which of the rival contenders for the crown might better maintain their power. Some months later, a substantial group of them had elected Szapolyai. Laski's mission was to gain the support of the sultan for his master, and in that he succeeded: a treaty promising Turkish aid to Szapolyai was agreed on 29 February 1528,

a few weeks after his departure. But he also found in Paolo Casali a
future agent at the Roman curia, and thus Paolo brought the
Casali their second royal patron. There is no evidence of English
involvement in Paolo's activities, but around the time that he was
leaving for Constantinople, in February 1527, the idea of offering
assistance to Szapolyai against Ferdinand was being touted in the
courts of England and France. It must have been known in
Constantinople, where there were foreigners aplenty, that Paolo
was brother to two of Henry's ambassadors. Perhaps, aware of his
English connections, the Szapolyai contingent made a deliberate
approach.[3]

Paolo returned to Italy in June 1528 with Rosello and twenty-two
horses, some of which were sold on to the Marquis of Mantua.
One may even have ended up in England, for the following month
Gregorio Casali solicited a Barbary horse for Henry VIII via the
Mantuan ambassador in Viterbo.[4] Literal as well as figurative horse-
trading had been central to Casali's early involvement in English
diplomacy when in 1519, barely out of his teens, he had embarked
on five years of travel between England and Italy, facilitating the
exchange of horses, hawks and hounds between Henry VIII and
the peninsular princes. Such presents were significant symbolic
markers of princely amity, and even amid the frenzied negotiations
over Henry's divorce, the routine of gift-giving continued. The
Mantuan envoy wryly commented that, things being what they
were in Italy, horse-racing was hardly a priority. But a royal request
was a royal request; it had to be passed on, and the marquis offered
Casali the pick of two mounts for his master.

Racehorses aside, there were bad tidings for Henry and his anti-
Imperial allies. Andrea Doria, the Genoese admiral who led the
French and papal fleets, had been in secret talks to take the Imperial
shilling. The news came to Gregorio courtesy of his agent Baptista
Sambuelo, who had been sent to hire two galleys from Doria for
Cardinal Campeggio's journey to England. Sambuelo, a cleric from
the northern town of Pavia, had a role of great variety in Gregorio's
service: his jobs ranged from cattle-herder and horse-deliverer to
embassy messenger. He was evidently well versed in rumour-
gathering, for while chatting to Doria's men, he discovered the

news of their master's imminent defection. It was a classic role for a member of an embassy household. In his treatise on diplomacy, Étienne Dolet recommended that the ambassador should have among his staff 'some one man who is cautious and versatile, who will wander about the city, joining in conversations and courting familiarity with a large number of persons, to gather every breath of rumour'.[5] The ambassador could thereby avoid direct involvement in spying himself. On Gregorio's staff, Sambuelo shared that role with others: Guido Gianetti, Gurone Bertani, and Giambernardino di Ferrara.

The news of Doria's defection reached the papal court on 21 July 1528. Casali had got his decretal commission just in time. Such was the butterfly effect of Italian politics in sixteenth-century Europe that the capricious Doria could unthinkingly send a tornado through English affairs. In a last attempt to avert the defection, cardinals Gonzaga and Sanseverino put up fifteen and seventeen thousand crowns (scudi) respectively as security for a payment of forty thousand to Doria; the remaining eight thousand was guaranteed by Gregorio and his Bolognese friends.[6] Once again he had to rely on his own credit in the interests of English diplomacy. Their efforts were in vain: the emperor had deeper pockets. The siege of Naples was faltering too. Typhus had taken hold in the League's camp; among those it had already killed was Casali's critic Robert Jerningham.

By 7 July 1528, Casali had left Viterbo to accompany Campeggio the thirty miles to Corneto (now Tarquinia), where he would begin his voyage to England. In the event Campeggio did not embark until the 25th, reaching Paris on 14 September and Dover on the 29th. The cardinal was still plagued by gout, and his journey was slow and painful. Gregorio, too, was suffering. He returned to court on 4 August and took to his bed with a fever, a consequence, so he said, of his efforts with Campeggio. His colleague Giovanni Gioacchino, an Italian diplomat in the French service, also succumbed. Contarini described Casali's illness as a tertian fever brought on by exhaustion; it could well have been malaria, a perpetual problem in Italy's mosquito-ridden summer heat, for it recurred periodically in the years to come. Malaria – the word

means 'bad air' in Italian – remained endemic in Italy until after
the Second World War. Only in the nineteenth century were
mosquitoes, rather than the bad air, established as its transmission
mechanism. In any case, whether or not Casali's fever was malaria,
it was apparently serious. It was not until the end of August that
he recovered sufficiently to retreat to convalesce in the hill town
of Loreto, famous for its shrine to the Virgin Mary, before moving
to his family home in Bologna. It would be four months before he
returned to court.[7]

At times like this the Casali clan came into its own. Having
returned from Constantinople, Paolo was now available to help
out in Viterbo, from where he sent on to Gregorio news of the
war. Later, he would be joined at the papal court by Giambattista
Casali, relocating temporarily from his post in Venice, and their
cousin Vicenzo. Vicenzo was 'prudent and expert' and had already
been instructed on the matter of Henry's divorce during Stephen
Gardiner's embassy, as Gregorio wrote to Pietro Vanni, Latin secretary to Henry VIII. It was one of the great strengths of the Casali
network that family members could stand in for one another in
this way, but it was by no means an exceptional arrangement. The
English crown – like other European powers – had long taken
advantage of the family networks known in Italy as *consorterie*.
Under Henry VII, the Gigli family of Lucca had acted as agents at
the papal court: first Giovanni Gigli, then his cousin Silvestro –
each in turn receiving the bishopric of Worcester as reward for
his services. The brothers Tommaso and Leonardo Spinelli of
Florence served the English and the papacy respectively in the early
part of the sixteenth century. Gregorio's colleague Girolamo
Ghinucci would enlist his brother Pietro in the campaign for
Henry's divorce. And the English were not alone in their use of
these family firms. Giacomo Malatesta, Mantuan ambassador to
Venice, asked his brother to substitute for him temporarily in August
1526; his counterpart in Rome, Francesco Gonzaga, brought his son
Girolamo into the family business. In a world dependent on ties
of fidelity, family relationships ensured a back-up should one sibling
be temporarily out of action.[8]

After the months of doubt, Wolsey was delighted that Gregorio had finally got Campeggio on the road, and wrote promising that 'at the first opportunity, which we expect to be soon, the king will confer a rich benefice on your brother'. It must have been welcome news for the family, for Giambattista was still excluded from his Venetian bishopric. Although the Pope had lobbied Gasparo Contarini in his favour, the Venetian ambassador observed dismissively that Clement's support for the Casali derived solely from compassion for these 'many brothers with limited means'. Giambattista would have to fight on for the possession.[9]

Wolsey, meanwhile, was also determined to reward Cardinal Pucci – the man who had refused the two thousand ducats – for his assistance in obtaining the decretal commission. He asked Casali to find out, by means of conversation with the cardinal's intimates, what sort of gift would suit best. A quiet chat like this with the entourage was often the way to get things done. Wolsey gave Casali a list of possible gifts – hangings, gold plate or horses – and further proposed a contribution towards the renovation of St Peter's basilica. Perhaps he thought the initial offer of cash had been a little vulgar (and it is true that cash was more commonly offered to the lower ranks at court). Casali, who probably had a more jaundiced view of exactly how helpful Cardinal Pucci had been, wrote back recommending a gift of silver plate.[10] Perhaps he thought that was all Pucci deserved.

As Campeggio embarked for England, Doria's defection was followed by worse news. The summer fevers that had left Casali in such ill-health were also to put an end to the League of Cognac's campaign for Naples. On 13 July, the French commander Odet de Foix, Sieur de Lautrec, contracted malaria. A little over a month later, on the night of 16–17 August, he died. Disease was severely weakening the French forces, and by the end of the month, the siege was all but over. Such was the rout that only one of the commanders, Count Guido Rangoni, escaped imprisonment or death. Less than a quarter of the thirty thousand men who had embarked on the enterprise four months earlier were able to walk away; as they did so, they abandoned their weapons, their supplies and their dying comrades. Even fewer survived the journey home. Some joined the Imperial army: it was a hazard of mercenary warfare that in such circumstances troops might readily defect. They would, at least, have food that way. When Naples finally opened its gates, a Spanish foot soldier dug up Lautrec's body and paraded the corpse through the streets before trying to ransom it to his family or compatriots.[11]

On 6 October 1528, Pope Clement VII returned to Rome after almost a year of exile. The city was only slowly recovering from the Sack. The Rome into which he and his court rode was much smaller than the city we know today, its population concentrated in the district known as Campo Marzio, across the Tiber from the Vatican (Plate 1 gives an impression of its size). Beneath its buildings the lines of the ancient city still circumscribed its precincts: the old chariot-racing arena gave Piazza Navona its outline; the walls of the Theatre of Pompey shaped the palace of the Orsini family at Campo de' Fiori. The ancient forum was all but ignored, except by the handful of artists who had started to investigate the rich wall-painting of Nero's Golden Palace, buried beneath the surface of the Renaissance city. The old fortified homes were gradually giving way to new palaces, like the Cancelleria of Cardinal Raffaele Riario; new roads like the Via Giulia of Pope Julius II were beginning to change the urban plan. But it was a slow and haphazard process, and the wartime devastation was still apparent. 'There are countless houses without their owners,' wrote Francesco Gonzaga, Mantuan ambassador, 'the attics and roofs destroyed. They lack doors, windows and the like, to such an extent the heart is touched with compassion to see so much destruction. I used to know many people in times past, Romans as well as foreigners. Now I do not see any of them here. When I have inquired about them, I learn that almost all of them are dead, especially the Romans, among whom one can hardly track down anyone. They have all succumbed to the pestilence. I am absolutely stunned by the sight of such a wilderness amid the ruins. It could be that, since the Curia is here, at least the population will increase, and consequently the houses will be restored, but I hardly hope to see this very quickly, because there will be so much to do before things can be brought back to their former state, for to tell the truth the ruin has been overwhelming.'[12]

The grand ceremonies of the papal court were now subdued,

if not abandoned altogether. Clement still wore the long beard he had grown during his six months of imprisonment the previous year, a sign of mourning for the devastated city, often personified as bride of the Pope. Travel was not yet safe; even in peacetime, bandits still haunted the byways. On the road to Rome, troops loyal to Napoleone Orsini stole baggage from Gregorio Casali and horses from Cardinal Gonzaga. Orsini might have been a friend during the Sigismondo affair, but his men were not always under control – in which, to be fair, he was not exceptional.[13]

A few days after Clement's entry into Rome, Campeggio arrived in London to a mixed welcome. He was, according to a second-hand account written up by the papal legate in France, welcomed by the gentlemen and nobles of the court, but had a hostile reception on the city streets, where the queen enjoyed popular support and Campeggio's arrival was thought to threaten the ruin of the kingdom. The apocalyptic motif of ruin – whether of England or Rome – peppers the diplomatic letters of these years. Whatever the truth of this tale, it was the one that reached the papal court, and it must have given those in Rome who were wary of Henry's divorce plans grounds for hope and fuel for their campaign. And so, for now, the action in the king's great matter moved decisively to England. There, Campeggio's first tactic was simple and expedient. The queen, he proposed, should be persuaded to enter a convent. But Catherine would have none of it. Campeggio, under orders from Clement to drag the business out as long as possible, was in no hurry to comply with Henry and begin the trial.[14]

In Rome, meanwhile, Giambattista, Paolo and Vicenzo Casali continued to eavesdrop on rumours, collate news and lobby colleagues. There was no let-up in the war to the north. The couriers dispatched from Rome with the ambassadors' reports struggled through, avoiding the most direct roads, taking circuitous routes to avoid Spanish troops. Their longer journeys entailed higher costs, for post horses and, no doubt, for the bribes and fees to be paid to local postmasters. By late November, the situation had so deteriorated that escorts of papal troops were required for safe passage through the towns north of Genoa. Reliable – and brave – couriers were vitally important in diplomacy. These were expert

horsemen who knew the roads well enough to begin their journeys before dawn and end them after twilight. We know only a
little about them. Taddeo and Alexander were the principal
messengers between London and Rome. The latter may have
been the more senior of the two, for he had the title 'messenger
of the Chamber', while Taddeo was known only as 'courier'.
This pair would carry crucial messages throughout 1529. Others
served too. One such was Barlow, a priest in service to Anne
Boleyn's father; in return for his services, both Anne and her
father wrote letters to Wolsey lobbying for a benefice for him.
Hercules Missolus, a relative of Bishop Stafileo, and John Davye,
a messenger in the service of Giovanni Gioacchino da Passano
(another Italian freelance diplomat), brought letters from France;
the wonderfully named 'Robin the Devil' took them back there.
Though their lives are often elusive, without couriers the political
world would not have functioned.[15]

Gregorio remained in Bologna through the autumn, convalescing
from his illness. Short of money, on 20 November and again on the
21st he wrote to Pietro Vanni. There was, he wrote, great scarcity in
Rome, and he hoped the king and Wolsey would assist him. He
was expecting a thousand crowns, promised by the king. The
courier Taddeo had been put to such expense in his arduous travels
that his costs had been nine hundred gold pieces – which Casali
had had to supply. He asked, politely, that the sum be repaid through
his banker Antonio Bonvisi, a Lucchese merchant with a base in
London.[16] Once again he was expending his own money in Henry's
cause.

As Campeggio dragged his feet, Wolsey sent the envoys in Rome
back for a renewed attempt to lobby Clement. There was resentment
in England at Campeggio's efforts to persuade Henry against the
divorce, and the king demanded that the ambassadors discover
whether he was acting on personal initiative or papal direction.[17] With
Gregorio recovering in Bologna, the task fell to his brother. On 16
December, Giambattista had an interview with the Pope, which he
dramatically recounted in a letter to Wolsey. 'Why,' asked Giambattista,
'did Your Holiness give the King such hope, only then to frustrate
and disappoint him?' A furious Clement laid his hand on the

ambassador's arm, forbidding him to speak further. He had been deceived, he said. And indeed he had: by Gregorio Casali, in the manoeuvre over the decretal commission that Wolsey thought so prudent. Clement had plenty of reason to complain about Wolsey, wrote Giambattista. 'He had granted the decretal bull merely to be shown to the King, and forthwith burnt.' That was all the English had asked of him, and he could prove it with Wolsey's own letter. 'And I would that they had asked for more,' the Pope told Giambattista, 'for then I might have readily refused it, nor would I be repenting so; I would give a finger, if I could, to revoke what has been done, seeing what evil is likely to follow from it.'

When Giambattista enquired of Clement what could induce him to change his mind, 'he grew angrier and more excited'. Giambattista pointed to the 'harm, ruin and heresy' that would ensue if he persisted. If treated badly by the Pope, Henry's goodwill towards the Holy See would be transferred elsewhere. It would be a bad thing to agree to the king's demand, and a poor example for the future, but it was the lesser evil. On his knees, Giambattista begged Clement to consider the consequences. If the friendship between the papacy and England vanished, 'we will be contemplating certain ruin'. What Giambattista was threatening here, however, was not the all-out break with the Church that would eventually take place. Rather he referred to the prospect of a political rift between England and Rome, of alliance between Henry and Clement's enemies, of withdrawal of English subsidy for papal wars and English support for the Pope's claim to Ravenna and Cervia.

Giambattista was not afraid to accentuate the drama if that would serve his purpose, and he continued with a vivid description of the Pope's anguish. 'Hereupon, tossing his arms about, and in the greatest distress, showing his agitated mind, he said, "I do consider the ruin which now hangs over me; what I have done torments me. If heresies or other evils arise, am I to blame? I have a clear conscience. Neither you nor Wolsey has cause to complain. I have done what I promised."' Henry could, said the Pope, send Campeggio back to Rome, then do as he pleased. But Clement had suggested such a remedy before, and Henry, determined that the legitimacy of his heir be irrefutable, had said no. On another day,

Giambattista recounted, when he asked again whether the secret decretal commission might be shown to some of the king's councillors, Clement once more refused. On his arrival in Rome a few days later, Gregorio too tried everything he could. Clement would not be moved.[18]

News of the English troubles was now all around town. The Venetian ambassador, Gasparo Contarini, heard it from the Pope himself. 'His Holiness had a good few words to say on the matter,' he reported, 'saying that it was a bad thing, because that king was so stubborn and obstinate in his opinion that even Cardinal Wolsey, who, as is well known, is of the highest authority, didn't dare contradict him; even if at night he imagined doing so, in the morning he'd say whatever pleased the king, even though the Cardinal knew it would be his ruin.' Clement feared that if Charles V put sufficient pressure on his aunt Catherine to agree to a divorce, then he might win Henry over to a renewed Anglo-Imperial alliance. But Contarini doubted that this would be possible. It was too much to hope that they could convince a queen to become a commoner. Clement was unnecessarily worried. Charles might have supported the proposal for Catherine to take religious vows that Campeggio had advocated on his arrival in London, had the queen been prepared to agree to it. But once Catherine had made plain her rejection of that or any other scheme, the emperor was consistently supportive of his aunt – to the point that in January 1530 he told his brother Ferdinand that a marriage between Henry and Anne 'whether or not by the Pope's consent would be a great evil and sufficient cause for a new war'. Whether that support flowed from genuine family feeling or from the observation that Henry's marital troubles usefully served to weaken England on the European stage must remain an open question.[19]

In late December 1528, Gregorio, now recovered sufficiently to take charge of matters, dispatched his cousin Vicenzo to England with a message that 'could better be explained in words, than sent in a letter'. He was to tell the king and Cardinal Wolsey of Casali's private opinion: that they should not rely on the Pope, but start to think of other arrangements. It was already clear to our man in Rome that English chances of success in the king's great matter

were slim indeed. Vicenzo could explain that in person, and as he
did so he could work his charm, ensuring that the Casali family
would not be blamed for failure. When Vicenzo left on the dangerous
post road he travelled with a papal official, Francesco Campano,
whose companionship would afford him some protection against
attack by Spanish troops, if not from the bands of angry and
desperate peasants, victims often of equally desperate but better-
armed soldiers, who waited to rob unwary travellers. Moreover,
the arrangement meant that he could keep an eye on Campano's
activities. By 27 December, the pair had crossed the Alps to reach
Chambéry, and a few days later reached Lyons, where William
Knight and his companion William Benet were waiting to ascertain
whether they should join in a new embassy to Clement. They
thought Vicenzo 'a young man of a gentle nature and apt to show
the truth', but he must have given a pessimistic report, for the pair
wrote to Henry that 'if what Vincent says is true, our going to
Rome will be in vain'.[20]

There was indeed new trouble ahead for Henry. Up until now,
he and Wolsey had relied on the argument that the dispensation
granted by Pope Julius II to allow him to marry his brother's widow
had been inadequate. That dispensation was contained in an official
legal document known as a papal bull. But the king had reckoned
without his wife's determination. Catherine of Aragon had plenty
of support: uneasy courtiers, some leading churchmen, and her
nephew, the most powerful man in Europe. She was educated and
resourceful, set on defending her own and her daughter's honour.
Now she played her trump card. She produced what she claimed
was a copy of a papal brief providing the dispensation for
their marriage. Like the papal bull, it was an official document,
but it was worded differently, and the differences worked in
Catherine's favour. Henry and his party cried forgery, but this was
an eventuality for which they had not planned. It was time for a
new embassy to Rome.

5

The Vicar of Hell in Rome

Back in Rome, in January 1529, Gregorio Casali awaited the arrival of Sir Francis Bryan and Pietro Vanni. With Henry's hopes for divorce in turmoil, the prospect of hosting the third English embassy in eighteen months must have been daunting. But at least this time he would be able to entertain his visitors in style, in his own family house. In that, he had a rare advantage over his fellows in the diplomatic corps, most of whom relied on renting or borrowing accommodation. Casali and his brothers, in contrast, had inherited a large property with halls, chambers, dining rooms and kitchens, not to mention a garden and stable; the family rented another eight properties to tenants. Just off Piazza Farnese, not far from the River Tiber, the family home, located on what is now Via Monserrato, was largely demolished in the 1540s when Pope Paul III decided to improve the view from his grand new Palazzo Farnese. It is likely, though, that it had the typical layout of a palazzo of the period, with rooms arranged around a courtyard and the principal apartments upstairs on the *piano nobile*. Its garden would have been a particularly desirable feature: al fresco dining and entertainment were rather fashionable in the warm Roman summers. But for now, during the winter, the main hall would be fitted out for entertaining, while the plate that Casali had pawned two years earlier, in the days before the Sack, would have to be redeemed and put out on display. A sideboard loaded with silverware was an essential piece of furniture in any upper-class Renaissance dining room. The family must have been thankful that their maternal relatives, the Caffarelli, had survived the Sack with their finances remarkably intact, to the point that they were in a position to offer loans to others less fortunate.[1] Gregorio might have to ask for some favours, but as the King of England's ambassador, he was relatively creditworthy.

Sir Francis Bryan, the new chief ambassador to Rome, was a man to be reckoned with at the Tudor court. An intimate of the king and half-cousin to Anne Boleyn, he was known as the 'Vicar of Hell'. He and Casali had probably already met during Casali's first visit to England in 1518–19 and at Wolsey's summit meeting in France in the summer of 1527. Famed for his love of hunting and gambling, and for the eye he had lost while jousting, Bryan was the Henrician courtier par excellence. He was skilled in military pursuits but equally at home penning poetry. A gentleman of the privy chamber, the select group of courtiers responsible for personal service to the king, he commanded authority as a diplomat because he was known to be among Henry's favourites. The fact that his loyalties lay firmly with Anne meant that for the first time in the diplomacy of the divorce, the Boleyn family had one of their own in Rome. Bryan's appointment was an indication, perhaps, that Wolsey's authority was on the wane, for while Gardiner and Fox, and even Casali, owed much of their success at court to the cardinal, Bryan did not. He was accompanied to Rome by Pietro Vanni, known usually in England as Peter Vannes, but originally from the Italian town of Lucca. Latin secretary first to Wolsey and later to Henry, Vanni was the man responsible for the polished translations of English letters dispatched to foreign rulers. He also put Casali's periodic Italian dispatches into Latin summaries for consumption in London.[2] Like Casali, he had made a career in foreign service. Unlike Casali, though, he had tied himself definitively to the Tudor court, settling in England for the long term.

Just as the English made use of Casali's standing at the curia to their own ends, so Wolsey now proposed to exploit Vanni's. Four years earlier, when Gregorio had first gone on a diplomatic mission to Rome, John Clerk had observed that he was 'better believed' by his fellow Italians when he spoke of Henry VIII's virtues, because he was 'of their own nation', and consequently had 'more credit'. Thus, as Vanni departed for Rome in 1529, he found that his draft instructions included the injunction to pretend that he 'as of himself', that is, as if on his own behalf, should speak 'frankly' to the Pope about the king's great matter, on the basis that 'being an Italian' he had a 'more fervent zeal' for the welfare of the Holy See.[3] The instructions went on to set out in some detail precisely what he should say to the Pope: the comments he was to make 'as of himself' were in reality a product of English direction. Henry could play on the fact that Vanni, like Casali, was seen as 'one of us' at the papal court. For now, the English still saw advantages in employing Italian diplomats.

Bryan set out for Rome with a confident plan to employ, in his diplomacy, 'fair words, large offers of money, or pension, or bishoprics'. He continued: 'Or if all this will not serve, with some bold words, we shall win these men.' Optimism was vital, for his mission, if not quite impossible, was certainly approaching that. He and Vanni were to gather the evidence to establish that Catherine's brief, purporting to be the original, was a forgery; get an updated decretal commission taking that into account; prepare the ground in the hope that Catherine could indeed be persuaded to enter a convent; and raise once again the possibility that Henry might have two wives at once. It was an astonishing list. If the Pope demurred for fear of what might happen if he defied the emperor, the ambassadors were to offer him a personal bodyguard of two thousand men. But, as Casali wrote to his cousin Vicenzo, the pair 'could not have come at a worse time'. For as they arrived, Rome was plunged into chaos with the rumour that Clement was dead.[4]

Accompanied by their twelve-strong entourage, Bryan and Vanni had set off for Rome in November 1528, and would be joined there by Stephen Gardiner in February 1529. Like Gardiner and Fox the previous year, they met King Francis in Paris; he sent a letter with them ordering his own diplomats to support the English in their suit to the Pope. At Bologna they met Uberto Gambara, former nuncio to England and now papal governor of the city, and discussed the matter of the king's marriage. But they suffered so many delays en route that an increasingly impatient Cardinal Wolsey took them to task, marvelling at their 'small diligence' in getting to Rome. Like the earlier couriers, they had to marshal political influence to negotiate the roads through northern Italy. In this they succeeded, but 'owing to the shortness of the days and the bad state of the roads and innumerable problems with the sea crossing and their horses', they still could not travel with speed. The ambassadors had good reason to be worried that amid the disorder caused by the tales of Clement's death, they would be at risk of robbery or worse. The price of bread in Rome was now so high that the poor could no longer afford it; Casali feared they would 'rise against the rich'. Bryan planned to leave Vanni in Orvieto with the king's letters and money, while he and a servant travelled the final eighty miles to Rome. But on their arrival at Orvieto they heard that the Pope was not dead, and so the party continued together, first to Viterbo and then to the next post stop at Ronciglione, where they met and dined with Cardinal Alessandro Farnese. The cardinal, well aware of the dangers of the road, offered the pair an escort to Rome.[5]

Approaching Rome from the north, diplomats would typically follow the road now known as the Via Trionfale into the city, descending from the top of Monte Mario, a hill about a mile and a half outside the walls. According to myth, Constantine, the first Christian emperor of ancient Rome, had had a vision of the Holy Cross over Monte Mario just before the victory at the battle of Ponte Milvio in the year 312 that confirmed his rule. As he caught his first glimpse of the city from the top of the hill, any ambassador with a smidgen of classical education (and most had some) would have been prompted to call to mind Constantine's victory, the triumph of the first Christian emperor over the pagans. It was an image with much resonance for diplomats tasked with maintaining peace and unity in Christendom, and managing the ongoing wars against the Turks.

After a steep descent, envoys would arrive at the tiny medieval church of San Lazzaro dei Lebbrosi and its leper colony, located safely outside the city walls. They would then progress through the fields that gave the name Prati to this quarter of Rome, past a house and vineyard once owned by Falcone de' Sinibaldis, where many diplomats stopped off for refreshment and a change of clothes before their formal entry into the city. Today, the vineyard is long gone, but its approximate location is marked by the Trattoria Antico Falcone on Via Trionfale, still serving refreshment even into the

twenty-first century. Finally, passing the churches of San Giovanni
Battista alli Spinelli and San Egidio, the ambassadors would enter
through the palace gate known as Porta Viridaria, to find themselves
in the piazza outside St Peter's – a St Peter's, though, in the midst
of rebuilding and as yet lacking Michelangelo's famous dome or
Bernini's colonnade. On 15 January, Gregorio met Francis Bryan
and Pietro Vanni outside the gates, with a welcoming party of 'nine
or ten gentlemen of his friends'. He regretted he could not give
them the splendid reception they deserved. Bryan was nonetheless
complimentary, writing that 'we be very well lodged'.[6]

Clement was hanging on to life, but his illness was serious. On
8 January, Paolo Casali told the Venetian diplomat Gasparo
Contarini that the Pope had a continuous *and* tertian fever –
something of a contradiction in terms, because a tertian fever, by
definition, waxed and waned – and that his condition was dangerous.
Meanwhile, the rumours of his death that had made Bryan and
Vanni's journey so perilous had reached none other than the Duke
of Urbino, commander of the Venetian army, who took them as
fact. His report found its way to Giambattista Casali in Venice, who
forwarded it urgently to England on 21 January. Five days later,
Giambattista sent word that he had been mistaken, along with an
apology to Wolsey. But by that time there was already a flurry of
excitement in England at the prospect of electing a pope more
amenable to Henry's cause – possibly even one Thomas Wolsey
(though several years later, Gregorio would write that Henry had
in fact preferred Cardinal Farnese over the alternatives). Detailed
schemes were drawn up, and it was proposed that Gregorio should
enter the conclave as the servant of one of the cardinals, the easiest
way for a diplomat to ensure his presence and influence as discussions progressed. Wolsey wrote to the ambassadors on 6 February
emphasising that it was vital the new pope not be hostile to Henry.
But by 19 February, the news had reached England that Clement,
if not entirely well, remained very much alive, and the plans were
shelved. Henry wrote to Clement expressing his delight at the
Pope's convalescence, though one imagines his teeth were firmly
gritted as he did so. And with no conclave to prepare for, the
ambassadors returned to Renaissance Rome's usual social circuit.[7]

Sir Francis Bryan was evidently impressed by Gregorio's lifestyle, and later wrote to Henry VIII describing 'The honour that Your Grace's Ambassador here does daily to Your Grace.' Gregorio's house, he continued, was 'furnished with gentlemen daily, and that of the best in Rome, and many times Cardinals, two at a time, taking him at dinner or supper, will sit down with him, and unlooked for they fare as well as they do at home'. He praised Casali's liberality, which, he said, would surely reflect well on the king's honour. The impact of a visit to Rome on an Englishman of this time, even a courtier like Bryan, must have been striking. Few English townhouses of the day could compare with the size and grandeur of Roman patrician palazzi. Classically inspired facades hid courtyards, fountains and elegant rooms painted with frescoes or adorned with lavish tapestries. Furniture, as in England, was still relatively minimal. Beds consisted of mattresses on planks and trestles, their splendour deriving from silk or taffeta hangings. Belongings were stored in wooden chests and boxes, often painted. The simple trestle tables for dining were easy to construct and move around, but they would be covered with fine linen tablecloths and napkins, and set with silver or colourful majolica crockery. The impression of magnificence was all-important, and the lavish table-ware was to be matched by an 'abundance of food'. One 1530 diplomatic dinner, described by the Ferrara dukes' major-domo Cristoforo da Messisbugo in a book of advice on holding successful banquets, consisted of six courses for a total of twenty guests, including the French ambassador and his entourage. The starter alone comprised mozzarella balls, strawberries, asparagus, caviar, anchovies and marzipan biscuits. (Modern distinctions between sweet and savoury were, as yet, unknown.) Three fish courses followed, the first featuring, among other dishes, sturgeon fried with orange, sugar and cinnamon, fresh eggs, and no fewer than fifteen crayfish per guest. The second and third were equally elaborate. The fourth course consisted of cherries, curds and whey, artichokes, olives, a 'soup' of muscardine pears, and whipped cream. The event was topped off with a final course of syrupy confections, sugar-coated chestnuts, pistachios and pine-nuts.[8]

Conviviality was central to the ambassador's role, and if offers of hospitality had been of necessity somewhat limited in Orvieto and Viterbo, now that the court was back in Rome the social wheels would once again be turning. The importance of entertaining is summed up in a quotation from Nicholas Hawkins, English resident ambassador to the Holy Roman Emperor Charles V from 1532 to 1534. While in Bologna for a meeting between Charles and the Pope, Hawkins became concerned that he was unable to match the standard set by others in the diplomatic corps when it came to entertaining. He wrote to Henry VIII's minister Thomas Cromwell: 'Truth it is, that the knowledge of such things which I should certify the King on, for the most part I must get it of the other ambassadors; and therefore must both invite them, and be invited.' This was the subtext to diplomatic hospitality. Étienne Dolet, Giambattista Casali's contemporary in diplomatic service at Venice, knew all about the practical advantages of maintaining a liberal comportment. Even the 'most upright men', he claimed, could be won over with a display of munificence. Nor should generosity be restricted to spies; it should be bestowed more generally, in the hope of winning hearts and minds, and receiving favours in return. 'By this practice of a lavish and splendid manner of living,' wrote Dolet, 'we place under obligation to ourselves both men of ample and men of slender means.' Niccolò Machiavelli agreed. In a letter to his friend Raffaello Girolami on his appointment as ambassador to the emperor, Machiavelli advised the diplomat to cultivate the court busybodies. 'The friendship of such men,' he wrote, 'can be gained by pleasing them with banquets and entertainments; I have seen entertainments given in the houses of very serious men, who thus offer such fellows a reason for visiting them, so that they can talk with them, because what one of them doesn't know another does, and much of the time they all together know everything.'[9] When Casali and Bryan entertained, they expected to get something out of it.

One man who regularly dined with them was Cardinal Ercole Gonzaga. He dropped in for an informal supper two or three times a week, and entertained Bryan in return. The cardinal, wrote Bryan to Henry, was 'a great friend' to the king: 'yours, body and soul'. Still in his early twenties, Ercole seemed content to let others take

care of his religious duties. Although later he would play a significant role in church reform, for now he concentrated his energies
on pursuits appropriate to a young nobleman, not least hunting,
and sent Bryan gifts of venison on an almost daily basis. But Ercole
Gonzaga was no accidental acquaintance. He had a long-standing
relationship with the Casali brothers, going back to his student days
in Bologna in 1524 and 1525, when Giambattista Casali, who had
graduated from the university there some years earlier, was also
living in the town. Giambattista corresponded with Ercole's mother,
Isabella d'Este, one of the leading art collectors of her day, and
sent political news to her son Federico, the cardinal's brother, who
had become Marquis of Mantua on his father's death in 1519. The
good relations between both Casali brothers and Cardinal Gonzaga
were noted by colleagues in the diplomatic corps: Ercole and
Giambattista were 'very cosy', said the Ferrarese ambassador; Ercole
and Gregorio were 'close friends', said the French secretary.[10]
Visitors to the Casali household – the de facto English embassy –
became a part of this friendship network. One of the attractions
of having a man like Casali on the spot was that new arrivals didn't
have to start from scratch: the introductions were easily made.

There were facilities for other types of introduction, too. Around
this time, a young man named Giambernardino di Ferrara occupied
the position of secretary in Casali's household, while simultaneously
working for Cardinal Benedetto Accolti, whose household he briefly
joined around 1532. According to Accolti, who was in a position to
know, Giambernardino was not in the business of providing traditional secretarial services. Rather he spent his time in the Casali
household procuring prostitutes. Given the importance of courtesans in the social life of the Roman elite, it would not be surprising
if this were at least partly true (though, as we will discover, the
cardinal had reason to slander his former employee). In fact, the
1517 census of Rome records the presence of a German courtesan
named Madona Paula living near the Casali with a 'male friend'
and renting a house from none other than Gregorio's mother
Antonina.[11] The Casali matriarch clearly had no scruples about
profiting, albeit indirectly, from the oldest profession.

Sexual services were easily accessible in Renaissance Rome. Pope

Clement VII – earlier in his life – was said to have enjoyed an affair with the courtesan Imperia, who was also mistress to the banker Agostino Chigi (Pope Leo X legitimised her daughter with the latter). Imperia's relationships, including one with the Spanish ambassador Enriques de Toledo, were of sufficient interest to be recorded in a popular book, as well as a number of diplomatic letters of the early 1500s. The gouty Cardinal Campeggio had had a much-commented-upon liaison with the celebrated Lucrezia da Clarice, better known as Matrema non vole (her name comes from a Roman phrase meaning 'Mother doesn't want me to'). In the early 1520s she was one of the city's leading courtesans, although she would later be eclipsed by Tullia d'Aragona, lover of the Florentine banker Filippo Strozzi. Numerous letters, poems and stories of the period describe the presence of courtesans on the Roman social circuit.[12] Such women were not simply prostitutes; they were more like a European variety of geisha, offering conversation, hospitality and entertainment as well as sex. They would have had excellent access to the kind of rumour and gossip that was the stock-in-trade of the diplomatic agent, and certainly numbered ambassadors alongside cardinals, noblemen and curial officials among their clients.

Sir Francis Bryan was a man who would have appreciated Giambernardino's organisational skills. It became part of his mythology that while in Rome he slept with a courtesan to gain intelligence. Pillow talk could be very useful to the Renaissance diplomat. Bryan wrote on another occasion to his friend Lord Lisle, the Governor of Calais: 'I perceive that in Calais ye have sufficient of courtezans to furnish and accomplish my desire, I do thank you of your good provision, but [. . .] I have called to my remembrance the misliving that ye and such other hath brought me to; for the which, being repented, have had absolution of the Pope.' Of course, diplomats were often advised against frequenting prostitutes – but presumably only because such conduct was common enough to merit the warnings. Confirmation is to be found in the fact that both Étienne Dolet and Ermolao Barbaro thought it necessary to counsel against it, the former writing: 'If, in the place where he is serving as ambassador, there is some vice which is freely indulged in (as in Venice and at Rome there is much recourse to harlots, both male and female), he should entirely refrain from it.'[13] It is safe to assume, however, that not all Renaissance diplomats refrained all the time; indeed, it would be more surprising to discover that Casali and his colleagues had never socialised with courtesans than to establish for certain that they did so. Moreover, these writers on diplomatic conduct saw fit to remind their readers not only of the perils of liaisons with women, but also of the dangers of frequenting 'licentious youths', as Barbaro put it. Who knows how common, in these bachelor diplomatic households, same-sex relationships may have been?

But ladies (or gentlemen) of the night aside, Bryan and Vanni had work to do. One of their main tasks was to search the papal registers to try and prove that the brief produced by Catherine of Aragon establishing the legitimacy of her marriage was a forgery. And they had money to ease their way. They were to find a trust-worthy individual in the scribes' office, whom they could assure of 'a sufficient reward, be it in ready money . . . or continual enter-tainment', which Giambernardino could presumably arrange. The plan seems to have worked, for Bryan wrote to the king on 26 January 1529 to report that not only had Vanni been searching the papal registers for relevant books and copying them; but that they had 'found the means to have those books to our lodging privily'. No document, however, was found, which fuelled suspi-cions of forgery. At least one request went through the official channels, but the more illicit discussions are easily imagined: a handful of gold ducats and an evening with Madona Paula, in return for some dusty volumes of old papal briefs. Gregorio, in an enter-prising manoeuvre, managed to obtain written testimony from the governor of the Sauli bank in Rome suggesting that the dispensa-tion for Henry's marriage to Catherine had been obtained corruptly: the banker alleged that the Spanish had written off seventy or eighty thousand ducats owed to them by Pope Julius II in return for his co-operation.[14] One of these tactics, surely, would work to put pressure on the legate Campeggio.

On 27 January, a new Imperial ambassador arrived in Rome. Miguel Mai dispensed with the pomp and ceremony that would usually attach to a diplomatic entry. With the Sack of Rome such a recent memory, perhaps he felt that triumphalism was best avoided. Though he had much other business too, Mai would be a key rival for the English in their efforts for a divorce. A gentleman of Barcelona (though in Casali's wicked description 'big and fat, like a Fleming'), he had studied at the University of Padua, near Venice, and now stayed in Cardinal Colonna's imposing palazzo, the Cancelleria. Commissioned by the Casali brothers' childhood guardian, Cardinal Raffaele Riario, the building survives to this day. The Colonna, one of the major baronial families of Rome, and famously rivals to the Orsini, were long-standing allies of the Holy Roman Empire, and often hosted Imperial envoys.[15]

Not long afterwards, on 15 February, Stephen Gardiner returned to Rome to join his three colleagues. His had been a breakneck ride across the continent, taking just twenty-four days from Dover to Rome. It was not the fortnight a professional courier could manage, but given the time of year, it was impressive nonetheless. His journey took about half the time of Bryan and Vanni's, which perhaps lends some justification to Wolsey's irritation at their slow progress. But even as Gardiner was arriving in Rome, it was already clear to Gregorio Casali that English hopes were fading. On 16 February 1529, in a rare surviving letter to a relative, he asked his cousin Vicenzo, now in England, to break the news to Wolsey. 'As Peter [Vannes] writes to Wolsey of the King's affairs,' he wrote, 'I shall say nothing to you, except that here we spare no pains.' Although the Pope's illness meant 'nothing could be done', Gregorio was busily lobbying both Jacopo Salviati and the incorruptible Cardinal Pucci. Salviati, the Pope's secretary, was well known to be a French ally who could be counted upon to oppose the Emperor. He was also famed for his 'cervello di gatta' – his (devious) 'mind of a cat', as one Florentine diplomat put it. Lorenzo Pucci remained an important adviser to Clement. 'I do not know,' Gregorio continued, 'what to hope of Dr Stephen's mission, and how far the Pope ought to pronounce the brief produced by the Queen a forgery. I think His Holiness will do nothing; which you may tell Wolsey, if he asks for my opinion on the matter.' He must have suspected that Wolsey's position was tenuous, and he was obviously frustrated that Vicenzo had failed to convey accurately the serious-ness of the situation in Rome. 'I hear you have told him that if the Pope's fears were removed, he would do everything for the King, licit or illicit. But if you remember rightly, I told you that the Pope would do all that could be done; for there are many things which the Pope says he cannot do.' The fundamental problem was that Clement was afraid of the Imperial armies. 'They cannot remove the fears of His Holiness, not even with a guard of 2,000 foot.' This was Wolsey's proposal: an English-backed bodyguard for the Pope in Rome. Gregorio went on: 'If you remember, I commis-sioned you to tell Wolsey that one of the reasons I was sending you to England was so that the King and His Reverend Lordship would realize that they ought to make some other arrangement.' He could not have been clearer. As early as February 1529, he believed that English hopes at the curia were exhausted.[16]

Yet despite this pessimistic assessment, Gregorio carried on. Perhaps he thought that something might still be salvaged. In 1529, no one was yet seriously predicting an English break with Rome. Threatening it, yes. Putting it into action, no. Most likely he believed that the impasse would be broken by Clement's death. That the Pope was ill was well-known. His successor might broker the settlement that Clement could – or would – not deliver.

6

Neither Fair nor Foul Will Serve

Clement, however, did not die. He simply stayed ill, frustratingly too ill to receive visitors, and that held up English business. The ambassadors could do little but demand audiences, and their demands were in vain. In the meantime, they waited for the latest detail of Clement's condition. Everyone had spies in the household. The Imperial ambassador Miguel Mai had two. The English had Paolo Casali. He was close to the Pope, perhaps a personal attendant of some sort, and made sure they received inside information about Clement's fluctuating health.[1] Once again, the Casali family network proved invaluable.

Treatment of the papal fever relied on medical knowledge dating back to the ancient world, to Galen, a man of the second century AD, and before him, in the fourth century BC, Hippocrates. In the sixteenth century it was believed that illness was the product of an imbalance between the four 'humours' thought to constitute the human body: blood, phlegm, black bile and yellow bile. Cures focused on purging bad humours to restore the requisite equilibrium: letting blood and provoking vomiting were common remedies. As envoys played amateur physician, an extended commentary on Clement's condition ensued in the diplomatic letters. On 12 January, Paolo reported that the Pope, feeling better, had had dinner, but after an hour or so had vomited up all the food. Some observers thought that this was a good sign, others that it was a bad one. A week later Paolo wrote that 'the physicians, finding no pulse, gave him over for dead. Next morning he recovered. The disease is so diminished that the fever has now left him, and tonight his physicians will give him a purge.' On 3 February, he heard 'from a sure and secret quarter that the Pope's disease has increased to delirium and vomiting, and his life is despaired of'; the following day, however, Clement oscillated between being 'pretty well recovered' and 'worse than usual'. He took doses of rhubarb as a purgative, but twice in three days, thought the Venetian ambassador, was overdoing it. The discussion might seem bizarre, even comic, to a modern reader, but given the political importance of the papal succession, the diplomats' preoccupation with the Pope's health is hardly surprising.[2]

Early in February, having already waited three weeks for an audience, Bryan and Vanni were most irritated to discover that Miguel Mai, the newly arrived Imperial ambassador, had been admitted to the Pope's presence. So as not to show partiality, Clement was obliged to see the English too, and did so on 6 February, but the envoys were limited to presenting their credentials and exchanging general pleasantries.[3] Entering the papal suite on the second floor of the Vatican Palace, the English ambassadors would have found themselves in a sequence of stunning frescoed apartments, still visible today to visitors to the Vatican Museums and known collectively as the Raphael Rooms, after their principal artist. They would have waited in the old hall of the Swiss Guard, the Sala Vecchia degli Svizzeri. Here stood the papal officials known as *ostiarii*, guardians of the threshold, the men who ensured that no one entered without an invitation. Awaiting their audiences under the gaze of the classical figures on the painted walls, the diplomats often had ample time to swap news and gossip, and perhaps to eavesdrop, too, on their fellows' conversations. Once admitted, they made their way through the Camera del Pappagallo, so named, it was said, for a real parrot owned by Pope Leo IX, and later decorated with the bird's image. Here the popes were accustomed to hold their secret consistories, the formal assemblies of the College of Cardinals from which all outsiders were excluded. Passing through the Sala dei Palafrenieri, the envoys would arrive in the largest room of the apartments, the Sala di Costantino, decorated by Raphael's pupils with frescoes of the life of Constantine and used for grand banquets and ceremonial audiences. A smaller chamber, the Stanza di Eliodoro, followed. This had been frescoed by the master himself with the story of Heliodorus, who was sent by a Syrian king to take the treasure from the temple of Jerusalem, but who with God's help was defeated in his mission. It was here that working diplomatic audiences often took place. Next – if they were privileged to enter so deep into the suite – came the room intended as the Pope's private library, where they would have seen Raphael's famous *School of Athens*, the masterpiece portraying the philosophers, mathematicians and scientists of the ancient world – a notoriously pagan subject for the popes. During the Sack of Rome, some Lutheran loyalist or mischievous wit among the invaders had scribbled 'Luther' over the fresco on the opposite wall depicting a theological dispute over the Holy Sacrament. Finally they might be admitted to the dining room, known as the Stanza dell'Incendio di Borgo, where a portrait of Pope Clement as a young cardinal featured in a corner of Giulio Romano's depiction of the Battle of Ostia – a famous clash of the tenth century between papal and Saracen forces.[4] It was a sight that even the grandest of Henry's palaces, hung with glittering tapestries as they were, could not match. Beyond lay the Pope's personal apartments: an antechamber, bedroom and en suite bathroom. But even here he might receive visitors, for privacy was not a concept that Renaissance men were familiar with. Given that he was still convalescing, it is probable that Clement did not move far from his bed.

By the end of February, plotting had commenced at court in anticipation of Clement's death. 'It is thought that, for now, he is out of danger,' wrote Paolo, 'but it's doubtful that he has much longer to live; God knows what damage will come to this Court, especially as it seems that now there are more schemes than ever; no-one is admitted to see him, because the Pope's illness is very taxing; he can't bear the pain, and consequently no business is done.'

Late in February, as Paolo monitored the Pope's condition, Vicenzo Casali left London for Rome, bearing new instructions for his cousin Gregorio, Francis Bryan, Pietro Vanni and Stephen Gardiner. Having crossed the Channel and passed Paris, he left Lyons on 1 March. What happened to him after that is a mystery. He is never again mentioned in the diplomatic correspondence. All we know is that some time that year, 1529, he died, aged twenty-eight, on royal service, 'through the difficulty of the times and country'. But that report of his death comes only five years later. He was, according to his epitaph, a young man talented in arts and letters and 'beloved of the greatest kings'. Perhaps, for a long time, Gregorio did not know what had become of his cousin. In April he complained that he had never received a commission for money that was supposed to have been sent with Vicenzo, but several years on he would write that his cousin had brought letters detailing the king's preference for Cardinal Farnese over either Campeggio or Wolsey in the event of a papal election, so perhaps the instructions did get through. Yet a March journey over the Alps cannot have been easy, and on his return Vicenzo had no papal chamberlain to accompany him. He would also have been carrying money. Was he attacked by bandits? By mutinous unpaid troops? Did a blizzard suddenly descend? All those things are possible. It is less likely that this was a political assassination: Gregorio did not raise the possibility when he finally wrote of his cousin's death. Had there been such suspicions, they would have prompted at least some comment from the assembled diplomats, and none is to be found. Though Henry's divorce was already presaging ruin for more than one person, it was not yet threatening anyone with death. The more commonplace explanations are the more plausible. Gardiner and Fox had already lost their assistant Richard Herde to the vicissitudes of travel, while in July 1524, Gregorio and a companion had found themselves 'in great fear of their lives' at Geneva when they were caught trying to smuggle money past enemy soldiers. Fortunately another English envoy, Sir John Russell, had been on hand to help. He hid the money in piles of old clothes, trussed it up with some baggage, marked it with a fake merchant's mark and smuggled it out of town, while Gregorio made his escape by night. Accidents were another hazard. In March 1527, Sir John, returning from a mission to the Pope, was forced to turn back after breaking his leg. Another English associate, whom we know only as Simon, broke his arm in a fall on a journey to Bologna. But while the medical theorising of the papal physicians probably killed as many as it cured, Renaissance surgeons were certainly cognisant of the art of setting a broken limb.[5]

As papal infirmity held up the negotiations, the Venetian ambassador Gasparo Contarini renewed his campaign to convince the English to drop their opposition to Venetian control of Ravenna and Cervia, the towns the papacy sought to recover for itself. Again he focused his efforts on Casali, and again Casali seemed ready to co-operate. In the hope of pleasing Clement, Henry had sent letters 'full of threats' demanding the return of the towns. But when they arrived with his ambassadors in Rome, Casali tipped off Contarini, and sent Paolo to him with a copy. Moreover, he persuaded Bryan and Vanni to delay sending on the letters to Venice, citing the excuse of the Pope's illness (there being, presumably, no advantage to be gained until Clement was well enough to appreciate their efforts). According to Contarini, Casali told him 'that he had a huge row with the other new English ambassadors about this, but nevertheless persuaded them that until the Pope's illness was over, they should delay'. They had also discussed it with Cardinal Gonzaga, who had concurred with Casali. 'Indeed,' he added, 'in my judgement Your Serenity should be well satisfied with the Cavalier Casali's operations.'[6]

Whether Casali should be condemned for flouting his instructions on this occasion is a tricky question. But given the balance of forces in Italy, even if English pressure had convinced the Venetians to return Ravenna and Cervia to the papacy, that would not have been decisive in Henry's great matter. Clement was preoccupied with winning Florence for his family, and the two towns, though significant symbolically and financially for the papacy, were marginal to that goal. Defying Henry was a serious gamble, but Gregorio had good reason to take the risk if it helped cultivate Venetian patronage. As Contarini wrote encouragingly of the prospects of gaining Gregorio's support, Gregorio, too, wrote to Venice, penning a letter to his brother Giambattista, English ambassador there, to emphasise the 'good work' he was doing for the Venetian cause.[7] Their younger brother Francesco was in the Venetian military service, and if he could keep his job – or improve it – so much the better, while Giambattista himself would never succeed in extracting the income from his Veneto bishopric without the acquiescence of the Venetian authorities. And Gregorio had serious financial problems too. In a letter of 27 January to Stephen Gardiner, he lamented the lack of money from England. If funds were not forthcoming, he said, he would be forced to quit his own house and move into the nearby English Hospice, the old pilgrim hostel that had been, in the past, the only serviceable residence for English ambassadors in Rome. Under the circumstances, it is easy to see why he was keen to keep the Venetians sweet.

It was standard practice for Renaissance diplomats to draw on their own resources to fund their masters' activities: hence Gregorio's decision to pawn the family silver back in the days of the Sack. Although he seems to have been paid with reasonable regularity, as were most of his colleagues, his complaints suggest that he struggled to meet the cost of living in the hard-pressed Rome of the late 1520s, never mind the expense of gifts, fees and diplomatic entertaining. His daily stipend, or 'diet', which can best be characterised as a basic income more or less sufficient to cover the costs of his diplomatic work, was forty shillings (about eight or nine crowns) a day. It was more than most short-term ambassadors from England received, and perhaps reflected the additional expense of maintaining a suitably magnificent establishment in Rome. He had an annual pension of 500 ducats from the French king, arranged by Cardinal Wolsey, though he had trouble obtaining its payment, and an annuity of 200 gold crowns which came with his knighthood. Laments about late payment and financial difficulty are something of a motif in diplomatic correspondence, and Casali was by no means alone in his complaints. Still, in the context of shortages, price rises, the demands of Henry's divorce and the needs of his family, he had grounds to grumble. Now his problems were compounded by the collapse of a Venetian bank to which Antonio Vivaldi, an Italian financier in London, had dispatched bills of exchange for Henry's diplomats. Eight thousand ducats had been lost as a result, although Vanni was working to recoup whatever he could. A further two thousand ducats had been sent to bankers in Florence, but they were insisting on an exchange rate of sixty-three pence to the ducat, rather than the usual sixty (five shillings). Casali had particular problems, wrote Vanni to Wolsey, because he was 'compelled to live as the king's ambassador' – to keep up the liberal comportment that so impressed colleague after colleague. Vivaldi eventually sent a relative to salvage what he could in Venice and to arrange the payment of the missing eight thousand ducats. Presumably under considerable pressure from Wolsey, he also arranged for further monies to be paid in Rome. Yet these funds were not for Casali's personal expenses; rather they covered the extortionate fees that had to be paid at the curia to expedite important church business.[8]

No surprise, then, that Sir Francis Bryan and Stephen Gardiner continued to lobby for funds for Gregorio and benefices for Giambattista. After all, wrote Bryan, it would bring the king honour to reward his servants, 'considering the faithful, trusty and true service that the whole house of Casali has ever been ready to do Your Grace'.[9] The reference to the 'whole house' again makes clear that this was no one-man show. And Bryan was an important and influential counterweight to men like the resentful Jerningham, with his claims of indiscretion, and the contemptuous Tuke, who had castigated Gregorio for his 'lightness'.

Meanwhile, the manoeuvring over Henry's divorce continued. Cardinal Campeggio remained in England, but after almost six months the trial had still not begun. Clement was still ill in Rome, and refused to discuss controversial matters. On 14 March, he saw Contarini, but only 'as a private gentleman', not to transact business; on 20 March, he met the English ambassadors, but would not speak of the divorce, only the 'general peace'.[10]

The previous summer, Casali had obtained a promise from Clement that he would not revoke the secret decretal commission sent with Campeggio to London. But its arrival in England had been delayed. When it finally reached Wolsey, probably in early May, it proved so ineffectual in its wording that the cardinal immediately instructed the envoys to pretend it had been 'much defaced' by rain en route, and to try and trick Clement into signing a new version, amplified with 'other pregnant, fat and available words'. Inadequate paperwork was proving an important weapon for a papacy intent on delay.[11]

In the early stages of Campeggio's stay in London, Anne Boleyn had been away from court, staying with her mother at Hever Castle in Kent, while Henry kept up the appearance of marriage to Catherine of Aragon for the legate's benefit. But by December 1528, Anne was back at court, spending Christmas at Greenwich Palace with both king and queen. On 4 April 1529, she sent a letter to the diplomats in Rome. We might imagine her, handsome, dark-haired and fashionably clad in striking black satin or velvet in her favoured French fashion (Plate 6 shows her wearing a French hood), dictating its contents to a secretary in her suite. Addressed to Stephen Gardiner, it contained a present of cramp-rings for him, Casali and Vanni. Between the fourteenth and sixteenth centuries, it was the tradition for cramp-rings – often made of gold or silver – to be hallowed by the monarch on Good Friday (which in 1529 fell on 28 March, just before the date of the letter). The royal touch, it was believed, made the rings effective against cramp and epilepsy. Anne wrote that she 'will be glad to do them' – that is, both Gregorio and Pietro – 'any pleasure which shall be in my power'.[12]

It may be surprising to learn that this is Anne's only surviving letter to our men in Rome. Historians disagree about the extent of her role in the campaign for the divorce: was she was an active participant in the development of Henry's strategy, or did she stand back and allow the king to manage affairs?[13] As far as the diplomats were concerned, if she intervened at all, it was via her influence with Henry, or her friendship with individuals. Sir Francis Bryan, Anne's cousin, wrote to her separately (the letters do not survive), but his colleagues rarely refer to her in their correspondence, and how far she discussed politics with them on their various visits to England is hard to ascertain. That said, she had a long experience of international correspondence from her nine years abroad: as a teenager and young woman she had served first at the court of Margaret of Austria, aunt to Charles V and regent of the Netherlands, and later in the household of Queen Claude of France. Her father had been a diplomat: he had taken part in several missions to the emperor and spent a year resident in France while Anne was in Claude's entourage. The world of European diplomacy cannot have been altogether unfamiliar to her, but she would also have understood the unwritten rules of women's participation in it. In day-to-day diplomatic letters, there are few references to women, and ambassadors rarely cite a woman's opinion, although sometimes one wonders whether the anonymous 'source very close to' a certain individual is that man's mistress. With the important exception of queens, duchesses and the like, the role of women in the diplomatic world was strictly circumscribed and, insofar as it existed, went largely unacknowledged.

On 28 March, Pietro Vanni had bad news to report. Cardinal Lorenzo Pucci – the very same adviser who had refused to take English bribes – had been given responsibility for examining the Julius II brief produced by Catherine of Aragon in support of her case. The ambassadors still awaited a first substantive conference with the Pope. It was not until early April that they succeeded in obtaining an audience where they could talk business, but faced with English demands that he revoke the brief, the Pope, reported Gasparo Contarini, found himself 'most bewildered, and does not know how he can possibly satisfy both justice and the king'.[14]

Within a week, papal bewilderment gave way to confrontation. The scenes at court as the tempers of usually unflappable diplomats flared are not hard to visualise. Stephen Gardiner went to the Pope alone, and spelt out Henry's threats to join with the German princes who were now tolerating the Lutheran religion. We might picture the drama: Clement convalescing on a litter, harangued by an English ambassador with the temerity to suggest that his authority counted for little. As Gardiner dispatched his report of that meeting to London, Clement wrote to Wolsey that 'it is not usual for the Pope to admonish the Emperor'. But the real problem, as Casali wrote, was the situation in Florence, where opponents of the Medici held steadfastly to their republican government. Clement wanted Florence back for his family, and one man had the power to deliver it to him: the Holy Roman Emperor Charles V. Sir Francis Bryan summed it up. 'The Pope,' he wrote to Henry, 'will do nothing for you.'[15]

Casali was well aware that only military progress against the emperor's forces was likely to sway the Pope in England's favour. For all his stated scepticism about the prospects of English success, he kept a close eye on developments, sending trusted men to assess the situation on the ground. Pietro Cavallucchio, whom we first met sneaking out of the besieged Castel Sant'Angelo, went south to Puglia, the heel of Italy, where Francesco Casali was now fighting, to report on the balance of forces for his friend Gregorio. Cavallucchio was 'very expert in military matters', said Casali, and would provide reliable information for Wolsey. Cavallucchio also travelled on Casali's behalf to the lakeside fortress at Bracciano, where Napoleone Orsini, the man who had helpfully imprisoned Sigismondo the previous year, was resisting Imperial attack. Orsini's antics, however, were playing havoc with the League's strategy in the area, for his family feuding complicated already intricate military tactics. Casali set himself up as broker in the wrangling over Bracciano, which did not endear him to certain of the parties involved. Meanwhile he lobbied the French for a more forceful intervention in Italy. He did not mince his words to Montmorency. 'Everyone is cursing the Most Christian King,' was his acid obser-vation in one letter, as he decried Francis's failure to invade Milan. The English well knew that without pressure from France, Clement would never consent to Henry's divorce.[16]

On 27 April 1529, the Imperial ambassador, with the support of his Portuguese counterpart, formally protested to the Pope that the case of Henry's marriage should not be tried in England but in Rome. Scandal and disorder, they warned, would otherwise ensue. An anonymous Florentine letter picks up the story, describing their protest as 'very lively'. The Imperial ambassador got his way – or most of it. He dispatched to Casali's house a Spanish messenger bearing an official citation demanding that the English envoys appear before the Pope. The order infuriated the ambassadors – and the fact of its delivery by a Spanish rather than a papal courier added insult to injury. Nonetheless, a papal demand was not to be ignored, and on 29 April, Stephen Gardiner and Pietro Vanni went to see Clement. The incensed Gardiner had what would be called in diplomatic language an altercation with the Imperial ambassador. In plain terms it must have been an almighty row. Were it not for the fact that Renaissance rooms were usually sparsely furnished, it would be tempting to assume that furniture was thrown. There was still, though, no conclusion. Clement delayed again, refusing

to sign the commissions presented to him by Catherine's representatives. Sick of their argument, and not feeling particularly well, he
took to his bed and decreed that there would be no audiences with
anyone for another ten or twelve days. There were now real fears
in Rome about the potential consequences of Henry's actions. As
a Mantuan agent, Fabrizio Peregrino, succinctly put it, returning
to the diplomatic expression *de jour*, the affair threatened to 'ruin
Christendom'.[17]

The English had few qualms about playing that card. The envoys
had already hinted that Henry would join with the Protestant
princes of Germany. Now, they resorted to the 'bold words' promised by Sir Francis Bryan and began to talk about the 'solicitation
of the princes of Almain, and such other matter as should and
ought to fear the Pope's said Holiness'. The anonymous Florentine
correspondent wrote that the English ambassadors 'wanted His
Beatitude to go beyond his duty, and his office, and justice. But,'
he added, 'His Beatitude's will to satisfy His Majesty is tempered
by the duty not to exceed too far what is right.' He worried for
the consequences if the ambassadors reported proceedings to
Henry when they were in such an irate frame of mind.[18]

They did precisely that. On 5 May, Sir Francis Bryan summed
up the situation. 'We have,' he wrote, 'opened all to the Pope, first
by fair means and then by foul; but neither fair nor foul will serve
here. We be like men that hope to gather fruit on a rotten stalk.'
He praised his colleague Gardiner – 'Master Stevens, in the presence of the Pope, so answered for your Grace that he made the
Pope ashamed of his own deeds' – and went on, 'And whereas Your
Grace writes unto us, that the Cardinal Campeggio says he is your
servant, and that he will do for Your Grace in all things; Sir, his
fair words that he says to Your Grace is, because he would have
the Bishopric of D[urham].' Bryan had had enough of Rome and
its frustrations, and asked to return home, for 'I could tell you
more of my mind in an hour's talking than I can write in a week.'
Finally, he added, 'I dare not write unto my cousin Anne the truth
of this matter, because I do not know Your Grace's pleasure whether
I shall so do or no; wherefore, if she be angry with me, I most
humbly desire Your Grace to make mine excuse. I have referred to

her in her letter all the news to your Grace, so your Grace may use her in this as ye shall think best.'[19]

Clement's illness – or divorce-induced hypochondria – dragged on. On 4 May, a frustrated Stephen Gardiner wrote to Henry, commenting caustically that: 'By reason the Cardinal [Pucci] hath been sick and is every other day sickly, and for the most part when the Cardinal is whole the Pope is sick, we have yet no expedition of the said bulls.' And indeed, according to insiders, the situation was serious. Clement's health was deteriorating. 'Count Lodovico Rangoni,' wrote Gregorio, 'who often sees His Holiness domestically, tells me that he has a terrible choler, and that today it's worse than ever.' Again, Clement's choice of cures was greeted with scepticism. This time it was not rhubarb but a decision, 'contrary to the advice of all his friends', to take the waters at Viterbo. The town's steaming sulphuric springs and pale-green mud might be pleasant enough to bathe in, but to drink? Gregorio was unconvinced. 'These are bad waters and heat – indeed, burn – the liver of whoever drinks them, and will be especially harmful to the Pope, because his liver is already burnt by medications.'[20]

Wolsey assured the ambassadors that the king knew they had tried everything possible, and was grateful for their efforts. But there was nothing more to be done. On 12 May, even before their latest letters had been received, Henry recalled Bryan and Gardiner to England. They left, as Gasparo Contarini recorded in typically dry fashion, 'less than satisfied' with the court of Rome. In his courtesy letter to Henry of 31 May, written on their departure, Clement made himself plain: he 'could not proceed as the King desires without great reproach'. Gardiner drew the short straw and rode post to England with the bad news. Bryan, having taken his leave of the Pope, rode north, planning on Casali's advice to see Ferrara, Venice and Mantua. On 30 May, Casali wrote a charming letter of introduction to the Marquis of Mantua. He had encouraged Bryan to meet the marquis and see his city; he hoped that his colleague would receive a warm welcome, and not just because Bryan was so close to the king. Bryan expected to be in Mantua by 12 June, a lovely time of year (mosquitoes apart) to enjoy the lakeside city, tucked into the curve of a river, brilliantly defendable and beautiful. There he would see the richly painted ducal palace, its decorations including the famous *Triumphs of Caesar* by Andrea Mantegna, later bought by King Charles I and now at Hampton Court Palace. He might walk in the beautiful secret garden, recently completed for Isabella d'Este, or gaze on Mantegna's other master-piece, the *Camera degli Sposi*. And there would be time to hunt, out on the plain of northern Italy, to try out the fine horses of the marquis' stable and perhaps to purchase one or two. In Ferrara, Bryan would see the spectacular moated fortress, and in Venice – like so many visitors before and after him – he could glide down the Grand Canal in a gondola. Contarini had written ahead, advising his friends and masters in the city to give Bryan 'good cheer'.[21] He was close to the king: it would be in their interests. And with the English cause in such a pitiful state, any ambassador would need a boost. How fortunate that Venice was famed, as Dolet said, for its 'recourse to harlots'.

7

Livia Pallavicino, Heiress

As Bryan headed north in June 1529, Casali and Vanni were left to hold the fort in Rome. Ahead of them was one of their trickiest diplomatic tasks to date. After months of delay, the legatine trial of Henry's divorce was about to start in England. Cardinals Campeggio and Wolsey would preside. Our men in Rome had to ensure that no one at the curia trumped its proceedings with an advocation – effectively, a transferral of the whole process to the court of Rome. As the Imperial protests grew stronger, it was a race against time. If the London trial could be concluded quickly in Henry's favour, then the verdict – sanctioned by Campeggio and Wolsey's official legatine commissions – would be mightily hard to overturn. But fortune was not on their side. Whereas a year earlier the Imperial troops in Italy had faltered, they faltered no longer. Charles V, Holy Roman Emperor and nephew to Catherine of Aragon, was on the verge of victory in the Italian war.

The diplomacy was at once delicate and desperate. Skilled though Casali and Vanni undoubtedly were, with Gardiner gone, a replacement legal expert was required at the curia, and William Benet was duly dispatched. Benet, a lawyer and churchman, had studied at the University of Bologna, probably around the same time as Giambattista Casali. He had doctorates in both canon and civil law by late 1522, when he worked as a lawyer in Cardinal Wolsey's service, but although he was a canon of St Paul's Cathedral and held a number of ecclesiastical benefices, he never reached high church office. Unlike the other English ambassadors, Benet seems to have lodged away from the Casali house. By 1533 he was staying with one Bianchetti of Bologna, a relative of the Casali family who later became a spy for Thomas Cranmer.[1] Whether his choice of accommodation was a product of a simple wish to stay with an old friend or prompted by a desire to keep some distance from Casali is, for now, an open question.

Wolsey sent with Benet new, detailed instructions for Casali and Vanni. They were to tread carefully with Clement. 'It is no time,' wrote Wolsey, 'to come to any rigorous or extreme words with His Holiness, but in gentle and modest manner to show himself such words as be mentioned in my said last letters [. . .] and so without irritation of him, but with conservation of his favour to entertain His holiness in the best manner that may be.' The ambassadors should try their best to thwart Imperial efforts to revoke the Legates' commission, for doing so would alienate Henry and the English nobility from the Holy See. The precise tactics were left to their 'wisdom and discretion'. Wolsey still thought it might be possible to persuade the Pope to provide an improved commission, giving more extensive powers to himself and Campeggio, and told the ambassadors so. It was not the most realistic hope under the circumstances, but Wolsey had little choice but to persevere. If the Pope proposed to advoke the cause – that is, to move the whole trial of Henry's marriage to Rome – they should tell him that 'that is not the way to satisfy his Grace [Henry]' and 'with wisdom and dexterity order yourselves herein accordingly'.[2]

Benet was also given further, oral, instructions to communicate to his colleagues in Rome. Presumably these included exactly what 'order yourselves accordingly' would mean in the event of an advocation. The ambassadors' difficulty was that no one in England yet had a clear strategy for how to respond to such an eventuality. Henry and his counsellors were prepared to threaten a breach with Rome, but to proceed with one was another matter. In June 1529, as the ambassadors' instructions became increasingly radical, they baulked at the suggestion that they should question papal authority. Implying that the Pope was not the 'true Vicar of Christ' – as had been proposed – was going too far, and risked driving the Pope into the arms of the Imperialists. 'None would have more courage than we for this business,' they wrote, 'and' – surely this should be but! – 'we earnestly beg you to consider whether it is advantageous to your cause.' Up until now, the diplomatic effort had focused on technicalities. But while one could compromise around a technical error in an old papal dispensation, there was no compromise on papal power. Questioning it came perilously close to Lutheranism. Eventually the advice given by Casali and Vanni – not to push the 'true Vicar of Christ' argument – was accepted back in England. On 25 June, Stephen Gardiner, who had returned to London just three days earlier, wrote to agree that this 'might irritate the Pope'. He preferred instead 'dulce [sweet] and pleasant means' of negotiation, which would keep the Pope in 'good benevolence and favour towards the King's Highness'. Any advocation would be Wolsey's 'utter undoing'.[3]

By 4 June 1529, Casali was lamenting that he had received no money from England since the previous September. Bryan and Vanni could attest to the costs he had incurred. The best solution was a substantial benefice for Giambattista, and Gregorio tried to manoeuvre the English into providing one. As he solicited help from the cardinals for Wolsey's ambitious plan to reorganise the English dioceses (a scheme that necessitated papal backing), he spread the tale that one of the cathedrals would go to his brother.[4] Wolsey did not take the hint. From England, there was nothing. Yet even as he bemoaned his lack of English financing, Casali was quietly sorting out an alternative solution: he would resolve his money problems with a lucrative marriage to an heiress. To do so he needed the help not of his English patrons but of the Pope and cardinals. It was hardly the most comfortable timing. Still, on 2 June, just after Bryan and Gardiner had departed, Gregorio Casali was betrothed to Livia Pallavicino, the daughter of Polidoro Pallavicino, member of a large landholding family with branches in Genoa, Parma and Piacenza, and his first wife Samaritana Giovenale. Samaritana's brother Latino Giovenale de' Manetti, Livia's guardian, was an important adviser to the influential cardinal Alessandro Farnese.

As ever in Casali's affairs, there were complications. Although Livia was a wealthy woman, her fortune was the subject of a ferocious dispute between various branches of her family. In the early years of the century, her father's attempts to sell off parts of the family property had aroused the anger of his brother Rolando, who tried repeatedly to have Polidoro declared of unsound mind. Whether or not this was justified (some years later a Ferrarese ambassador would describe him merely as 'none too bright'), in February 1513 Rolando succeeded in his aim. With Polidoro in jail, Livia, then aged just three or four, came under the guardianship of her maternal uncle, Latino Giovenale. Ten years on, in 1523, she would have been around the age at which a girl of her class would marry, and Latino Giovenale began to make arrangements for her betrothal to a man who was both 'suitable and respectable'. The choice of husband was important. The Pallavicino family lacked male heirs to take control of their family castles, strategically positioned near a bend of the River Po around the halfway point of its four-hundred-mile course east from Turin to the Adriatic Sea. These fortresses would fall instead to the men who married Livia and her cousins, a potent and attractive combination of marital fortune with martial influence. (Plate 7 shows the castle that would become known as the Rocca Pallavicino-Casali, in Monticelli d'Ongina.) Clement VII, with an eye to the balance of power in northern Italy, took a personal interest in the Pallavicino marriages. He was less than impressed in 1525 when Rolando Pallavicino, without the appropriate permission, married off his daughter Barbara to Count Ludovico Rangoni. By May 1524, Livia was engaged to Sciarra Colonna, a commander in the Imperial army and illegitimate son of Fabrizio Colonna, Grand Constable of Naples. But with an eye to a better prospect, Sciarra broke off the engagement and, after an audacious but unsuccessful bid to wed the widowed Duchess of Camerino and thereby win himself a dukedom, married Margherita Chigi, his brother's widow and daughter of one of the richest men in Rome. It was a small world, and Gregorio evidently knew his fiancée's former betrothed, for in April 1529 he held discussions with Sciarra about a possible defection from the Imperial to the French service.[5]

Polidoro died in August 1527, leaving his daughter and his second wife, Lucrezia Borasca, who was due to give birth. But Lucrezia's baby died, and Livia, now in her late teens, came into the family property near Piacenza. Her inheritance was controversial, because a provision in her grandfather's will had excluded women from the succession, though the legality of that clause was arguable – and indeed would be debated for decades to come in a legal marathon rivalling in length and intricacy the fictional Jarndyce and Jarndyce. (It began in 1530 and finished in 1630, although related issues were still being thrashed out up until 1695.) But that was not the only problem. The old conflict between Livia's father and uncle lived on, and when Rolando died in 1529, his daughters, Livia's cousins, became players in the Pallavicino disputes. Thus Gregorio had to contend with two other husbands of Pallavicino heiresses: Counts Ludovico and Guido Rangoni, the former married to Rolando's daughter Barbara, and the latter to Argentina, daughter of another paternal uncle.[6] Nonetheless, the Pallavicino–Casali engagement – not least from Pope Clement's point of view – solved a number of problems in a very satisfactory way. The Casali were not, as a family, a big baronial house whose acquisition of Livia's strategic property might alter the distribution of power in the region in a manner detrimental to the papacy. The income from the holdings would go some way towards helping Gregorio keep up the appearance appropriate to a royal ambassador in Rome. And by permitting the marriage at all – for his agreement was needed for Livia to marry outside Parma – Clement might hope to gain a favourable hearing from Casali in future.

We have no record of what the English made of Gregorio's marital plans but, his financial prospects looking decidedly healthier, Casali ploughed on with Henry's business. His task now, with Pietro Vanni, was to prevent the advocation of the divorce case to Rome. Their strategy was simple: they pretended that the trial in England had not begun. If there was no trial, there was no need for an advocation. All they needed to do was to prevent news of the trial's commencement reaching the papal court. So, they lied; or, to use the Renaissance euphemism, 'dissimulated'. This was, after all, perfectly honourable practice. Machiavelli had famously advised his diplomat friend Raffaello Girolami: 'And if, to be sure, sometimes you need to conceal a fact with words, do it in such a way that it does not become known, or, if it does become known, that you have a quick and ready defence.' Étienne Dolet, airing a rather disingenuous French moral superiority, wrote in his treatise on the office of ambassador: 'If he has some business to transact with the people of Venice or the Pope at Rome or other princes of Italy, inasmuch as they are past masters of pretence and dissimulation, he should likewise pretend and dissimulate, and should let his speech be greatly at variance with his thoughts.'[7]

So, pretend and dissimulate our men in Rome did, and given the difficulty of communication with England, their task was not as impossible as it might sound. At the very least they could generate some plausible doubt about the reliability of Imperial claims that the trial was indeed under way. Thus began a series of deceptions and interceptions. First, Casali lied about the content of his correspondence, producing an anodyne fake to show the Pope, and sending his real news to England in a separate ciphered letter. He forwarded both on to Wolsey and asked him to reply in similar form, with one letter for official consumption, and another with secret instructions. He and Vanni also made plans to intercept any letters that might be sent out of Rome against Henry's interests – especially those citing the king to appear at the papal court in person – promising to use 'all our vigilance, diligence and attention' to ensure they did not get through. Moreover, they asked the Pope to take painstaking care that no news should leak either from himself or from the curia that might irritate the king.[8]

Could their trickery succeed? It seemed ever less likely. It was now common knowledge that Charles V planned to come to Italy – a sure sign of Imperial victory. He would be crowned in a ceremony confirming his unique status in western Christendom as Holy Roman Emperor, protector of the Church. There was not yet a peace treaty, but that was only a matter of time. Charles had won. And if Charles had won, were Henry's hopes for divorce not lost? As the English worried at the prospect of advocation, the ambassadors seized on any offer of help. On 7 June, the young cardinal Benedetto Accolti, who two years earlier had been besieged with Gregorio in the Castel Sant'Angelo, wrote to Henry and Wolsey to offer his services, citing Stephen Gardiner as a referee able to testify to his good offices. Of an age with Casali, Benedetto was the nephew of one of the most learned and wily lawyers at

the curia, Pietro Accolti, the man who had drawn up the original
dispensation for Henry's marriage to Catherine in 1506. If he could
sway his uncle in Henry's favour, that would be good news indeed
for the English, who by now were probably desperate enough to
entertain any proposition forthcoming, even from such a surprising
quarter as the young Accolti, who received two pensions from the
Imperialists. (That was not in itself a reason to refuse his services:
all sorts of people, including many of Henry's courtiers, received
pensions from foreign powers; it was no secret, and did not neces-
sarily entail reciprocal service.) It still should have prompted more
questions than the English seem to have asked, but with Henry's
situation looking increasingly precarious, there was no turning
down even the unlikeliest of offers. With the promise, no doubt,
of ample reward, Benedetto Accolti was recruited to the king's
cause.[9]

On 16 June 1529, William Benet arrived in Rome to join Casali
and Vanni. As the three envoys began the tedious wait for a papal
audience, they compared their instructions and sketched out a plan.
Back home, meanwhile, there were dramatic scenes as, on Friday
18 June 1529, almost a year after Campeggio first embarked for
England, the trial hearings began. Unexpectedly, Catherine of
Aragon appeared in person. The scene made famous by dramatists
from Shakespeare onwards was originally described by the French
ambassador Jean du Bellay, a reminder of the importance of diplomats in writing – and sometimes embroidering – the stories we
know of history. Du Bellay did not see fit to adorn the essentials
with visual description, but we might imagine Catherine dressed
as befitted her status as queen, in costly fabrics, rich and dark, black,
perhaps, or purple (Plate 3 shows her in about 1525). Often she
dressed in Spanish style, but sometimes in English: on this occasion
the latter would undoubtedly have been the diplomatic choice.[10]

Last Friday, wrote Du Bellay, the cause was brought before the
judges. The queen appeared in person. She refused the judges'
authority, and questioned the decision to hold the trial in England.
Henry appeared too, and made his formal request that the legates
determine the validity of his marriage. From the start, he said, he
had felt a perpetual scruple about it, and judged both on his own

account and by the testimony of good and learned men that it was
null and void. To that, the queen replied that she was dumbfounded
that he should have kept his doubts to himself for so long. Henry
excused himself, citing the great love he had for her. He desired,
above all else in the world, that the marriage should be declared
valid and his conscience relieved. He remonstrated that the queen's
request for the removal of the cause to Rome was unreasonable,
considering the emperor's power there, which would prevent the
matter from being judged freely. England, in contrast, was a secure
place, where the queen was rightly loved and esteemed and could
not be pressurised, having had her choice of counsel, whether
prelates, lawyers or others.

Finally, Du Bellay recounted, Catherine fell on her knees before
Henry. She begged him to consider her honour, her daughter's and
his own. He should not be displeased that she did her duty to con-
serve and defend the honour and welfare of her daughter, and he
should consider the reputation of her nation, her relatives and her
friends, who would feel marvellously offended in this affair.[11]

As Catherine made her plea, Henry's ambassadors at Rome had
an audience with the Pope, but discussed only generalities. On 22
June, Wolsey wrote to Casali and Vanni. As he beseeched the
ambassadors for their aid, it became clear that his fate now depended
on their success or failure. His tone was strained. An advocation
would bring 'high dishonour' to Henry, Campeggio and himself.
The men in Rome must do all they could to prevent it. It was their
last chance to show that they were 'of some reputation there'. If
the advocation were granted, the Pope would not only 'lose the
king and devotion of this realm from him and the See Apostolic,
but also utterly destroy me for ever'.[12] Wolsey knew that his career
and reputation depended on his ability to deliver the divorce. That
in turn depended on Casali and his colleagues.

There were other preoccupations in Rome. William Benet
worried that it was in the Italian interest to move the trial there.
He wrote to Wolsey warning that the lawyers and advisers retained
for the king thought it would be to their advantage if the case was
advoked. Moreover, they had been boasting in secret of the 'lucre'
they hoped to obtain from such a move.[13] Benet did not mention

either Casali or Vanni by name, and there is no evidence he intended to refer to them. But it would not be hard for those in England suspicious of their activities, as Jerningham and Tuke had been, to conclude that the comment extended to them too.

As the three envoys tried desperately to cling to their lie, Casali put his personal reputation in Rome on the line. He and Vanni maintained that the legatine trial had not yet begun, and that Henry wanted instead to come to a deal as part of a more expansive European peace treaty. Repeatedly the three stressed to both the Pope and his secretary Jacopo Salviati that advocation would be highly damaging. Gregorio – so his fellows claimed – was particularly persuasive; Clement believed he was acting 'very sincerely indeed'. That art of dissimulation, the ability to walk the stage in masks, redounded to the diplomat's credit. But on 22 June, Francesco Campano, papal nuncio to England (the man on whom Vicenzo Casali had earlier been tasked with spying) arrived in Rome and announced that the legates had formally opened proceedings on 31 May, the date on which the process of summoning witnesses had indeed begun. Salviati – he of the devious mind – was no fool, and when the ambassadors enquired of him what he had heard from Campano, he told them bluntly that he knew exactly what was going on in London. Benet protested that Campano's reports were based on 'conjectures', but in private conversation, Salviati told Gregorio he was 'amazed that we kept denying it'. Gregorio tried his best: 'I assured him that I knew for certain from Dr Benet, and from Peter [Vanni], and from letters from England that there was nothing going on, but that I reckoned it had to be taken into account that Campeggio was a man most partial to his own distinction and exaltation, and to the favour of princes, and that he had promised the king wonders in this cause.' But now that Campeggio found himself unable to make the desired ruling, an advocation would give him an honourable exit. He could maintain he had done everything possible, and would have ruled in Henry's favour, but that it was simply out of his hands. Hence, Gregorio told Salviati, the legate's reports were specifically aimed at encouraging a move of the case to Rome.[14]

Alongside their constant lobbying, the ambassadors tried less respectable tactics. For some time now, English couriers had taken papal correspondence to France in order to avoid its interception by the anti-Medici party that controlled the Republic of Florence. While apparently doing Clement a favour, the English had taken advantage of this arrangement to steal the papal letters and send them on to Venice, where expert code-crackers could be employed to decipher them. But their contacts in Venice proved unreliable, for copies now made their way back to Salviati. The English envoys made their excuses – and presumably Salviati was not particularly surprised, for intercepting letters was part of the bread-and-butter business of diplomacy. Still, it was an awkward embarrassment at a bad time. The ambassadors had to confess to Wolsey, who must have been furious, and advise him that Henry should deny all knowledge.[15]

It was easy enough to break ciphers, for although Renaissance scholars knew about sophisticated polyalphabetic methods of encoding, for day-to-day correspondence diplomats stuck to simple substitution methods instead. The system was based on replacing one letter of the alphabet with another, though additional special symbols or combinations might be used for common words (Pope, and the like). In 1474, Cicco Simonetta, a Milanese secretary famed for his code-breaking skills, had written a tract on cryptanalysis containing thirteen rules for cracking such ciphers, and although some more complex variations were developed, they were easily solved by the experts, men like Marco Raphael and Zuan Soro of Venice, who, according to Clement VII, 'could decipher any cipher'. More secure systems were unwieldy and slow. Almost two centuries on, polyalphabetic codes, 'invented by professors in a University and upon rules of Algebra or Arithmetick', would still be considered impractical, time-consuming and difficult by the famous theoretician of diplomacy, François de Callières. Henry's ambassadors did not even take the precaution of changing their ciphers regularly. One long-serving diplomat, Tommaso Spinelli, used the same cipher for over fourteen years; the Imperial ambassador in London, Eustace Chapuys, employed the same one for twelve, even though it was broken halfway through his tenure. But the fact that codes could be cracked did not much matter so long as ambassadors understood that their letters were far from secure. Even a half-baked cipher would provide temporary protection from the spying eyes of frontier officials and embassy servants (if they were denied the time to copy it), and mixed cipher/non-cipher dispatches could be shown, albeit briefly, to others at court. Truly confidential messages were only ever sent orally.[16]

Their embarrassment at the code-breaking fiasco set aside, the following day, 29 June, Casali and his colleagues wrote with news of the war. It was bad. The Imperialists and their Roman allies the Colonna had had success in Lombardy. The French commander St Pôl had been captured; the King of France was resigned to making peace. Wolsey must see, they wrote, that in such times, and with such iniquitous events, their hopes for the king's matter were daily diminishing. Wolsey already knew it. On 3 July, Jean du Bellay, French ambassador to England, reported that the cardinal was in hiding at Hampton Court, with 'nowhere else to go'. He had fortified his gallery and garden, and allowed only a handful of people to see him. Wolsey was a prescient man. On the very day of their letter, although the ambassadors would not yet have known it, the Pope and emperor had made peace, concluding the Treaty of Barcelona. Charles was to restore Medici rule in Florence, and ensure that the papacy received the lands it had lost to Venice and Ferrara in the course of the war. There was no mention of Henry in their pact – the trial of his marriage was still continuing – but Clement must have known what was expected. And on 5 July, as the Imperialists began peace talks with France, Catherine of Aragon's protest against the proceedings of the legatine court arrived in Rome.[17]

On the same day, things began to look up for the Casali family. Giambattista Casali was confirmed by Consistory – the official assembly of Pope and cardinals in council – as the rightful Bishop of Belluno. After eighteen months he had beaten off the rival claim of Giovanni Barozzi, favoured by the Venetian authorities. Like his brother's marriage, this benefice would be an alternative source of income – if the Venetians could be persuaded to accept the ruling. Perhaps Clement, sympathetic to the 'many brothers with limited means', had realised that their English patronage might now be in jeopardy. Giambattista's victory in court was backed up with a friendly letter to the Venetian authorities from Gasparo Contarini – perhaps reward for Gregorio's sympathy to the Venetians in the Ravenna and Cervia affair. 'The Magnificent Cavalier Casali,' he wrote, 'who has behaved most modestly throughout this whole case against Giovanni Barozzi, now that he has had the sentence in his favour, has asked me to beg Your Serenity to give the possession to his Reverend brother. I certainly know that they are all excellent gentlemen, and also have always done the best of service to the Glorious Republic.'[18] Unfortunately, Contarini's pleas were in vain. The Venetians were not inclined to do the Casali favours. The dowry of Livia Pallavicino was the family's best prospect.

8

The Fall of Cardinal Wolsey

As the ambassadors' mission reached its climax in the heat of the Roman summer of 1529, Gregorio's younger brother Francesco was fighting a last-ditch action in Puglia, the heel of Italy. These were the final days of the war. Imperial troops were closing in. The French, defeated in the north at Landriano, near Milan, on 21 June, were close to abandoning their Venetian allies, for whom Francesco led a hundred light horse. On the flat coastal plain, troops clashed in ambush, assault and skirmish. Francesco was captured. He may have been among the hundred and sixty soldiers taken when a daring ambush on 24 June went wrong. Arriving just too late to surprise a party of Imperial light horsemen lodging outside Ruvo di Puglia, they found themselves trapped between two bands of Imperial troops – those in Ruvo and others stationed barely four miles to the north-west in Corato. Some observers said they simply gave up, allowing themselves to be taken 'like women'. Vettor Soranzo and Camillo Orsini, the Venetian commanders in the camp, scrambled to blame one another for the humiliation. A ransom of two thousand ducats was demanded for Francesco's release – two thirds of Gregorio's annual English stipend.[1]

In Rome, the ambassadors were trying desperately to avert the advocation of Henry's cause with a mixture of personal pleas and shameless deceit. Gregorio played all he could on the favour his family enjoyed with Clement. Over the years, the Casali had served the Medici well. Giambattista had spent time in the papal household. Francesco had been appointed to the equestrian order of Pope Leo X while still in his teens. In 1523, Gregorio had spent six and a half months in London with Gabrielo Cexano, Clement's secretary, staying at the Throgmorton Street house of the Florentine merchants PierFrancesco Bardi and Giovanni Cavalcanti, who had an important role in liaising between the Medici family and the English crown. And from these early days, Clement had done much for the Casali. He had appointed Andrea Casali to the Bolognese senate and made Giambattista Casali a papal nuncio. He had approved Gregorio's marriage and granted Giambattista his bishop-ric in the face of Venetian opposition. It was a change in fortune for the family, for a generation earlier, Gregorio's uncle Catellano and his future guardian Cardinal Raffaele Riario had been caught up in the infamous conspiracy of the Florentine Pazzi family to murder Cardinal Giulio's father and uncle. In 1517, Riario had again been accused of plotting against the Medici. Then, only a collective effort by supporters in Rome – including Gregorio's Caffarelli relatives – had saved him.[2]

Jacopo Salviati, papal secretary, was getting bored with English excuses and denials. He told Gregorio bluntly that the ambassadors' collective pretence that the trial of Henry VIII's divorce had not begun was pointless. Campeggio had reported 'all the actions and plans of the King's Majesty'. Clement, however, unprepared to force Henry's hand, vacillated. His indecision over Henry's divorce was to define his reputation for centuries to come, perhaps unfairly, for as a diplomatic tactic, delay has a fine pedigree. When it came to Florence, and his family interests, the Pope was decisive enough.[3]

In a final attempt to play for time at the legatine trial, the English diplomats in Rome devised a stratagem for delay. 'Wherein I promise your grace,' wrote Benet to Wolsey, 'Mr Gregory has used great diligence and taken great labours. At this time, we can do no more for our lives.' Early in July, at English prompting, Salviati proposed sending a courier to London to establish the facts of the trial's progress. After 'much doleful conversation' with Gregorio, the Pope agreed. It would buy them a month. When the Imperial ambassadors baulked at the suggestion, Gregorio went back to Clement, telling him firmly that 'it was not his duty to consider what the Imperialists wished, but what was right and proper'. Increasingly insistent, the Imperialists demanded that the advocation be granted the following Saturday. But the messenger left nonetheless, albeit bearing a letter in which Clement told Wolsey that he could not gratify the King 'without incurring manifest danger'. Though the English envoys recounted these events with considerable restraint, the Mantuan ambassador reported that Clement had turned the air blue with his blaspheming over Henry's 'obstinate desire', denouncing the king's 'devilish inspiration' – an expression with real resonance in a world where belief in the Devil was commonplace – and declaring that the divorce would cause chaos. And this on a day when, according to the ambassador, Clement was in 'quite a good mood'![4] Gregorio never admitted it to Henry or Wolsey, but it would hardly be surprising to find that he had been on the receiving end of some choice papal phrases too.

As they awaited the courier's return, Pietro Vanni renewed his efforts to intercept correspondence. Given the unreliability of the post, it was usual for all manner of letters from London to be sent to Rome care of the English ambassadors, who would then distribute them to their addressees. Having failed to get away with the theft of outgoing correspondence, Vanni now turned his attention to incoming letters. When he discovered in the English parcel a letter from Campeggio to his brother, he opened it to find the legate declaring that he would not be sorry if the case were advoked. To conceal the fact that he had stolen the letter, Vanni devised an elegant cover story. Relying on the convention that diplomatic letters would often be shown to others at court, he wrote to Wolsey in a mixture of plain text and cipher. In the plain text, visible to all, he falsely claimed that letters sent to him in Rome had been opened. His implication was clear – someone, but not him, was spying on English correspondence. In the ciphered section he then explained: 'What I said above, about the open packet, was not true: but I wrote it for safety's sake, so that your Most Reverend Lordship can read that clause to Campeggio, if he complains that his letters have not been delivered.' It was a plausible bluff. The following month, Brian Tuke, Henry's master of posts, confirmed that he could find no means of sending unciphered letters to Rome without their being read en route. Local postmasters would often take advantage of their position to open couriers' correspondence, acquiring valuable information along the way. Letters from the papal court had lately been opened at Florence, Genoa and Lyons. Others, too, played the game. In September 1531, the Imperial ambassador to Rome heard from the Pope that the Duke of Ferrara had forged ciphered letters from Clement, then 'deciphered' them and sent them on to the emperor to give the impression that Clement was secretly negotiating with England and France.[5]

Even working 'night and day' on Henry's great matter, as Vanni put it, Gregorio was careful to keep up his acquaintance with alternative patrons. With the English cause in trouble, other princes might prove more profitable masters. Now, he exploited contacts his brother Paolo had made in Constantinople the year before to gather news of the war in central Europe. Sultan Suleiman the Magnificent and his army had left the city in May 1529, heading for Hungary and thence Austria. As they advanced west, a secret agent of the sultan's ally King John Szapolyai of Hungary arrived in Rome. In July he was received at the Casali house, and it may have been around this time that Paolo Casali, who had met Szapolyai's agents during his stay in Constantinople, began acting as an agent for the Hungarians at the curia. Szapolyai, with the backing of a sizeable portion of the Hungarian nobility (the realm was, traditionally, an elective monarchy), was fighting for the throne of Hungary with the Imperial candidate Ferdinand of Habsburg, Charles V's brother, styled King of the Romans. Ferdinand, Gregorio reported, was under serious pressure from the Hungarians, all the more so because on another flank the German Lutherans were even now arming themselves to go to the aid of their Protestant fellows in Switzerland. Presumably he calculated that news of trouble for the Imperialists would be well-received in England.[6]

On 12 July, Pope Clement VII told Gasparo Contarini that he still did not know whether or not he would advoke Henry's case. He was under pressure from the Imperialists to do so, he said, but had told them that it would be better to put everything on hold until peace had been concluded. But now he had heard that things were proceeding at great haste in England; he had heard about the queen's appearance, perhaps from Du Bellay's account; and

Catherine had written personally to him swearing that her first marriage had never been consummated, a key point of contention in the legatine trial. Clement bemoaned his dilemma to Contarini, but within a week his mind was made up. On 16 July, the case was advoked. Cardinal Pietro Accolti made the formal recommendation to the cardinals' assembly, Consistory. His nephew Benedetto's offers to the English had, for now, come to naught. Two days later, Clement penned letters of apology to Henry and Wolsey, but his expressions of 'sorrow' at having been 'compelled' to advoke the case must have sounded hollow to his readers. The ambassadors tried to get the news back first, before the official papal letters arrived, but the only way to evade the attention of inquisitive postmasters was to send their letter secretly, by a private courier and on an unsafe route.[7]

The ambassadors in Rome had one remaining tactic, with at best an outside chance of success. They would try to ensure that the official letter bringing news of the advocation to Cardinal Campeggio did not arrive. Even a couple of days of delay might make time for some manoeuvring at the trial. Pietro Cavallucchio, now returned from reporting on the state of affairs in Puglia, was dispatched on a new military mission. With a band of cavalry and infantry, he headed for the border area between Brescia and Verona, where the territories of Milan, Mantua and Venice adjoined and the flat plain of northern Italy gives way to the Alpine foothills. The Mantuan ambassador Giacomo Malatesta thought Cavallucchio had gone to steal correspondence arriving in Rome from Catherine of Aragon, which is possible, but he had probably misunderstood the direction of the letters Cavallucchio was to intercept. The English also put pressure on the Venetian authorities to prevent the news getting through, but to no avail. Others were in the interception business too. Their request to Venice fell into the hands of an Imperial captain, who handed it over to his diplomatic masters.[8]

On 3 August 1529, Charles V, Holy Roman Emperor, and Francis I, King of France, made peace. Known as the 'Ladies' Peace', the Treaty of Cambrai had been negotiated by Francis's mother, Louise of Savoy, and Charles's aunt, Margaret of Austria. It was a treaty on Charles's terms. Francis had to pay a ransom of two million crowns, withdraw his troops from Italy, surrender the remaining towns he held on the peninsula, renounce his claims to Flanders and Artois, and more besides; in return, Charles made some minor concessions and released the French princes he had held as hostages since 1526.[9]

It would have been easy to think that with Imperial victory, English hopes for a divorce were over. Perhaps Gregorio did. He took to his bed, sick. His brother Francesco remained a prisoner of war. In Venice, Giambattista Casali appeared to be ignoring English business entirely. He occupied himself instead with commissioning a mirror for his patron Isabella d'Este, Marchioness of Mantua, and was pleased with the results. Clear and true, the mirror was encased in an elegant box made from a type of wood resembling ebony. But his artistic enterprise was abruptly interrupted when he heard news of Francesco's capture, and he turned for help not to the English, but to Isabella and her son Federico, the marquis. Both wrote letters in Francesco's favour to Isabella's younger son Ferrante, Federico's brother, who commanded Imperial forces in Puglia. No matter which side a mercenary captain found himself on, he could always find friends on the other. In the event, Francesco had no need of the letters. Somehow – perhaps with assistance, perhaps not – he contrived to free himself from his chains and escape. In a rare religious moment, Giambattista Casali attributed his liberation to the power of the Holy Spirit. More probable, if more mundane as an explanation, is that Francesco had found the wherewithal to buy his way out of jail.[10]

A week after Francesco's escape, the Casali situation began to look up. On 21 August 1529, Gregorio's fiancée Livia Pallavicino was granted papal permission to marry outside the district of Parma – a crucial next step on the way to formalising their marriage. Ironically, the man who wrote out the papal brief permitting the marriage was none other than Casali's old adversary in Henry's divorce negotiations, Cardinal Lorenzo Pucci. In addition, moves were probably already afoot for the papal treasury – known as the Camera Apostolica – to intervene in the Pallavicino property dispute, potentially in Livia's favour. On 30 October, it would formally take control of the disputed territory of Monticelli d'Ongina.[11] Clearly, Clement's frustration with the English over Henry's marriage did not extend to personal antagonism towards the king's ambassador. But what prompted Clement's willingness to dispense such favour to Gregorio? Was this an attempt to break down his loyalty to England? Or an effort to compensate him for the service for which Henry and Wolsey had so patently failed to reward him?

Despite the advocation, Clement was in no hurry to hear the divorce case or make a decision that would risk losing England's obedience to Rome. On 29 August, he issued a papal brief suspending further hearing of the king's cause until Christmas. Gregorio tried to push him further, drafting a promise that three months after the advocation he would pronounce a sentence of divorce.[12] Clement, however, would not go that far. The peace treaties concluded, the Medici Pope could turn to his plans for his family, and his 'infinite desire' for the city of Florence, still in the hands of his opponents.

Some time after 15 August, Casali left Rome for Florence. The official line was that he had gone to the baths. And indeed he may have done: there were some pleasant enough spas in Tuscany, which was a traditional summer retreat, and perhaps he sought a cure for his health problems. On the other hand, the baths – mentioned only in an official diplomatic letter that would have been checked by papal officials – may have been a cover story. For Gregorio also went to meet the Florentine rebels as they anticipated Imperial attack, and to advocate a settlement, perhaps another ruse to win papal favour for himself and his master. He returned in mid-September in the company of a Florentine agent to report that the city was well supplied with troops and its citizens in good spirits. They would need to be. At the end of October, the Imperial siege of Florence would begin.[13]

As the emperor's armies prepared to take on that last pocket of resistance on the Italian peninsula, at the papal court attention had turned to planning a coronation for the victorious Charles V. The event, to be held in the northern city of Bologna, would also facilitate negotiations for a general European peace, and would be an

opportunity for theatrical display of the new unity between Pope
and emperor. It was traditional that the emperors should demon-
strate their loyalty to the papacy by submitting to the ritual of
crowning, thereby acknowledging papal supremacy. But there
had been no such coronation since 1452, when Pope Nicholas V had
crowned the Emperor Frederick III in the more usual venue of St
Peter's in Rome. Now, St Peter's, half-demolished ahead of
rebuilding, was in no state to host such a ceremony. The mythical
site of the apostle's grave at the basilica's west end was covered
with a temporary pavilion, and visions of a new dome existed only
in the imagination of architects. Besides, it must have been ques-
tionable whether the Roman populace, their memories of the Sack
still raw, would have welcomed an Imperial visit. On 25 September,
Gregorio, always alert for opportunities to promote his family,
wrote to Wolsey suggesting that Giambattista might be accredited
as English ambassador for the papal–Imperial meeting. But on
5 October 1529, probably before Gregorio's letter had even arrived
in England, Girolamo Ghinucci was re-appointed to the papal court.
Ghinucci, Bishop of Worcester, had been Gregorio's colleague in
Rome during 1525–6 before being posted to Spain. Now he was
back to join Gregorio and William Benet.[14]

Even as he prepared to be crowned, Charles V had pressing
problems. Although war in the west (Florence excepted) was over
for now, in the east Suleiman and his army had arrived in August
1529 at the town of Mohács, located on the Danube river close to the
modern-day border between Hungary and Croatia. On 8 September,
Ottoman troops had taken the city of Buda (modern Budapest)
and were advancing on Vienna, less than a hundred and fifty miles
to the west. On the night of 26–7 September, the siege of Vienna
began. According to some, the sultan had with him over a hundred
thousand men. Although after three weeks the Turks would retreat,
Suleiman's offensive gave his ally John Szapolyai charge of much
of Hungary. The 'threat of the Turk' – often hoary diplomatic
rhetoric – thus became a card to play in the game of Henry's
divorce. On 7 October 1529, Clement wrote to Henry reiterating
his decision of 29 August to suspend all hearings until Christmas.
'Besides,' he wrote, 'we implore you, as Defender of the Faith, to

imagine – amid this crisis of Christian faith, where now the Turkish tyrant, enemy of the very name of Christianity, with his army, would destroy our Christian accord – what calamity the discord of the Christian Princes over this marital contention might bring.'[15]

Clement's reference to Henry's style 'Defender of the Faith' was pointed, a reminder to the king of his professed loyalty to Rome, loyalty that now, apparently, was ebbing. The title had been granted in October 1521 by Clement's cousin, Pope Leo X, just weeks after the presentation of Henry VIII's pamphlet against Martin Luther, the *Assertio Septem Sacramentorum* (*Defence of the Seven Sacraments*), at a special meeting of Consistory. The Medici–Tudor friendship had been firm through the years, and the title was part of a much longer series of exchanges of gifts between the two houses. In 1513, following his victory against the French at Tournai, Henry had been given the Holy Sword and Cap of Maintenance by Leo X. In return, the king had given Giulio de' Medici (the future Clement VII) the cardinal-protectorship of England, and made Giuliano de' Medici, Pope Leo's brother, a member of the Order of the Garter. Only Henry's bizarre insistence on divorce now threatened to divide them.[16]

In the next months, Clement extended further favours to the Casali. On 28 September, Gregorio received news that his younger brother Paolo would be sent to England as papal nuncio, and on 6 October Paolo was formally accredited. He was the second Casali brother to hold the post: Giambattista had been nuncio to England in 1525, when he had been thought by the Pope to be 'acceptable unto the king's highness and your grace for his brother's sake', a reference to Gregorio, by then already in Henry's service. Blood mattered to our men in Rome. Officially Paolo went to England on a mission to gain support for the war against the Ottoman Empire, a job for which his personal knowledge of Constantinople might have made him a good candidate, although it is surprising that his liaison with the agents of John Szapolyai was not perceived to be a problem. But whatever the explanation for the appointment, it was undoubtedly very convenient for the Casali to have a family member in England at this time – one who could work to smooth things over, to assure Henry that everything possible had been done in Rome, that his ambassadors could not have tried harder. Paolo travelled via Paris, where he spent a good week or so, arriving in England some time in early or mid-November. There he found a pungent change in the political environment. Cardinal Wolsey was gone from government, and that made Paolo's presence in England even more crucial for his family.[17]

At the heart of Wolsey's fall from power was his failure to deliver Henry's divorce. Had the legatine trial gone differently, he might have survived. As it was, the king had no more use for him – except as a new means to put pressure on the Pope. As cardinal-legate, Wolsey was the highest representative of the Roman Church in England. By bringing low a cardinal, a prince of the Church, Henry could perfectly convey to Clement that he would not tolerate further excuses in his great matter. For the Casali family, this dramatic change in Henry's government must have been worrying indeed. Wolsey had been their patron, their principal tie with the English court, the man central to the running of the diplomatic service. The risk was that his agents might now fall with him.[18]

On 9 October, Wolsey was indicted for *praemunire* – the offence of promoting papal authority against the English sovereign. There was a second indictment on the 20th, and two days later the cardinal acknowledged his guilt. In the meantime he surrendered the Great Seal and with it his office as Lord Chancellor. Wolsey feared life imprisonment. Dozens of charges were made against him, many of them concerning his conduct of foreign policy. But there were other allegations too: increasing rents, having an 'arrogant demeanour' in council, unlawfully suppressing religious houses, all manner of corruption, and several grievances concerning his conduct in specific legal disputes.

Near the top of the list, in third place, was one charge that implicated Gregorio Casali directly. The cardinal was accused 'For having, when in France, commissioned Sir Gregory de Casalis, in the King's name, to conclude a treaty with the Duke of Ferrara without any warrant from the King.' Another charge claimed that he had been 'writing to ambassadors abroad, in his own name, and without the King's knowledge, and causing them to write again to him, so as

to conceal their information'. The first charge is immortalised in
Shakespeare and Fletcher's *Henry VIII*:

> Item, you sent a large commission
> To Gregory de Cassado, to conclude,
> Without the king's will or the state's allowance
> A league between his highness and Ferrara.[19]

There is no question that in 1527 Wolsey did give Casali powers to
conclude with both the duke and the Marquis of Mantua. Nor is
there any question that Casali corresponded directly with the
cardinal. Henry had not objected at the time, but if an early-modern
king wished to apply retrospective justice, there was little to stop
him.

Yet the Casali did not lack cards to play. There was no great
interest in England in dispensing with their services, and finding a
suitable ambassador for Rome was no easy matter. Some of the
obvious candidates, like John Clerk, who had served there earlier
in the decade, were too close to the queen for comfort. Other
diplomats, experienced in France or Spain, lacked the detailed
knowledge of curia protocol that Gregorio Casali could offer.
Moreover, Gregorio had won over many of the special envoys sent
to Rome in the past few years; not all of them were in the Wolsey
party, and even those who owed their careers to the cardinal were
quickly jumping ship.

A few months before Paolo's arrival in London, Eustace Chapuys
had taken up the post of Imperial ambassador at Henry's court.
Originally from Savoy, he had studied law in Italy, and in the 1520s
worked for the Imperial commander Charles de Bourbon, a position that brought him into the diplomatic service of Charles V.
On 6 December, Chapuys reported that he had met Paolo Casali
in the street. Paolo had promised to call on him but had not yet
done so. 'Whatever his mission may be, he has certainly arrived
under a bad constellation,' wrote Chapuys, and he was right. But
if anyone could smooth things over for the Casali family it was
surely the 'young, virtuous and lovable' Paolo. He found new
friends, among them the Duke of Norfolk, Thomas Howard, Anne

Boleyn's uncle, now establishing himself as England's most influential nobleman. Paolo did a good job of stringing Chapuys along too. On 9 December, their paths crossed at Norfolk's lodgings. Paolo told Chapuys that Gregorio 'had always been sincerely attached to the Imperial service' and, at Gregorio's suggestion, floated the possibility of re-establishing an Anglo-Imperial league. Chapuys thought the latter proposal most implausible, but the former may have been half-true, for when Gregorio had first entered the English service, England and the Empire had been allies. He would not have been alone among Henry's diplomats in favouring an Imperial alliance. Moreover, Gregorio's maternal relatives, the Caffarelli, were long-standing Imperial supporters in the city politics of Rome and the curia.[20]

During Paolo's stay in England, Henry was spending much of his time with Anne Boleyn at Greenwich Palace, eight miles or so downriver from Westminster. Developed by Henry VII at the turn of the century, and perhaps modelled on the palaces of the Burgundian dukes, Greenwich boasted a splendid frontage along the River Thames with a convenient watergate for river travel. A grand edifice of brick surrounding a courtyard, its lack of a moat made clear that this was no defensive castle, but a leisure palace for the new Tudor dynasty. We might picture Paolo Casali being rowed downriver to attend on Henry here, joining in the great feasts and making merry with the royal courtiers. At one such 'splendid' dinner, he joined the Imperial and French ambassadors. The king was, as Chapuys recounted, 'very familiar and jovial with all of us, and never ceased, except when the music of several instruments sounded, to address us on all manner of subjects'. Their common language, most likely, was French. Such occasions presented Paolo with opportunities to meet the king, and the gentlemen and players of the English court. Still only in his twenties, he worked hard to re-establish himself and his family in the changed regime.[21]

Paolo Casali left England on 15 December, having stayed for only about a month. He apparently suggested to Chapuys that he would shortly return, but for whatever reason he did not. During his last days in London, Chapuys had tried in vain to win him over, but his efforts had been stymied by Henry's lavish promises to the Casali family if the divorce could be successfully concluded. 'I have not,' wrote Chapuys, 'the least doubt that both the Nuncio and his brother, Messire Gregoire, will pursue the affair heart and soul; for this king, as I am told, has promised the latter a very fat bishopric in this country in case of success. Should however, the affair turn out otherwise than they expect, it is to be presumed that neither he nor his brother will get any reward.'[22] On the first point, Chapuys was obviously a little confused, for the layman Gregorio would have little use for a bishopric: presumably it was to go to either Giambattista or Paolo, though the latter had not yet taken holy orders. But there was no such confusion in his assessment of the consequences if the Casali failed.

9

A Coronation and a Wedding

As Paolo was arriving in London, two new English envoys were on the road to Italy. Sir Nicholas Carew and Dr Richard Sampson had been sent to meet Charles V, who was due to arrive in Bologna for his coronation by the Pope. Carew, Henry's master of horse and like Sir Francis Bryan a gentleman of the king's privy chamber, was married to Sir Francis's sister Elizabeth. The two men had been close friends for more than a decade, and Carew, like Bryan, would have met Casali when he was first in England back in 1518. Another of the stylish young men about court who surrounded the king, Carew was famed for his skill in jousting. His companion Sampson, dean of the Chapel Royal, was a lawyer trained in Italy and France, with wide experience in diplomacy. He had acted for Henry in the divorce trial hearings. Sending him to the emperor was a provocative move.

Theirs was a leisurely journey, in some ceremonial style, and was memorialised in an account by Thomas Wall, Windsor herald, who accompanied the pair. The vivid description of food, games and spectacle in this chapter is largely his.[1] Carew and Sampson were at Calais on 12 October 1529, but did not arrive in Bologna until 2 December: a total of fifty-two days on the road. This was no post-route dash. They had fine horses to bring with them, gifts from Henry to the princes of Italy, and such steeds were not to be exhausted. Besides, there was business to be done en route. In Paris they took supper with Bryan, now ambassador to France. On 23 October they met King Francis, and the following day they saw his mother, Louise of Savoy, she of the Ladies' Peace. Further along their route, Paolo Casali, on his way to England, joined them for supper at Carew's lodgings. Three days later, on Sunday 31 October, they met Pietro Vanni at La Charité, a town on the Loire. Vanni, returning to England by post, would have been able to give his colleagues the latest news of developments in Rome, and it must have been a sorry tale to hear. Still, the journey cannot have been altogether unpleasant. Along the way, they were presented with wine – the traditional civic gift of welcome – in towns including Boulogne, Abbeville and Nevers.

Gregorio, as usual, acted as fixer. Carew and Sampson sent to him from Lyons for accommodation and assistance; they received a general safe-conduct, special letters to Milan and Pavia, and letters from the Pope to the officials of Piacenza and Parma. Gregorio 'daily doeth us much pleasure in this scarce and desolate country', wrote the ambassadors to Henry. In Turin, the pair met the Duke of Savoy, who sent them 'a goodly present of raw wildfowl that is to wit six capons, four pheasants, twelve woodcocks, twelve partridges, twelve quails and six rabbits'. Wildfowl had a particular cultural significance in Renaissance Italy. For most people, consumption of fowl was thought to be unhealthy: it would heat the blood and lead to the sin of lust. For princes, however, and others who exercised political power, it was a suitably noble food; in Florence, members of the ruling council were required to eat it.[2]

Some miles further on, Carew and Sampson dined with the governor of Piacenza. On their arrival at Reggio nell'Emilia, close to their destination, Basilio de Zobolis, a nephew of Gregorio Casali, put them up at his house, 'preparing very well both our supper and breakfast the next day for us at his cost'. The charges of diplomacy fell not only on Gregorio but on his extended family too. There, Carew and Sampson received from the Duke of Ferrara a gift of twenty capons, twenty partridges, four hares, two Parmesan cheeses, twelve bottles of wine, two barrels of olives, six boxes of marmalade and confectionery, six torches and twenty-four candles of virgin wax. This was ducal one-upmanship in action: the rulers of Savoy and Ferrara vied to outdo one another in their generosity to the representatives of a foreign prince, and, by implication, to that prince himself.

The luxurious presents belied the fact that the Italy through which Carew and Sampson travelled had been shattered by war. Prices, they discovered, had soared, and they wrote to Henry bemoaning the 'importune charges here in these parts'. Their letter described in graphic terms the 'utter destruction' of the land around them. What had once been 'the most goodly country for corn and vines' was now 'desolate'. Only a handful of 'miserable persons' were left to work the fields, and vines had been allowed to grow wild, for there was no one to harvest the grapes. Vigevano, once 'one of the goodly towns of Italy', was 'all destroyed', and likewise Pavia. 'And great pity,' they wrote, 'the children crying about the streets for bread and yea dying for hunger.' The population had been devastated by 'war, famine and pestilence'; Italy would take years to recover. It was not just the Imperialists' fault, the ambassadors added; 'they say that Monsieur de Lautrec destroyed much where as he passed'. This was the way of war in Renaissance Italy. Troops took their food where they could find it: often, the country people starved.[3]

It was in this inauspicious setting that Clement made his entry to the Papal States' second city on 24 October. On 4 November, Charles arrived in grand style to meet him, making his way from the western gate of San Felice past a series of specially constructed triumphal arches, their imagery evoking the ancient emperors of Rome. For the victors in the Italian war, if not for the rest, this would be a feast of colour and spectacle.[4] A city of splendid red brick, Bologna was known as 'Boulogne la Grasse' – Fat Bologna – bloated with mercantile riches to fill the papal coffers. Its palaces were dressed with terracotta friezes, while the Asinelli and Garisenda towers teetered above the centre of the city, the smaller of the pair looking as if it might topple at any moment, as it does to this day. The huge unfinished basilica of San Petronio stood in the central square, commemorating the city's first bishop, a man of the fifth century.

Carew and Sampson arrived in Bologna on Thursday 2 December 1529. Gregorio met them outside the city walls with a company of thirty to forty of his friends and kinsmen. Bryan and Vanni, arriving in Rome some months before, had had a welcome from just nine or ten gentlemen: the prestige of the coronation embassy

1. The brutality of the Sack of Rome is apparent in the foreground of this near-contemporary image, which also depicts some of the city's most famous landmarks.

2. This miniature shows Henry VIII aged 35 and can therefore be dated to 1526 or 1527.

3. Catherine of Aragon was six years her husband's senior. She turned forty in December 1525, after which her prospects of bearing a male heir looked increasingly remote.

4. Giulio de' Medici was elected Pope in the conclave of 1523 and took the name Clement VII.

5. Ferry Carondelet, an ambassador for the Holy Roman Emperor at the papal court, wears the fine clothes expected of sixteenth-century diplomats.

6. This late sixteenth-century portrait of Anne Boleyn is a copy of an earlier original.

7. The Rocca Pallavicino-Casali, Monticelli d'Ongina. Through his marriage to Livia Pallavicino, Gregorio Casali gained access to strategically important property in the Po Valley.

8. This portrait of Charles V was commissioned by his brother Ferdinand during Charles' 1532 visit to Bologna.

9. The Casali family commissioned this painting from Filippino Lippi.
The Casali coat of arms is depicted on the stonework to the top right.

15

POPVLORVM ORATORES

10. A group of diplomats on horseback portrayed in a festival book
commemorating the procession after Charles V's coronation in Bologna.

is immediately apparent. Such out-of-town welcomes were a tradition harking back to classical times, and in better days were notorious as an opportunity for competitive splendour, as ambassadors vied to show off their trains. When four Venetian ambassadors had arrived in Rome in 1492, they had brought with them two hundred horses, or thereabouts, and eighty pack-saddles. That was pure ostentation: eighty or so horses was a more usual number.[5] As Carew and Sampson approached the city gates, the emperor's guard lined up, 'well horsed and appointed', to greet them; as they continued through the colonnaded streets, yet more gentlemen welcomed them. Gregorio ordered 'a plenteous supper', at which they were joined by Monsieur du Prat, great chamberlain to the emperor, Benedetto Accolti, Cardinal of Ravenna, and another dozen gentlemen. During supper they were entertained by trumpeters and other minstrels, dancers, and 'diverse others to pass the time'.

The Casali house, where this entertaining went on, was located in the centre of Bologna, on the corner of Via Castiglione and what is now Via Farini, just around the corner from San Petronio.[6] Although the palazzo no longer survives, the location of the Casali cross (now displayed in San Petronio) is still marked by a plaque on Via Farini, just over the road. The family owned most of the block, renting out the smaller properties. Their palace was, in the words of one contemporary, most beautiful; it was also eminently suitable for entertaining. A substantial building arranged around a courtyard, its loggia was decorated with fifteen painted coats of arms, and would have been an ideal location for dining, though not during Carew and Sampson's stay: the Bologna winter can be unpleasantly chilly. Its ground-floor rooms provided both accommodation for guests and space for business encounters, and here our chief ambassador might have slept in a bed hung with taffeta drapes in striking green, red or yellow, with contrasting lining. Devotional images of the Virgin and saints kept watch over the bedchambers; typically, such artworks would be hung above doorways. There were some 'profane' paintings in the house, too. One, in the 'French style', featured 'a nude woman in the middle and other figures in a bath', perhaps the goddess Diana or the biblical temptress Bathsheba at her toilette.

The main hall, where the diplomatic banquets would have taken place, was upstairs on the *piano nobile*, and equipped with a pulley system to raise water from the lower storey. The furnishings throughout were lavish, showing a cosmopolitan taste. In line with convention, the family arms were liberally displayed around the house. Such display – of coats of arms, prestigious gilded artworks, secular art and exotic objects – was central to establishing social status. Also notable is the existence of a chapel in the family home. Laymen required a special licence to set up a private chapel, and the fact that the previous generation of the Casali had been able to do so points eloquently to their standing in the city. With images of the Virgin Mary and St Bernardine, and a Flemish altarpiece of the Virgin Mary and the three Magi, in a frame of fine gold, the chapel was well-equipped. The ambassadors may have heard Mass there.

On their first full day in town, Friday 3 December, Carew and Sampson went to meet the emperor and the Pope. There is no record of what was said, but most likely it was nothing more than an exchange of pleasantries. Protocol dictated that serious discussions wait for another day. On Saturday 4 December, the ambassadors went out to see the *jeu de cannes*, an eccentric game fought on horseback between two teams of Spanish cavaliers dressed in elaborate Moorish costumes, with heart-shaped shields covered in taffeta. Their masterful horsemanship in the crowded central piazza could be observed by the emperor from the Palazzo Comunale. The game itself took the form of a fight with sticks, which were twirled then thrown at opponents. The canes were hung with golden tassels and had pennants at the top, and the sight of dozens of them thrown into the air – to the accompaniment of music from trumpets, fifes and drums – must have been striking. One topped the roof of the Palazzo Comunale before falling into the courtyard.

On Sunday, the assembled diplomats attended Mass at the Church of San Domenico. The saint himself, founder of the Dominican Order, had been buried there, his marble sepulchre decorated by such luminaries of medieval art as Pisano and later adorned with statuettes, some by the young Michelangelo. Just to the right of the high altar, the gathering crowd would have seen the Casali family chapel, and inside it *The Mystical Marriage of Saint Catherine*, commissioned around 1500 by Gregorio's uncles Francesco and Catellano, the latter a Dominican himself, from Filippino Lippi, a pupil of Botticelli (Plate 9). Still dominating the chapel today, it features the Casali family arms in the decoration towards its top right corner.

Such a grand ceremonial occasion as an Imperial coronation was bound to be an opportunity for some diplomatic squabbling over precedence, for its every aspect was governed by detailed protocols dictating which prince outranked which other. Contesting this princely pecking order had always been part of the day-to-day diplomatic routine. The papal master of ceremonies, Biagio Martinelli, presided over affairs, procuring order amid the jostling for power as envoys demanded he bend this or that rule, or grant this or that favour. A month earlier, he had been dispatched by Clement to remind the King of Hungary's envoy that while at the Imperial court Hungarian representatives might precede the English, at the papal court it was the other way about. (The King of Hungary under discussion was Ferdinand Habsburg, rather than his rival John Szapolyai.) Martinelli resented having to worry about this when he had plenty of other things to do, but eventually he persuaded the Hungarian envoy to concede, on the rather technical basis that Henry VIII claimed the kingdom of France (the English had, after all, ruled a swathe of that country in the previous century) and that therefore the Hungarians would be giving way to the French, about whose precedence there was no argument. Such were the manoeuvrings of the curia's ritual world.[7]

The Sunday of the San Domenico Mass was also the occasion for the start of a joust, hosted by twenty-four gentlemen of Bologna against all comers. Gregorio's cousin Andrea had a track record in jousting, having come a respectable second in a city tournament in 1514, but whether he took part on this occasion is not recorded. Carew – a star jouster of Henry's court – probably did not participate either, but one of his attendants, a certain Master Parker,

squire of the king's stable, did enter the lists. He 'did run at the
tilt four courses and broke two spears and gave one attaint', that
is, one blow to a rival. Parker's principal job on the embassy,
however, was to see to the horses that Henry had sent with Carew
for distribution as gifts, notably to the Marquis of Mantua. On
looking them over, however, Gregorio Casali was unimpressed. Of
those supplied, he wrote to the marquis, 'I find none appropriate
for Your Excellency save for a bay gelding, which runs very well.'
He added that Henry, who amid his matrimonial troubles still had
time for racing, had given his ambassador 'the hottest commission
ever' to find Barbary horses; Gregorio hoped that, should his
colleague make it to Mantua, the marquis would 'have ready those
two Barbary horses about which you spoke to me'.[8]

On the same day he penned that letter, Monday 6 December,
Gregorio Casali concluded the second stage of his marriage to Livia
Pallavicino, signing the marriage contract. Given the expense of
hosting an embassy during the coronation celebrations, it must
have been a relief to him to know that a small fortune was in the
offing. Perhaps his improved prospects gave Gregorio a reason to
indulge in some particularly lavish entertaining, for the following
evening Sir Nicholas Carew hosted a grand diplomatic dinner at
the Casali palazzo. The affair was not entirely a success. Although,
as the embassy herald recorded, it was a 'sumptuous supper', 'many
lords and gentlemen of the Emperor's . . . for great business could
not come'. Perhaps that was their way of communicating displeasure
at Henry's treatment of his queen. The English ambassadors had
to settle for their counterparts from France and Hungary, along
with 'diverse Italian noblemen', and fourteen 'ladies of the town',
maybe Gregorio's relatives; his cousins had married well into local
patrician families like the Lupari, Sampiero, Gozzadini and
Aldrovandi. They enjoyed a twelve-course dinner featuring 'all
manner of wildfowl possible to be gotten' and entertainment until
past midnight. 'And before the said supper,' wrote Thomas Wall,
'during the same, and especially after supper there was playing on
diverse instruments as sackbuts [a predecessor of the trombone],
cornets, viols, crooked pipes [crumhorns], virginals, with also men
and children singing. And thus after supper they danced, with

BRITISH LIBRARY

Using our Reading Rooms

Discover the world's knowledge

Important information about our services

- Only general reference works and current science and business collections are available on open shelves in the Reading Rooms
- Most items in the Library's collection are kept in storage. Delivery of items from storage areas to Reading Rooms normally takes between 70 minutes (onsite) and 48+ hours (offsite) depending on where they are held
- Items stored onsite must be requested before 16.00 for delivery the same day
- You cannot borrow items from any of our Reading Rooms
- You can use the Library's free WiFi service throughout the St Pancras building and outside on the Piazza and Terrace
- Most Reading Rooms have self-service photocopiers and microfilm reader printers which are operated on an account based system. An account is automatically created when you log in at a copier, printer or cash terminal. Some Reading Rooms have dedicated Copying Service Desks, for assisted copying, and a self-help Digital Scanning Service is now available. There are network printers in all the Reading Rooms and printing can be purchased in the same way as photocopies.

Which Reading Room?

Whilst you can consult the majority of our collections from most Reading Rooms, it helps to use the appropriate area for your research. Staff will be happy to advise you which Reading Room you should use.

- Use the **Humanities** Reading Rooms for history, literature, art and culture; in print and online
- Explore **Manuscripts**, **Rare Books & Music** and **Maps** in their own dedicated Reading Rooms
- The **Asian & African Studies** Reading Room contains a wide range of material in western and oriental languages, with access to online resources and collections of prints, drawings and photographs
- Study international law, economics, management and politics in our **Social Sciences** Reading Room
- Our **Science** Reading Rooms provide easy access to current literature on all aspects of science, technology and medicine, including journals, books, conference papers and online databases
- Experience **Sound Archive** recordings in the special sound and vision units, or listen to popular sounds at the **SoundServer** desks in Humanities – floor 2
- For anyone wanting to develop their research into a commercial proposition, our **Business & IP Centre** provides free access to patents, market research reports, directories, industry, financial and company reports, and a range of online databases.

other pastimes, as with morris dancers and men that leaped sovereignly.'

As his diplomats partied, Henry VIII mulled over Paolo Casali's advice on the divorce. Casali had told the king that Cardinal Alessandro Farnese thought that Charles could be persuaded to compromise. Farnese, a member of an illustrious Roman family and the future Pope Paul III, was friendly to the Casali; his secretary was Latino Giovenale de' Manetti, Livia Pallavicino's guardian. Henry believed that the cardinal's offer had 'good likelihood of some fruit and effect to ensue thereof'. In a letter to Carew and Sampson, he expressed the optimistic opinion that they might be able to talk the emperor into agreeing to a settlement whereby Catherine would enter a religious house. He went on, 'what with the Turks on the one side and states of Italy combining themselves against him on the other [Charles] had never so much need of our amity as he now hath at this present time'. The Italian states, however, were doing nothing of the sort. With the exception of Florence, they were preparing to make their peace. Henry's hopes for a diplomatic settlement were destined to be dashed.[9]

The cosy relationship between Clement and Charles was evident to every visitor. The pair had adjoining chambers in what is now Bologna's town hall, the Palazzo Comunale, next door to San Petronio on the city's main square. Girolamo Ghinucci wrote from Bologna that only a single wall divided the two apartments, and that a door in it enabled them to visit each other with ease. Their proximity conveyed potently their determination to show unity, and demonstrated papal acceptance of Charles's contrition for the Sack of Rome. At stake in Clement's meetings with the emperor was the chance to restore Medici rule in Florence. Not just restore, in fact, but inaugurate, for in past times the family had governed only as the city's leading oligarchs, maintaining the trappings of republican government. Now, they might be its dukes. Clement's candidate for the throne was Alessandro de' Medici, perhaps his own bastard son, though more likely the illegitimate offspring of a Medici cousin, Lorenzo II, Duke of Urbino. Known as 'il Moro' – the Moor – Alessandro was the child of a maid, Simonetta da Colle Vecchio, very likely African, who worked in the Medici household. He was a rare black prince in Renaissance Europe.[10]

Back in England, in the aftermath of Wolsey's fall, Anne Boleyn and her family were cementing their ascendancy at court. On 8 December 1529, her father Thomas was created Earl of Wiltshire. In Bologna, amid the rounds of feasting and entertaining, the months running up to the coronation were interspersed with intriguing meetings with the emperor. The English archives for this period are sparse; perhaps record-keeping suffered in the months immediately following Wolsey's removal from office. Thomas Wall's account maintains a studied secrecy on the English diplomats' discussions with Charles: not a hint of their contents finds its way into the leaves of his manuscript. And his textbook discretion (for diplomatic secretaries were always suspects when information leaked) leaves the tenor of Carew and Sampson's talks with the emperor a mystery. Eustace Chapuys was confident that Carew was a secret supporter of Queen Catherine, who had told him that Sir Nicholas was 'very affectionately inclined' towards her. How far that coloured Carew's discussions in Bologna – whether with Charles or with his fellow diplomats – is impossible to know. A second-hand report would later claim that certain of the king's ambassadors at Bologna advised Giambattista Casali 'to hinder and trouble these the king's causes, as much as he might'. William Benet was accused of being one of those who secretly opposed the king. Perhaps Carew was too.[11]

On 10 and 11 December, there were further meetings between the English ambassadors and the emperor, and on Sunday 12th another round of the *jeu de cannes*, this time to celebrate the birth of Charles's son. It was held in the town marketplace and featured a hundred Spaniards on 'light genettes' – small Spanish horses – fifty in white, yellow and black, and fifty in white, yellow and blue, all damask and taffeta. 'It was a goodly sight and much good sport,' wrote Thomas Wall. On the afternoon of Friday 17 December, the ambassadors 'rode about in the town a sporting'. The young men who formed embassy entourages could be notoriously badly behaved on such occasions, but this time there were no reports of trouble. Ten years earlier, however, Carew and Bryan had conducted themselves so outrageously on a mission to France (riding through Paris with King Francis hurling eggs, stones and other missiles at the locals) that they provided Wolsey with an excuse to expel them from court (though they soon returned). In 1538, a party of young men (five under nineteen and seven 'slightly over') accompanying Stephen Gardiner on embassy to France proved so rowdy that the French complained.[12]

On 20 December, the English ambassadors once again met the emperor, and on Christmas Eve Charles sent for them to attend on him at evensong. It was traditional to fast, so they would not eat until midnight. They paraded to church: the gentlemen and noblemen first, 'in good order', the Pope's cross, then twenty-four cardinals, 'all arrayed in red camlet, furred with miniver'. Gregorio carried the train of the papal cope, a highly symbolic act, for ambassadors' performance of such duties was a demonstration of their princes' loyalty to the pontiff. The Pope sat to the right of the altar, the emperor before him on a stool equipped with cloth-of-gold cushions. It was a spectacular display: bishops in their copes and white satin mitres, cardinals in cloth of gold or richly embroidered tissue. At the close of the service, it fell to the Duke of Milan to bear Clement's train as the Pope processed from the church.

On Christmas Day, the assembled ambassadors gathered once again to attend Clement – a point Gregorio did not neglect to mention in his dispatches.[13] Into the great basilica of San Petronio crowded papal officials in scarlet, cardinals in rich cloth of gold with mitres of white damask, and the Pope himself, in a sedan chair of crimson velvet borne on the shoulders of eight attendants. Clement wore a cope covered in pearls and a tiara 'of gold and stones right oriental'. Six further attendants held a canopy above him. Perhaps the tiara was less than comfortable, for at some point during the ceremony it was replaced by a mitre, 'very rich of gold-smith's work', and then again with a mitre of mere 'plain cloth of gold', before – at the close of the ceremony – the tiara again. As the Mass played out, a series of noblemen came forward to offer water for the Pope to wash his hands. Like carrying the cope, this was another intimate service that conveyed their fealty to the pontiff. It also made emphatically clear the pecking order at court, for the noblemen served in reverse order of precedence: first a Spanish marquis, second Alessandro de' Medici, the man Clement hoped would rule Florence, third the Duke of Milan, and finally the emperor himself.

The social round continued. On 28 December, Carew joined the Casali brothers' old friend Ercole Gonzaga, Cardinal of Mantua, for dinner; two days later, Cardinal Salviati, papal legate to France and son of the influential secretary Jacopo, entertained the English. On 2 January, Carew had Ercole Gonzaga and Benedetto Accolti to dinner; on 5 January, the ambassadors met the Pope; on 8 January and then again on the 11th, they hosted the Cardinal of Mantua. Like Sir Francis Bryan, Carew had evidently hit it off with the hunting-mad Gonzaga.

On 1 January, peace was proclaimed between the emperor and all of Italy except the Republic of Florence, besieged now for more than two months by Imperial troops under the command of Philibert de Châlon, Prince of Orange. On the very same day, Gregorio announced that due to 'certain events that have arisen', Carew had been forced to delay a planned trip to Mantua to present Henry's gift horse to the marquis, sending his servant Parker – he of the jousting – instead. Were negotiations with Pope and emperor progressing better than expected? Or worse? Reports persisted in Italy that Henry was planning to break with Rome – rumours fuelled by Imperial reports from London, and probably inflamed by English diplomatic hard-talk. On 8 January, the Mantuan ambassador Francesco Gonzaga wrote: 'His Majesty has let it be known that if and when the Pope refuses to declare that [the queen] is not his wife, he plans to withdraw the obedience of that Island from the Holy See; nor will he come any more to Rome for the expedition of benefices or any spiritual matter. It's almost as if he's threatening to join the Lutherans.' As the story spread, it grew like a Chinese whisper. The Ferrarese ambassador to Venice wrote dramatically on 13 January: 'In this second hour of the night, news was brought to my house that the King of England and all His Majesty's dominions have converted to the faith of Martin Luther.'[14]

Gonzaga, however, was conflating two propositions. Henry

would indeed shortly propose that English affairs – which included his marriage – should be subject to English jurisdiction. That did not imply that he was about to throw his lot in with reformed religion. In terms of his personal beliefs, the king was quite orthodox. He thought Luther a heretic, and in November 1529 had told Chapuys so. The reformer, he said, should have stuck to criticising the 'vices, abuses, and errors of the clergy', instead of attacking the sacraments of the Church'. Had he done so, Henry would have defended him. But in fact the king maintained a ban on Lutheran books, issuing a proclamation in May 1530 that required crown officials to take an oath to stamp out the heresy.[15]

On 17 January, the ambassadors dined with Campeggio, who had arrived a few days earlier from England. After the months of wrangling in London, a return to his home town must have been a palpable relief. One can imagine he put aside diplomatic discretion and told some colourful tales. If Clement had turned the air blue in frustration with Henry, Campeggio had as much, if not more, reason to curse the English king. And he could also report an important turn in Henry's political approach: to anti-clericalism. In November 1529, Henry had called the Parliament that would come to be known as the 'Reformation Parliament'. In its first session, it had passed a string of measures circumscribing church power, restricting traditional taxes, prohibiting clerical engagement in trade and farming, and clamping down on non-residence and 'pluralism' – the practice of holding more than one benefice. He had played on lay hostility to the Church to do so, on the feeling of the Commons, as the Tudor chronicler Edward Hall put it, that 'the spirituality [clergy] had before time grievously oppressed them, both contrary to the law of the realm and contrary to all right'. Indeed, had the king wished, the Commons would happily have gone rather further in their campaign against the Church. But Henry's ambassadors were keen to reassure allies like Francis I that the king's activities were not intended as an attack on papal authority, where such authority was legitimate. As with Wolsey's disgrace, it was all part of a strategy to crank up the pressure on Clement.[16]

On 30 January, Livia Pallavicino arrived from Venice and Gregorio

Casali's marriage was finally solemnised. 'There was at supper,' wrote Thomas Wall, 'great feasting and many ladies and gentle-women.' Among them may have been Isabella d'Este, who was in Bologna at the time and had attended the wedding of Gregorio's sister in Rome four years earlier. Though we have no description of Gregorio and Livia's celebrations, an account of the sister's wedding by Francesco Gonzaga hints at how they might have looked: a grand dinner with the diplomatic corps in attendance, dancing both before and after the lavish meal, with the accompani-ment of tambourines, flutes and harp. Perhaps the bride wore some of the rich jewels in the family collection: gold necklaces and bracelets garnished with pearls, diamonds and rubies.[17]

What Livia made of her new life we can only speculate. Aged over twenty-one, by the standards of the day she was old to marry, but she would have grown up to expect an arranged match such as this. Her upbringing had been far from simple, and the family travails can hardly have been comforting. Now she had brought to her marriage a substantial and politically sensitive inheritance that many of her relatives wanted to take away. Perhaps she rose to the challenge of the dispute. Perhaps she found it a burdensome responsibility.

Two days after the wedding, on 1 February, Sir Nicholas Carew and Richard Sampson took their leave of the emperor. They were rewarded in the traditional manner with presents of lavish gold chains. Carew's weighed two thousand ducats, while Sampson's was half that weight. Such gifts could easily be exchanged for money if necessary, or individual links removed and sold. Carew may have cashed in his chain, for a list of royal plate made up three years later records his sale to the king of a 'great chain of gold' with a hundred and one links. Their herald and secretary, Thomas Wall, was presented with a hundred crowns of Venice. On 7 February, the ambassadors left Bologna. It was a precipitate depar-ture, two weeks in advance of Charles's coronation. It had not been the intention that they should stay a long time, but that they did not remain for the coronation smacks of a deliberate snub. Casali, Ghinucci and Benet did stay, but they were accredited to the Pope, not the emperor.[18]

It is possible that Carew and Sampson were due to be replaced in time for the coronation by a new group of ambassadors, led by Anne Boleyn's father, which left London with a commission dated 21 January.[19] But for travel across the Alps in winter that was cutting it very fine, and the English must have known it. Formally, the Boleyn embassy's commission was to treat for a general peace with the Pope, emperor, kings of France, Portugal, Poland, Denmark, Scotland, Doge of Venice and dukes of Milan and Ferrara. Henry accredited not only Thomas Boleyn but also John Stokesley, Edward Lee and William Benet. The reality of their mission, however, is illustrated by the fact that among their entourage was one Thomas Cranmer, a leading light in Henry's new strategy for the divorce, of whom and which more later. Even as they were departing, the Imperial ambassador in London, Eustace Chapuys, was dispatching Catherine's pleas for support to the emperor. 'The treatment of the Queen,' he wrote, 'is worse than ever. The King keeps away from her as much as possible; he is always here with the Lady [Anne], and the Queen away at Richmond. [. . .] He has renewed his attempts to persuade her to become a nun, but is wasting his time, for she will never consent. The continual trouble and annoyance which she undergoes constrain her to persevere in importuning Your Majesty, both by her own letters and by mine; nor will she cease to do so, until her suit is brought to a final conclusion.' Catherine was in need of Charles's support, and was anxious that her nephew not abandon her in the face of a greater political interest – an alliance against the sultan, at which Henry had hinted in his letter to Carew and Sampson.[20]

The first part of Charles's coronation was scheduled for 22 February 1530, the second for the 24th. That would be his thirtieth birthday and the fifth anniversary of the Battle of Pavia, when Imperial forces had routed the French and captured King Francis. The basilica of San Petronio had been especially prepared for the occasion, and temporary chapels set up to replace those altars that would have been used had the event taken place in the traditional venue of St Peter's in Rome.[21] In the first chapel on the left, that of San Abbondio, with its century-old frescoes of Christ's triumph over the synagogue and the Tree of Good and Evil, Charles donned

the Imperial mantle before his crowning. The next chapel was that
of the Three Kings, where on the left a graphic fresco of Hell
includes a rarity of church iconography: the image of a damned
Mohammed, a reminder to the assembled Christians of their
ongoing battle with the infidel. As with the rest of Charles's stay
in Bologna, the coronation was a spectacular occasion. (Plate 10
shows ambassadors in the procession that followed.) The crowds
were garbed in satin, velvet, damask and fine linen, the participants
in cloth of silver and gold. By submitting to the ritual of anoint-
ment, oration, prayer and coronation, the emperor acknowledged
the very papal authority that Henry VIII was now beginning to
question.

The new English embassy had not yet arrived, but Gregorio
hoped that the emperor, due to leave on 17 March, would wait for
them. On 12 March he expected the ambassadors to arrive on the
13th or 14th, but it was the 19th before they finally turned up. Unlike
Carew and Sampson, Thomas Boleyn and his party did not enjoy
a spectacular welcome. The papal master of ceremonies, Biagio
Martinelli, commented that they arrived 'without any honour'. He
was referring to the lack of ceremony on their entrance, but that
was surely a reflection of the increasingly strained relations between
England and the papacy. Clement granted them an audience, but
his attitude is evident from the fact that on 23 March he wrote to
Charles V asking what answer he would like to be given. Charles,
in turn, refused to discuss the divorce with Boleyn, insisting that
it should be left to the legal process.[22]

Yet even amid the English troubles, Gregorio Casali did not
neglect his family interests. The latest beneficiary of his diplomatic
contacts was a young relative – the Italian term 'nepote' covers a
variety of relationships – Ludovico Crescenzi, a connection of his
sister Giovanna's second husband. Ludovico made his way into the
service of Federico Gonzaga, formerly Marquis and now, with
Imperial patronage, raised to the station of Duke of Mantua.[23]

10

The Scholar Croke Cries Foul

Although the more excitable members of the diplomatic corps believed that England was about to break with Rome, the threats to do so – however convincingly conveyed by Henry's ambassadors – were not yet put into practice. Domestic politics precluded a quick schism: neither clergy nor nobility were convinced of the need for it. And so, as Carew and Sampson pursued discussions with the emperor, the English began another, parallel, strategy for the divorce: a quest for academic opinion in support of Henry's position. The authorship of the new strategy is widely credited to Thomas Cranmer, a Cambridge don who had already served Henry as a junior diplomat. Some time in the late summer or autumn of 1529, he suggested that rather than focus his efforts on Rome, the king might seek the support of university theologians. His idea caught the attention first of Stephen Gardiner and Edward Fox, and subsequently of the king himself.[1]

There had long been two arguments for Henry's divorce. The first was fairly typical as a means to secure a papal verdict of nullity, and focused on the technical inadequacy of the papal bull granting Henry dispensation to marry his brother Arthur's widow. To date, on Wolsey's instruction, his diplomats had emphasised this first problem. The second argument related to the Biblical text on which Henry's concern for the validity of his marriage – his 'Levitical scruple' – was founded. This was the prohibition in Leviticus against marriage to a brother's wife. Chapter 18, verse 16 reads, 'Thou shalt not uncover the nakedness of thy brother's wife: it is thy brother's nakedness'; a further section (chapter 20, verse 21) suggests that a man who does so will remain childless

(Henry's scholars re-interpreted this as 'have no sons'). Matters were complicated by the seemingly contradictory injunction in Deuteronomy, chapter 25, verse 5, which required that 'When brethren dwell together, and one of them dieth without children, the wife of the deceased shall not marry to another: but his brother shall take her and raise up seed for his brother.' The essential question for Henry's envoys as they embarked on the new campaign was whether the Pope could dispense from the Levitical prohibition. Questioning papal power to dispense, however, implied a challenge to the authority of Rome. With hindsight, this was the beginning of English Reformation diplomacy. For our man in Rome, it would have been a surprising turn, but he may not have foreseen that it presaged an all-out break with the papacy; indeed Henry himself did not yet conceive of it that way. It was equally possible (and perhaps more palatable) for the king and his diplomats to continue in the belief that the quest for opinions was a strategy to increase the pressure on Clement: more bravado, more 'bold words'.[2]

The leading universities of Italy were those of Bologna – famed for its legal scholarship and the alma mater of both Giambattista Casali and William Benet – and Padua. It was to these that the ambassadors now turned their attention. The former, founded late in the twelfth century, was in terms of faculty the largest in Italy: in the 1520s, about half of its hundred professors taught law. The latter had suffered badly in the aftermath of a city rebellion against Venice in 1509, but was gradually recovering; still, its law professors were accustomed to provide – for a fee – advice to foreign princes on legal questions of import.[3] And so our story moves from the grandeur of Bologna's imperial ceremony to a world of universities, scholars, archives and libraries. The campaign for Henry's divorce became a quest for patristic justification and for legal precedents that might be brought to bear on the case. Alongside soliciting opinions from university faculties, the king's agents turned to the writings of the church fathers, men like Saints Basil and Gregory, who back in the fourth century had joined in the furious debates as the numerous Christian factions thrashed out an orthodox religion. These men had written in their native tongue, Greek. Experts on the Old Testament were in demand too, and here Henry's agents sought out Jewish theologians, learned in Hebrew, who might shed light on the nuances of scripture. Venice, with its sizeable Jewish and Greek communities and scholarly connections, was an obvious starting point.

While Gregorio stayed on in Bologna, it fell to his brother Giambattista to facilitate business in Venice and nearby Padua. Once again, the Casali family consortium came into its own. Giambattista was probably the elder of the two brothers, although he had been the second-born son. The eldest Casali brother, Girolamo, had died in 1510, still in his teens. Of Giambattista's childhood we know little, but he attended university in Bologna, graduated in 1519 and became an apostolic protonotary (a high-ranking curia official) while still in his early twenties. In January 1525, he went to England as papal nuncio. Later the same year, shortly after Gregorio was made English ambassador to Rome, he became England's ambassador to Venice, arriving there on 26 January 1526, 'clad in a rochet and purple cope', with an entourage of twelve, soon to increase to eighteen. At first he took lodgings at San Giorgio Maggiore, but by mid-1528 he was staying in Ca' Dandolo, a grand house on the waterfront near St Mark's, now the Hotel Danieli. The Venetian diarist Marin Sanuto, who for years penned and copied lively, if not always accurate, reports of political affairs in the city, was unimpressed with Giambattista's diplomatic debut, observing that he was 'very inept and not prac-tised in statesmanship'. But that had been five years earlier, and in the meantime Giambattista had won himself friends in the ruling circles of Venice. Those friends, however, were not univer-sally favourable to Henry VIII's divorce.[4]

Dispatched to join the Casali brothers were Richard Croke, an unofficial agent, who arrived in Bologna in December 1529, and John Stokesley, accredited as ambassador to the emperor on 21 January 1530, as one of the Boleyn mission. Both were eminently well-qualified for the task at hand. Stokesley had attracted the praise of England's leading scholars for his learning, had studied in Rome before, and was skilled in Latin, Greek and Hebrew. Now in his fifties, he had held a string of royal offices and would soon become

Bishop of London. Croke, somewhat younger than his colleague, but at forty-one still at least ten years Gregorio Casali's senior, had an international reputation as a scholar of Greek, which he taught at Leipzig and Cambridge. He had also lectured in theology. But while Stokesley had spent enough time at court to appreciate the niceties of political manoeuvring, Croke was anything but a diplomat.[5]

There now began a sorry comic tale of embassy politics, for Richard Croke proved to be the colleague from hell. He left a letter book full of vitriol, much of it aimed at Giambattista and his brothers (though he fell out with almost all his fellows during his months in Italy), a collection that puts the historian in something of a quandary. How far should one credit correspondence that often reads as paranoid rambling? Is there a grain of truth, sometimes, in what Croke himself described as his 'long and tedious loquacity'?[6] Given that his letters are the main source for this period of the diplomacy, it seems foolish to ignore them altogether, but we need to take care.

As the diplomacy had played out in Rome, back in England Henry's advisers had put together a series of manuscript 'king's books'. Collections of arguments for the divorce, they included much of the material that finally appeared in 1531 in the collection of European university opinions on the case known as the *Censurae*. John Stokesley had been one of the major contributors. The ambassadors showed these volumes to those from whom they requested opinions, but guarded them jealously for fear that with advance sight of Henry's arguments, Catherine's lawyers would be better able to refute them. Needless to say, the Imperial ambassadors devoted considerable energy to getting their hands on the texts. Such was the apprehension about spying that Henry's envoys were even wary of sharing the books with one another. Girolamo Ghinucci was most frustrated to discover that Richard Sampson had not brought a copy to Bologna, and complained that although he had heard that Paolo Casali had brought one back from England, he was refusing to let it out of his sight. It was an inharmonious and inauspicious start to Henry's campaign for the Italian universities.[7]

Amid the discord, Richard Croke arrived in Bologna on 19 December 1529, with the summit meeting of Clement and Charles still in full swing. His journey had been taxing, and he was horrified at the cost of living, which, at more than three ducats a day, was in no way covered by the money he had been supplied. Unofficial agents like Croke did not enjoy the stipends allocated to ambassadors, most of whom received a daily allowance of 26s. 8d (closer to six ducats). Gregorio Casali got forty shillings a day, which amounted to eight or nine ducats. Croke had two cover stories. Sometimes he pretended to be a Flemish merchant enquiring on behalf of a friend with a marital quandary that by coincidence bore remarkable similarities to that of the King of England. On other occasions he claimed to be collecting books for an English ecclesiastical library.[8] Given the publicity surrounding Henry's cause, it seems highly unlikely that he could have sustained either false identity for long. That did not stop him trying.

Croke arrived in Venice in January. The houses of the lagoon city, then as now, were accessible only by boat, their facades elaborately decorated, glistering in the winter sun or hazy behind the fog, their windows of prized local glass dramatic above the canals. The more grandiose residences boasted private watergates from which residents could be ferried to and fro. Croke took accommodation separately from Giambattista Casali, the better to conceal his activities from the authorities. For official liaison, however, he was dependent on his colleague. His target was the library of St Mark's cathedral and its rich collection of patristic manuscripts, and we might imagine him making his way past the extravagance of domes, gilding and glitzy mosaics in his book-collector persona, passing by the Palazzo Ducale with its double colonnade and pink-and-white facade glimmering against the water. Croke's house, he admitted to Stokesley, was not as elegant as Casali's, but it was more suitable for transacting the king's business. Secrecy was paramount: when the agent invited his colleague to visit, he proposed discussions in the gardens, churches and porticoes of Venice, beautiful but anonymous places away from prying eyes and listening ears of the sort that four years earlier had exposed Gregorio's secret talks with the French.[9]

Within days of arriving in Venice, Croke evinced a dislike for the Casali family. In a letter of 18 January, he denounced Giambattista Casali's 'pride and fraud', fanning the flames of the rivalry between the Ghinucci and Casali families.[10] The two clans contended for the status of preferred Italian *consorteria* at Henry's court, each offering a network of agents on the peninsula to serve the king. Girolamo Ghinucci held the bishopric of Worcester, a more generous reward than the Casali had from the English; he was Giambattista Casali's most prominent rival for an English-sponsored cardinal's hat, and his reappointment to Rome after a spell with the emperor in Spain might well have been perceived as a slight to Gregorio. Moreover, Ghinucci held the papal office of Auditor of the Camera Apostolica (the papal treasury), and thus wielded considerable influence in the dispute over Livia Pallavicino's inheritance, influence that he could use for or against the Casali. Perhaps it suited the English to maintain competing Italian agents, for then one could always be employed to spy on the other. It was part of the logic of dispatching ambassadors in pairs that co-envoys could each be tasked with monitoring the other.

On 11 February, Ghinucci wrote a diplomatic reply to Croke's stream of correspondence. He regretted Giambattista's unhelpfulness, but advised Croke to avoid arguing with him. He did, however, fuel Croke's suspicions by suggesting that Casali had lied to him about a particular letter in Greek that Croke was seeking. Croke was convinced that Giambattista was sabotaging his efforts. It was Casali's fault, he wrote, that he could not get a notary to endorse a transcription of a letter by Diodorus of Tarsus, a fourth-century theologian, that disapproved of a man marrying two sisters. (Only with notarial authentication were copies of documents legally valid.) Croke wrote repeatedly to his friends in England, telling them to trust only in Ghinucci and his brother. Casali, he claimed, was secretly hindering the king's cause, or even betraying it, by saying that Henry sought the divorce only because of his 'love for a girl'. Moreover, Casali had told those Croke sought to win over that the people of England were opposed to their king. Day by day his indignant tone rose. By 21 February, he was writing furiously to Stephen Gardiner that even three sheets of paper would not suffice to detail Casali's 'daily frauds'. Such was Croke's paranoia that he feared 'poison, or the dagger' and claimed to John Stokesley that 'the king's honour has been all but prostituted by these Casalis'. In Giambattista's defence, Croke's antics were probably enough to inspire even the mildest of men to threats, and it is not hard to conceive that in an intemperate moment he might have vowed to 'murder that Croke' with poison, dagger, or whatever blunt instrument came to hand.[11]

One major problem confronted Henry's diplomats in Italy as they embarked on their new tasks. After years of war, the Italian powers – with the exception of Florence – were now at peace. But it was a victor's peace, and the victor was Charles V, Holy Roman Emperor. No one wanted to test his patience, especially when his troops were even now besieging Florence. Neither the Venetian authorities, nor the Duke of Ferrara, nor the newly promoted Duke of Mantua, nor anyone else wanted to express open support for the divorce on Charles's territory. Croke himself acknowledged that in Venice it was 'dangerous to be concerned in public matters without the permission of the Senate'. Already forced to return territory to the Papal States – including the towns of Ravenna and Cervia for which Contarini had lobbied so hard – the Venetians had no desire to antagonise Charles further. This was the challenging context of the English operation in Venice. To be fair to Croke, Giambattista Casali, despite his need to operate officially, could probably have done more to facilitate his colleague's discreet (or underhand) opinion-gathering. Giambattista, however, had personal motives not to rile the city authorities, for the only chance he had of extracting a living from his bishopric was to reach agreement on the legitimacy of his appointment. Like Gregorio in Rome, he had the expense of maintaining an eighteen-strong diplomatic household and living in suitable style, and matters were made worse by the Venetian decision in April 1530 to withdraw various privileges from resident foreign diplomats, notably rent-free furnished accommodation. Unlike Gregorio, Giambattista also had the problem of a position in the church hierarchy that he owed directly to Clement VII. He was, as the Imperial ambassador to Venice succinctly put it, a vassal of the Pope. That made for an increasingly difficult balancing act as the English strategy began to question the extent of papal authority.[12]

As the quest for academic opinion began, the formal divorce process slowed to a virtual standstill. Clement was unhappy at the English tactics, but reluctant to force Henry's hand. In late March, he offered to delay hearing the king's cause until September 1530 – more than a year after the original advocation. Catherine's supporters must have been furious, but Henry, playing for time, accepted the papal offer. In an effort to constrain the English campaign, however, in May 1530 Clement issued a mandate forbidding anyone – on pain of excommunication – to write or advise on the question of Henry VIII's marriage, 'contrary to his conscience, in the hope of rewards, prayers, hatred, fear or favour'. While giving the appearance of favouring open and conscientious debate, Clement thus aimed to clamp down on the expansive bribery in which both sides were engaged.[13]

Gregorio, meanwhile, was taking care to maintain relationships in England. He had dispatched his man of affairs, Gurone Bertani, to London, perhaps with Paolo, perhaps after him, to ensure that the family had a caretaker and lobbyist at Henry's court. It was common practice for nobles away from court to do so: in an era of personalised government, there was no substitute for direct intervention with the king and his ministers. Of an age with Gregorio, Gurone, a native of Modena, proved a highly capable diplomat in his later career, and was entrusted with sensitive negotiations between England and Rome even into the 1560s. He also helped his master with some discreet arm's-length lobbying for the French. Keeping his patronage options open, in March 1530 Gregorio wrote to Anne de Montmorency, chief minister to King Francis, that he 'would never tire of serving the Most Christian King', whether in Rome or in England ('Most Christian King' was the French equivalent to Henry's 'Defender of the Faith'). Montmorency was evidently keen for Sir Nicholas Carew to take over as ambassador to France, and Gregorio ensured the request was passed on to London, although in fact it was Sir Francis Bryan who returned to reside there from late 1530 to the end of 1531. For Montmorency's benefit, Gregorio played up his good relations with the post-Wolsey regime. The Duke of Norfolk was 'very much my lord', he wrote, 'and my man much confided in by the said duke'. If Montmorency needed the duke to intervene on any point, he should let Gregorio know.[14] We can only speculate whether Gurone – and indeed Paolo – had really worked such wonders with Henry's nobility. Perhaps Gurone showed some early promise as a diplomatic agent, though it is safe to assume there is a little exaggeration for effect.

Besides managing relationships with England and France and keeping an eye on the latest developments in the divorce, Gregorio also had to contend with the conflict over Livia's inheritance. On 12 March 1530, he wrote to Montmorency about Pallavicino family manoeuvrings over some Lombardy property, where one Cagnino Gonzaga (husband to Luisa Pallavicino, a distant cousin of Livia) was causing him trouble. Gregorio hoped that pressure from France might help him in his claim to the property. Thus did interests of state and family mingle in his daily life. He must have been reassured when, on 13 March, the deputies of the tiny town of Monticelli – where Livia had inherited her castle – swore allegiance to her, accepting the legitimacy of her claim. Within a few weeks he was on his way to survey the lands of which he was now lord. It was as well that Gregorio was asserting his right to Livia's dowry, for it looked very much as if his brother Giambattista was losing favour with the English. It must have worried Gregorio when, on 28 March, Henry wrote lobbying for a cardinal's hat for Girolamo Ghinucci – omitting any mention of his other potential candidate, Giambattista. Had Croke's constant criticism undermined the family's claim to promotion?[15]

While Gregorio and Paolo had been quick to work on re-establishing the family's credit with the new post-Wolsey regime, Giambattista had barely contributed to the collective effort. In a letter to Henry dated 5 April 1530, he openly admitted that of late he had not written to the king, 'as I received no directions'. He had kept his brother and the ambassadors at Bologna informed as to his activities, and had written to Norfolk and to Gurone Bertani, with whom he would correspond again in the event of having further news. But that was all. And given that it was an ambassador's job to provide a steady stream of information – Machiavelli

recommended letters every eight or ten days and a full report on
the political situation every two months – failing to communicate
directly with Henry seems somewhat careless, if only in the sense
that it left Croke to tell the story of events with no counter-reports
favourable to Giambattista. To be fair, it is likely that following
Wolsey's fall, no one had picked up the intricate pieces of his
diplomatic network, and that Giambattista had indeed lacked advice
from England. Yet his comportment, in the circumstances, was less
than astute. Although his name was included in a subsequent letter
from Henry lobbying for cardinals' hats, dated 9 April 1530, the
king made it clear that he was second choice to Ghinucci.[16]

By 9 April, Gregorio had reached Monticelli, perhaps on his
return from Milan, to where he had escorted the Earl of Wiltshire
and his colleagues following their brief stay in Bologna. The tiny
riverside settlement was dominated by its huge fortress, now the
Rocca Pallavicino-Casali (Plate 7). Following the local deputies' oath
of allegiance, a personal visit would allow Gregorio to assert his
lordship against potential rivals. From Monticelli he wrote to
his brother with an update on his efforts in Milan to persuade friars
to write in the king's favour and pen their opinions in a manner
acceptable to the English (that is, not conceding too much to papal
power). He also took the opportunity to scold Giambattista for
grave negligence in his dealings with Croke. The king, wrote
Gregorio, wanted everyone to work together. True, he agreed,
Croke was 'crazy'. But the warring had to stop.[17] Gregorio's criticism
is understandable. The Casali relationship with England depended
on their provision of a reliable family network. If Giambattista did
not play his part, they would all be in jeopardy.

On his return from Monticelli d'Ongina, Gregorio spent much
of the next three months, from April to June 1530, in Bologna,
where he and his cousin Andrea co-ordinated the search for
supportive scholars. Giambattista and Richard Croke, meanwhile,
led the campaign in Venice and the nearby university town of
Padua. Croke, however, was getting no friendlier. Everywhere he
saw plots, conspiracies and betrayals. He now blamed not only the
Casali, but Girolamo Ghinucci too for failing him, and implied that
Giambattista had threatened to kill him. In England, however,

Croke's reports were not given a great deal of credence. Edward Fox wrote to him with a warning not to 'meddle' between the two ambassadors. And Ghinucci, despite his relative favour with Croke, believed that his colleague's insistence on working outside the official channels was creating problems of protocol. Giambattista Casali was the accredited ambassador at Venice, and to act without him might raise suspicions that they were operating outside Henry's orders.[18]

Yet even as he penned his diatribes, Croke also faced diplomatic troubles. His plan to work undercover began to miscarry as those from whom he solicited opinions discovered, one by one, the truth of the matter. Warned off writing in favour of the king by 'many Venetian nobles', Gianfrancesco Marino, provincial minister of the Franciscan Order for Venice, sent for Croke and tried to return the money he had been paid in return for an opinion supportive of Henry. Although in May 1530 he was given a personal copy of the papal authorisation to speak or write freely on the subject according to his conscience (provided, of course, he did not take bribes), he said he would do so only with the Venetian authorities' approval. Giambattista was wary of taking matters to the Senate, for to do so risked an explicit ban on open comment that would only make the situation worse.[19]

By spring 1530, the campaign for opinions was in no little disarray. Such was the breakdown in communication between Henry's various agents that none of them appeared to know who had engaged which theologians to write for them. At the beginning of May, Richard Croke finally wrote to Girolamo Ghinucci suggesting that they should compare lists, but he still managed to work in an accusation that one or other of Gregorio Casali and Ghinucci's nephew Andrea must have been making up names. Even Ghinucci now treated Croke with disdain. In a letter of 21 May, he told his colleague tersely that he had been instructed by the king to work together with Gregorio: neither one was to act without the other's knowledge. Ghinucci and Casali were, after all, as near as one got in their day to being professional diplomats. Both had been in royal service for ten years. Croke's amateurish interference must have been tiresome.[20]

Though Croke's paranoia often appears embarrassingly comic, there is reason to ask whether it had any basis in truth. Giambattista Casali hardly threw himself with enthusiasm into the king's new campaign. In early May of 1530, as his colleagues busily sought pro-Henry opinions, he was occupying himself with the tricky question of where his sometime patron Isabella d'Este, Marchioness of Mantua, might best be accommodated in Venice. He and his friend Jacopo Malatesta, the Mantuan ambassador, had evidently spent some time working through the options: putting up a fussy marchioness and her forty-strong household was an organisational chore.[21] Under more normal diplomatic circumstances, such liaison with the influential mother of a neighbouring prince might well have been thought entirely appropriate. An ambassador's usual role was to maintain a magnificent style of living in honour of his prince, and to facilitate negotiation as he was instructed (usually, in Venice, on matters of trade relations). But times had changed, and Giambattista had failed to adjust.

Put together the circumstantial evidence, and there are plenty of clues as to the kind of lifestyle Giambattista Casali aspired to enjoy in Venice. It was one recommended by the Venetian diplomat Ermolao Barbaro in his treatise on the office of ambassador, in which he wrote that the diplomat's enthusiasm for the arts should inspire the performance of entertainments, painting, writing and singing in his household. Giambattista seems to have taken the model to heart. As we know, he had studied in Bologna alongside Isabella's son Ercole Gonzaga, now a cardinal. He commissioned art objects for Isabella herself, not only a mirror but also decorative plasterworks (*stucchi*). He invited some of Venice's leading musicians to his house for a discussion of ancient Greek music theory. (This throws into doubt, if not conclusively, an attempt by Ghinucci to discredit him that depended on his not knowing Greek.) Indeed, his cultural reputation was such that he appeared as a character in a best-selling Venetian book of the second half of the century, Giovan Francesco Straparola's *Le Piacevoli Notti* (*The Pleasurable Nights*). First published in 1550, it took the form of a series of stories told in the company of Lucrezia Gonzaga, a well-known lady of letters, and her attendants. 'Casal of Bologna, bishop and ambassador of the king of England' was the first-named of the 'many noble and most learned men' who 'joined this sweet and honest company'. Next in line was 'the learned Pietro Bembo'.[22]

Bembo is notable because he featured in a list of members of 'the Imperial faction' in Venice to whom Richard Croke claimed Giambattista was overly close. One of the most celebrated intellectuals of his time, a poet and philologist who had edited the work of Petrarch and Dante, Pietro Bembo also knew politics: he had served in Pope Leo X's secretariat. Now in his sixties, and living away from the curia in the relative quiet of Padua, he had just been commissioned to write the official history of the city of Venice. Giambattista corresponded with him, and was likely to have frequented Venetian intellectual circles alongside his sister-in-law's cousin Argentina Pallavicino, who was in contact not only with Bembo but also with Pietro Aretino (a satirist later famed as the 'scourge of princes' who had left Rome for Venice amid a flurry of scandal) and probably Titian too. Another significant acquaintance of Giambattista's was Henry VIII's young cousin Reginald Pole. They were of a similar age, and in 1526, his first year as English ambassador to Venice, Casali went to visit Pole in Padua, where the latter was studying. Pole left Italy shortly afterwards and did not return until the autumn of 1532, but in the Italian context, his trajectory on the divorce is telling. Having initially supported Henry's cause, he then picked up contact with precisely the circle of reforming churchmen in Venice – Gasparo Contarini among them – whom Croke accused Giambattista of frequenting. Eventually he switched sides. All told, it is not hard to imagine that Giambattista, with his predilection for artistic enterprise and intellectual chat, might have seemed something of the dilettante to Richard Croke, especially if his friends were genuinely unconvinced of Henry's case for a divorce.[23]

II

The Daily Frauds of the
Brothers Casali

By May 1530, Croke had added corruption and betrayal to his
compendium of Casali wrongdoing. His friends believed, so he
said, that Giambattista Casali was a papal spy, while Gregorio was
demanding money to pay scholars whose services he, Croke, had
already retained. His suspicion was fuelled by reports from Girolamo
di Vicenza, Bishop of Vaison, who had lodged with Giambattista.
The bishop told Croke (or so the latter wrote) that 'the Casali had
often told him that they regretted that the king had embarked on
this cause and that they had always opposed it'.[1]

If Giambattista had actively been hindering the king's cause, one
person who should have been interested was Rodrigo Niño, Imperial
ambassador to Venice. Yet Niño's reports on the matter are far
from conclusive. Initially, in June 1530, he was rather enthused by
Giambattista's apparent distaste for Henry's activities. The pair had
met at the annual festival marking Ascension Day, when the Doge,
elective ruler of Venice, celebrated the city's ritual marriage to the
sea. It was a spectacular event dating back to Byzantine times or
perhaps even beyond. After a Mass in San Marco, the Doge sailed
out on Venice's flagship, the state barge known as the *Bucintoro*, to
the church of Sant'Elena, followed by a procession of lavishly
decorated boats carrying the worthies of the city. There, the patri-
arch of Castello waited in a gilt-trimmed barge to give his blessing;
bells rang and the chapel choir sang. The Doge then sailed to the
port of San Nicolò, which marked the channel between the lagoon
and the sea, where he threw a gold ring into the water in the
culmination of the rite, saying, 'We espouse thee, O sea, as a sign
of true and perpetual dominion.'[2]

Such occasions were often convenient for informal discussion among the ambassadors who accompanied the Doge, and this one was no exception. Niño reported that Giambattista had made 'great excuses' for himself and his brother, declaring their disapproval of the king's proceedings and how they had fallen into disgrace with Henry for telling him so. Moreover (and in confirmation of the Casali–Ghinucci rivalry), Giambattista had blamed Ghinucci and his colleagues in Bologna for 'all the mischief'. The emperor should believe, wrote Niño, that every day, the Casali 'find themselves more embarrassed in this odious business'. But later, in a letter of 28 June 1530, Niño backtracked. Giambattista, he now said, had been 'very active in promoting the king's interests', although he added the rider: 'though owing to his being a vassal of the Pope suspicion generally attaches to him'. A month on, he reported a further conversation with Giambattista, in which the latter implied that he was unhappy about the divorce business, but begged Niño 'for the love of God' to keep the knowledge to himself, for fear that the king 'would have his life and his brother's' if this (and likewise their Ascension Day conversation) became known.[3] This last picture of Giambattista swerving between loyal service and indiscretion, perhaps genuinely unable to make up his mind about Henry's great matter, seems a convincing one. Many others among the king's servants shared such an attitude: uncomfortable with their master's obsession, disturbed by the increasingly explicit defiance of papal authority, but reluctant to defy the king for fear of losing income, position and patronage. There were few martyrs-in-the-making at the Henrician court.

On 9 June, Gregorio, still in Bologna but about to leave for Rome, wrote to Henry. His letter was polite enough, but conveyed nonetheless more than a little irritation at his master's handling of the matter. 'I do wish,' he wrote, 'that it had pleased Your Majesty to entrust this business to me, while the Pope and Emperor were here, for then it might have been managed more commodiously, more fully, and more expeditiously.' In particular, he could have prevented the Imperialists from obtaining subscriptions from some of the Dominican friars.[4] Bearing in mind that Casali's uncle had been a member of the Dominican order, and that the family were patrons of one of the most prominent chapels in Bologna's Dominican church,

Gregorio might well have exerted some influence in Henry's favour. But the fact that he had to write this letter at all illustrates the incremental marginalisation of his role in English diplomacy. Back in 1527, under Cardinal Wolsey, things had been very different.

Yet if the Casali were somewhat out of favour, so too was Richard Croke. For revealing the 'long infidelity and negligence' of the king's enemies, he wrote to John Stokesley, he had been labelled a 'brabeller', though he did not say by whom. The Casali, he continued, had 'beguiled' their colleagues. Only Croke would 'plainly utter the untruth of these Italians', even if that proved unwelcome. In less than three years, the Italian diplomats of Henry's service had gone from praiseworthy facilitators of English affairs in Rome to 'untrue' foreigners. The dissimulation of which they were such masters, thus making them accomplished diplomats, now counted against them. And Croke's criticism presages a broader shift in diplomatic practice. Up until now, the general assumption in the period had been – as one historian has put it – that 'foreign nationals could be expected to serve as loyally as would a Middlesex man'. Like mercenary troops and commanders, they could move between the service of different sovereigns, choosing or rejecting ties of allegiance. What mattered was their loyalty to their adopted ruler. Some scholars have even suggested that foreigners – by virtue of their lack of interest in domestic rivalries – made rather better diplomats, though one can take the argument too far. But as Henry turned to the rhetoric of English custom to justify his challenge to papal authority, things were about to change.[5]

Croke continued his attacks on Henry's Italian diplomats in a letter of 9 June. 'There was never noble Prince so abused by craft and malice of them whom He putteth in trust,' he wrote to Henry, 'as Your Highness is, in this your most just cause.' 'Giambattista,' he went on, 'is familiar with the Emperor's Ambassador.' He warmed to his theme of untrustworthy Italians, who used 'cloak and colour' to hinder Henry's cause and told the Pope 'of every man's doing'. For a king who saw evident distinctions between his own men and the Italian agents recruited by Wolsey – as had been apparent even three years before, when he dispatched William Knight – Croke's accusations would only serve to confirm him in his belief. The Casali already had detractors in England, the likes of Tuke, who had spoken of Gregorio's 'lightness'. Croke's language – 'light dissimuler' is his choice description of Gregorio – reflects theirs. And, of course, the divorce still seemed as far away as ever.[6]

Croke knew, however, that the Italians – both the Casali and Ghinucci families – had their spies at the English court. 'Certain men' would advise them 'of all things that I and other do write unto Your Highness, insomuch that to the great prejudice of your matters here all their faults be cloaked'. Through his agent Gurone in England, who maintained a separate line of communication with courtiers, Gregorio ensured that he had an assessment of developments independent from that conveyed in his official instructions. In a postscript to another letter, Croke alerted Henry that the Casali knew they were under suspicion at the English court. Giambattista Casali had told him of Gurone's report that 'your Highness should speak words of challenge as well against Sir Gregory as him'. Giambattista knew, moreover, that Gurone had defied royal orders not to tell the Casali of Henry's criticism. But although Croke's attacks largely focused on his Italian colleagues, they were not his only targets. He later turned his fire on William Benet, suggesting that he was not only obstructing the royal cause, but had advised Giambattista to do so as well. Benet, claimed Croke, had been fraternising with the emperor's chancellor while they were both at Bologna. There were untrustworthy Englishmen too.[7]

Reading Croke's account, it would be easy to conclude that the campaign for university opinions had been an utter failure. Not so. On 26 May, the Imperial ambassador Miguel Mai wrote with his worries that the English were making headway. Henry's ambassadors had money, he said, for bribes. He was clearly fretting that they might win people over. And they did. On 10 June, the ambassadors successfully obtained endorsement of Henry's cause from the University of Bologna, and on 1 July the University of Padua likewise supported the king, a decision assisted in no small part by the lobbying of the philosopher Niccolò Leonico Tomeo, a long-standing tutor and friend to English students at that university (who, however, fell out with Henry's agents in the process, claiming they had paid him with a lame horse). The king, gradually, was getting what he wanted. Gregorio, now back in Rome, ensured that Gurone Bertani was updated with regular accounts of his diligent work for Henry: entertaining 'certain friars' who might be persuaded to support the king, lobbying the French to secure favourable opinions from their academics, having off-the-record chats with Cardinal Egidio and trying to assure Clement that Henry was not – as the Pope suspected – assisting the besieged Florentines.[8]

Although Clement had agreed to delay the divorce hearing until September, time was ticking on, and Henry needed new tactics for delay. The diplomatic approach was eclectic. In mid-June, the nobility of England were corralled into signing an appeal for the divorce, which was then dispatched for presentation at the papal court. The ambassadors in Rome were instructed to threaten Clement with English subsidies for the besieged Florentine faction opposed to Medici rule. Casali had 'very bitter words' with the Pope about Henry's cause; he told Miguel Mai that the king would no longer be deterred by the threat of scandal. But although Henry was now seeking alternatives, his ambassadors continued to work on the basis that some compromise with the papacy might be found. William Benet, for example, confided in Mai that a papal nuncio was travelling to England to arrange a trial in neither England nor Rome but some different place. Finally the English representatives contrived to bounce Clement into a scheme whereby he would absent himself from Rome just as the legal year began, thus delaying progress in the trial until November.[9]

All this manoeuvring was motivated by what one historian has called a 'panic' in the English government, which by the summer of 1530 was manifestly apprehensive about the weakness of its own theological case, both for domestic consumption and for presentation at the forthcoming trial in Rome. Although they had won over a couple of universities, for all their efforts Henry's agents could find little in canon law to support the king's contention that popes could not dispense from the Levitical proscription against marriage with a brother's wife. Only a handful of authorities came down on Henry's side; there was much legal precedent against him. Perhaps the seriousness of the situation had some effect on Henry's envoys in Italy, who seem to have reached a temporary truce. Even Croke conceded that the Casali were getting down to work. In Bologna, the family network proved its worth as Gregorio's cousin Andrea Casali facilitated dealings in the city. Andrea, elder brother of Vicenzo and cousin to Gregorio and Giambattista on their father's side, was head of the Casali household there. In 1525 the Pope had appointed him a senator in Bologna, after what the then Bolognese ambassador in Rome described as some 'very efficacious lobbying' by Henry VIII and Wolsey. As the ambassadors set out to obtain an opinion in Henry's favour from the dons of Bologna, Andrea's position and contacts proved invaluable in a city where the balance between papal rule and patrician aspiration for authority had always to be negotiated. Useful too were the efforts of Girolamo Previdelli, a former tutor to the Casali children, who taught at the University of Bologna. He had dedicated his first printed work, a legal treatise on the plague, published in 1528, to Giambattista Casali, and his treatise on Henry's divorce, which includes prefatory and concluding dedications to Gregorio Casali, makes clear his debt to the family: 'What we are, what we have, what we are reckoned – if we are reckoned anything – is yours: and, in fine, we owe life itself to you and all of yours, and we have wished everything that is mine to be yours always.'[10]

Bologna was governed by a papal appointee, Uberto Gambara, Bishop of Tortona and a man well-versed in diplomacy, who had been legate to England in 1526–7, returning briefly in 1528. On 12 September, Croke wrote to Cranmer to report that Andrea Casali had successfully obtained confirmation by the college of Bologna of their June vote in Henry's favour. But the news had reached Gambara's notice, and he had called in every one of the friars involved, and some of the doctors of law. 'How the devil', asked Croke, had he learnt about it? In a letter to the king, Croke blamed Andrea Casali and Previdelli for leaking information. Gambara, he was horrified to discover, knew 'certain secret arguments and probations in defence of the Levitical law against Deuteronomy'. He also knew about the money used to 'reward' supporters, potentially in contravention of the papal mandate. And he was far from happy. On 4 August, the Pope had, after all, repeated his interdict against writing 'contrary to one's conscience' for reward.[11]

Yet for all Croke's frenetic letters, the picture painted by Stokesley was rather different. The Bologna doctors, he wrote to Henry, wanted more time to consider the issues, but they would be done by the end of September, and Henry's counsel at Rome would have their opinions early the following month. Previdelli's counsel was already completed and sent to Rome, with two 'authenticated transcripts' of the determinations of Bologna and Padua. Andrea Casali and Previdelli were 'diligently and effectually' soliciting an opinion from Bologna University. Gambara had made a 'shameful ruffle' and directed 'threats of impeachment' at some of the university theologians, but Casali and Previdelli would advise on whether his threats were carried out. Finally, said Stokesley, the Venetian authorities were causing difficulties. One friar was called before the Doge, and 'both he and his fellows were put in such fear that as yet they dare not meddle openly thereabouts. Howbeit, they have stood constantly in maintaining of their determination, notwithstanding great terrors of the said Emperor's ambassador and his agents.' In contrast to Croke's outpourings, it was a measured and positive report. And there was more good news when on 24 September the University of Ferrara voted in Henry's favour.[12]

As the agents in Bologna went about their work, in Venice the Imperial ambassador Rodrigo Niño was doing his best to thwart the English efforts. In July 1530, Niño successfully acquired some of the English correspondence leaving Venice and sent it on to the emperor. His spying would – in the long term – have serious consequences for Giambattista Casali, but that he had to spy on him in the first place rather gives the lie to any suggestion that the pair were hand in glove. Moreover, it puts a different spin on Croke's account of how Niño had got his hands on an opinion from one Tommaso Ognibene, a Dominican theologian of Venice who first backed Henry but later changed his mind.[13] While Croke had implied that Giambattista's disloyalty was to blame, the explanation could as easily have been Niño's dirty tricks.

The poisonous conflict between Henry's diplomats came to a head in the case of Canon Raffaele Venosta da Como, theologian of Padua. Some time before the end of July 1530, Venosta was approached by the English diplomats to write an opinion on Henry VIII's divorce, and his Determinatio, favourable to the king, was duly produced and

dated 30 July 1530. He gave the manuscript to Richard Croke, who
began to make a copy of it. Niño, however, was about to score something of a coup. By means of a Spanish canon, resident like Venosta
at the monastery of San Giovanni da Verdara, he convinced
Venosta to defect to the queen's side. Niño believed that Venosta had
seen the secret collection of arguments in Henry's favour and was
consequently in an excellent position to rebut them. Venosta asked
the English to give his pro-Henry manuscript back, telling Croke (or
so the latter claimed) that as soon as he got it he would 'immediately
set forth his work in the Queen's favour'. This prompted Croke to
insist to Stokesley that they should at least keep a copy, but Stokesley
was adamant that he should hand over both the original and his copy
to Casali for return to Venosta, which he did some time before 23
August. 'I told my lord what would come of it,' wrote the embit-
tered Croke later to his friend Thomas Cranmer.[14]

Raffaele Venosta proceeded to demolish his own arguments,
setting out his pro-Henry case alongside the case in favour of
Catherine. The new treatise, which he gave to Niño, was dated
Wednesday 17 August, just two and a half weeks after his first opinion,
and was printed by the 30th. To add insult to injury, Venosta noted
in his treatise that he had written the counsel for Henry merely 'as
an intellectual exercise'. Unaware of Venosta's about-turn, Croke
was, for once, rather complimentary about his colleagues, conceding
in a letter of 7 September that even Giambattista – from fear and
shame – was buckling down to work. If the Casali persevered in the
cause, he assured Henry, 'I shall as gladly report always their good
deeds as I have had good cause to report hitherto their bad.'[15] It
would be another month before Croke discovered what Venosta had
done. It is not hard to picture his fury – and Niño's delight.

On 14 October 1530, Richard Croke wrote to Venosta. He suggested
that the canon should beg the king's indulgence for his behaviour and
tell Henry that he had been pressured into changing his mind by the
Imperial party. Clement's mandates of 21 May and 4 August forbade
writing on the divorce contrary to one's conscience – on pain of
excommunication – but Venosta could avoid this penalty if he could
claim that he had written under duress. Venosta complied and wrote
to Henry, at least after Giambattista Casali paid him eight crowns to

do so. According to Croke his letter was delivered under seal, with the intention that it should not be opened until it reached the king in England. But Casali then went to a printer with Venosta's letter and a manuscript purporting to be his original opinion in favour of Henry, dated 30 July. It was Croke's belief that Casali had 'altered many things in the said epistle and work', and it seems very likely that he had, for the new opinion – allegedly 'reviewed, corrected and amplified' by the canon – is nearly twice as long as the pro-Henry section of the earlier treatise. Either the earlier opinion was drastically cut for printing, or someone substantially expanded this subsequent version. Internal irregularities in the text, such as the appearance of a 'Fourth Conclusion' without reference to a First, Second or Third, point to a rather hasty process of revision and amendment.[16]

On discovering what Casali had done, the suspicious Croke made enquiries of both Venosta and the printer. Venosta told Croke that he had not consented to the printing. The printer added that Casali had stood by as the copies came off the press. Afterwards he had personally broken the forms and told the printer that if he revealed to Croke anything of the business, 'he would cause him to be slain'. If Croke is to be believed, Giambattista was in the habit of threatening murder. Croke wrote that Venosta was 'angry with the printing of the epistle, and saith that he will testify in the preface of his book that he will be taken for no traitor to the emperor, nor that anything that ever he wrote for the king is his mind or opinion'. Given Casali's deceit, his anger is hardly surprising.[17]

On 18 November, Raffaele Venosta published a third book, *De potestate papae in dispensandis matrimoniis*, again opposing Henry. Once again he disowned his work of 30 July as 'an intellectual exercise' carried out at the 'instance and importunity' of the English agents. Well might Richard Croke denounce the canon as a 'light cloisterer'.[18]

As his mission in Italy came to an end, Richard Croke drew up a series of articles against Gregorio Casali and his brothers, to be proved 'partly with their own letters, partly with the letters of divers other men of good and substantial credence'. Among his claims were that Gregorio Casali 'had divulged at Milan that the question concerned the king', thereby scaring off potential supporters, and had delivered the secret king's book to Henry's enemies, who wrote against it. He accused Giambattista of misleading him with a 'false index' of St Mark's library, of printing the king's case in order 'to divulge the said cause' and of bringing to himself and Stokesley various of the king's enemies, 'pretending that they were the king's sure friends'.[19]

What of these claims? Was Henry really as badly served by his ambassadors as his agent would have it? There are three reasons to be sceptical about Croke's allegations. First, he had form. Earlier in his career, while at St John's College, Cambridge, he had accused his patron, John Fisher, of nepotism. Fisher had defended himself with an attack on Croke's own conduct.[20] Some of those who heard Croke's accusations against Casali may have reflected that they had seen it all before. Second, Croke's assumptions that it would be possible for him to work undercover and that anyone would have been fooled by his protestations that his mission had nothing to do with Henry VIII were indubitably mistaken. Third, his claims rest on an assumption that minds were already made up, that it was easy to draw a line between Henry's friends and Henry's enemies, to work with the former and not the latter. It was not so. Three years away from the schism, there were plenty of people who might have been swayed one way or the other by convincing argument, or who slowly formed their own view after months of study. Venosta was far from alone in switching sides.

Moreover, it is testament to the work of Henry's diplomats that the king ended up with official endorsements for his cause from three Italian universities – Padua, Bologna and Ferrara – and less formal support from academics at Vicenza. Given the political climate in Italy, it was hardly a bad result. To those he could add the opinions of lawyers and theologians at Orléans, Angers, Paris, Bourges and Toulouse. And unlike their English or Spanish counterparts, the French and Italian universities had the all-important appearance of neutrality in the matter. For purposes of domestic and international propaganda, Henry had what he needed. In spite of their infighting – and perhaps to the surprise of Croke's correspondents – our men in Bologna and Venice had delivered.

12

The Custom of England

As the campaign for opinions gathered pace, the Casali still had money troubles. Livia's dowry was certainly proving useful, but Giambattista remained unable to extract an income from his bishopric, and there is little evidence that Paolo's Hungarian connections were particularly profitable. In the summer of 1530, the Marquis del Vasto, an Imperial commander who was good friends with the youngest Casali brother, Francesco, offered him excellent terms if he went to fight for the Habsburgs in Hungary, where Imperial armies were gathering to take on the Turks. But Gregorio was most anxious to avoid such an engagement – not least because Henry had made it very clear that he did not approve of two brothers serving two 'less-than-friendly princes'. It had been fine for Francesco to fight for Charles V back in the early 1520s. But after 1525, when England had switched sides to ally with the French, things had changed. If Francesco took up the offer, Henry would undoubtedly be furious. But without it, what would he live on?

Francesco's story was a sorry one, but far from uncommon. Throughout the Italian wars he had been a mercenary captain, first in the Imperial service and later for Venice. When Camillo Orsini, the commander in charge, had left Puglia after the defeats of 1529, charge of both cavalry and infantry in the area had fallen to Francesco. He had had to hold his ground 'without money, only with promises', wrote Gregorio to Anne de Montmorency in a letter of 27 July 1530. On Francesco's return to Venice with the troops to whom he was now personally indebted on the Signoria's behalf, his erstwhile masters had declined to take responsibility, and Francesco, understandably, was 'most dissatisfied and discontented' with them. Gregorio had tried lobbying Gasparo Contarini, but to no avail. Like ambassadors, *condottieri* had to pay their own way, and reimbursement was not always forthcoming. Hence they had a persistent interest in booty, often unconducive to the efficient conduct of war. However, matters could, wrote Gregorio, easily be resolved if the French would only consent to employ Francesco in *their* army. As for his 'valour and sufficiency', he continued, 'you can have knowledge of it from everyone who ever fought in these Italian wars'. No French offer, though, ever materialised.[1]

The Casali family did manage to exploit other opportunities. Two years earlier, Napoleone Orsini, the lawless Abbot of Farfa, had helped Gregorio by holding hostage the Imperial messenger Sigismondo. Now Giambattista returned the favour. On 20 July, Orsini arrived in Venice, and Giambattista provided him with accommodation. Orsini's castle at Bracciano was under siege by papal troops, but he reckoned his men inside could hold out for two years. He confided to the Mantuan ambassador that the Pope was persecuting him for no good cause, for he had always been Clement's good servant, though Clement would probably not have seen it that way. As the manoeuvring over Bracciano went on, complicated by an intra-family feud, the Casali tried to take advantage. The latest proposal, reported on 8 August, was that some independent party should take interim control of the castle, and Gregorio Casali was one of Napoleone Orsini's three favoured candidates. (The others were the French diplomat Gabriel de Grammont, Bishop of Tarbes, promoted to the cardinalate just a few weeks before, and Renzo da Ceri, an Orsini relative, with whom Francesco Casali had fought in Puglia.) Napoleone did not want Cardinal Franciotto Orsini, a distant relative, to get his hands on the property. By 15 September, Casali, along with Tarbes, had succeeded in obtaining a pardon for Napoleone, and – much to the irritation of the Imperial ambassador – the sequestration of the Castello di Bracciano until such time as the dispute between the Orsini brothers about its rightful ownership could be resolved.[2]

As life in Rome slowly returned to normal three years on from the Sack, the last battle of this Italian war was fought at Gavinana in the hills north-west of Florence. There, on 3 August 1530, Imperial troops defeated the Florentines, and within two weeks the city capitulated. Thus began, to unquestionable papal satisfaction, more than two hundred years of Medici rule of Florence, a state of affairs that Clement owed to Charles V. Henry VIII had briefly thought to intervene in support of the city's defence, but his promises of aid were too few and came too late.[3]

By the end of August, Gregorio Casali was back in Rome on the social circuit, dining with the French Cardinal Grammont, with whom he had to discuss the fate of Bracciano. With one eye still on Francesco's future employment, he lobbied the cardinal in person about a French job for his brother. Talks about the divorce continued. On 18 September, Gregorio wrote to Henry to report an intriguing development. The Pope, he said, had secretly proposed that the king might be allowed to have two wives. It was a suggestion that had been floated and rapidly dropped right at the start of the divorce business, in late 1527. Casali, so he claimed, had been told by Clement not to speak of the proposal, but had ignored the injunction. For Henry, though, bigamy was legally too risky, for it left the succession unclear.[4]

Casali was aware that his position in the English service was delicate. It was an open secret. Even the Imperial ambassador, Miguel Mai, knew of the rumours. 'The king of England,' he told Charles V in a letter of 2 October, 'has written to his ambassador, Gregorio Casali, that he has been told that he has not used due diligence in this matter, which the king does not believe, and he commits the matter to his care and promises great rewards for it; Casali is very sharp and for his honour has written, so I hear, a very long and discreet letter, telling the king the truth of matters here and warning him not to be deceived.' With Croke preparing to return to England, Gregorio needed to pre-empt any rumours he might spread.[5]

By the summer of 1530, Henry's opposition to any compromise that might acknowledge papal authority to determine the divorce was hardening. But his views were far from universally shared by his subjects. In order to put pressure on the Church in England, in July the king had fourteen clerics arrested and charged, as Wolsey had been, with *praemunire*, the offence of introducing foreign (in practice, papal) authority into England in preference to royal authority, an accusation related to their dealings with Wolsey. Among them were John Clerk, Bishop of Bath and a former ambassador to Rome, and John Fisher, Bishop of Rochester, both known supporters of the queen. It was a manoeuvre intended to make clear that any hint of loyalty to Rome was a risk. In the autumn, Henry followed this up with instructions to his ambassadors to appeal his case to a future General Council of the Church. This was a controversial move because in 1459 Pope Pius II had outlawed such appeals, condemning them as 'a horrible abuse' and threatening anyone who questioned papal authority with excommunication. The backdrop to Pius's bull, known as *Execrabilis*, had been the series of four church councils held in the first half of the fifteenth century in an attempt to resolve the schism that had bitterly divided the Catholic Church since 1378. Rival popes had ruled – one in Rome, another, backed by the French, in Avignon. For a while there had even been a third. Matters were finally resolved in the 1440s with the re-establishment of a single papacy at Rome under Nicholas V, and from then on the popes had taken care to consolidate their power. Now, with the Lutheran heresy to contend with, there was once again pressure for a council. It would, however, be another fifteen years before the Council of Trent was finally convened, and a further eighteen before its proceedings concluded, in 1563.[6]

The ambassadors demurred at their master's request. They wrote querying the order to appeal to a General Council and requesting new instructions, and enclosed copies of two papal bulls prohibiting such appeals. Henry was unimpressed at his ambassadors' collective timidity. On 7 October 1530, he wrote insisting on the 'custom and privilege' of the Realm that Englishmen should not be compelled to go to law outside England'. This was, he told the envoys, not something to be kept quiet, but to be put openly and in earnest to the Pope. Henry had hinted at similar beliefs in the past. In 1515, when it was proposed that a dispute over the independence of the English Church should be heard at Rome, the king had refused, explicitly stating that 'kings of England in time past have never had any superior but God only'. But by introducing the argument now, Henry raised the stakes. Although the ambassadors had long argued for the settlement of the matter in England (through the issue of a decretal commission), hitherto the question of English custom had not been to the fore. And as with Croke's untrue Italians, Henry's language now reflected a certain English 'nationalism', although the king's concept of the nation was certainly not the same as the understanding of the word today. To the men and women of sixteenth-century Europe, nations were more akin to ethnic communities, often of merchants or tradesmen, carrying on their business in a foreign city. One spoke of the Florentine or the Genoese nation in Rome, or of the Flemish nation in London. The word still had more than a remnant of its Latin meaning – tribe, or breed, the group into which one is born. Only later, in the nineteenth century, did the 'nation' become the abstract, imagined community of people who might be drawn together to form the modern nation-state. Nonetheless, Henry's appeal to the 'custom of England' certainly hints at some concept of an English nation beyond his own person as monarch.[7]

As Henry attacked Clement's authority, on 27 September 1530, the Pope celebrated the feast of the early martyrs Cosmas and Damian, adopted by the Medici family as patrons. After a solemn Mass, the cardinals and ambassadors of the court were invited to a sumptuous lunch, though not an excessive one; so wrote the Mantuan ambassador approvingly, his observation more likely a reflection of the classical belief that moderation in all things was appropriate than an objective assessment of the quantity of food involved. Eating at the Belvedere, so-named for its beautiful view from the top of the Vatican hill, the diners would have found themselves surrounded by cypress trees. The small *palazzetto* here in the Vatican complex was one of the earliest examples of a Renaissance rustic villa in Rome, built in imitation of the classical model. Adorned with pastoral scenes by artists including Andrea Mantegna and Pinturicchio, its northern aspect made it a pleasurable environment for summer luncheons, and citrus trees grew in its central courtyard, where a fountain helped cool the air. Under Pope Julius II, the groves had been filled with ancient statues, among them those of Laocoön and Venus Felix, now in the Vatican Museums. In his brief reign, Adrian VI had notoriously denounced the Laocoön group as 'idols of the ancients', but his successor Clement had no such objections to pagan iconography. The al fresco lunch was followed by music, and His Holiness spent the day, so it was reported, in pleasant conversation.[8] It was a momentary escape from the increasingly vexing problem of the King of England's marriage.

In October and November 1530, Gregorio was back in Bologna. Miguel Mai reported on 21 October that he had gone there to fetch his wife. Perhaps Livia was now to take up a role as diplomatic hostess in Rome. But Gregorio was probably also busy engaging theologians and lawyers in advance of the expected divorce hearing in Rome. It was a good time to be out of the city. In early October, the Tiber burst its banks, its floodwaters reaching their peak on the 8th of the month, an event still marked by a plaque on the church of Santa Maria della Minerva near the Pantheon. The flooding was 'so great that it ran through every street in Rome', explained William Benet to Henry, 'and in many streets it was above two fathoms deep'. Even the Pope could not get to his palace. It was two days before the waters subsided sufficiently that men could ride through the streets.[9]

On Saturday 4 November, just three days before he should have been enthroned as Archbishop of York, Cardinal Wolsey was arrested for treason. Accused of 'sumptuous sinister practices made to the court of Rome' and intriguing with foreign powers, he was dispatched to London. He did not reach the Tower. On 29 November, still on the road south, he died at Leicester Abbey. What prompted his arrest is an intriguing but probably unanswerable question. It may have been yet another device in Henry's campaign to bring pressure to bear on Rome. It may have been occasioned by indiscreet contacts with foreign monarchs. There may have been suspicions about how Wolsey might use his enthronement. We will probably never know. News of his arrest, though not yet of his death, reached Rome on 6 December, but there is no record of the ambassadors' reaction.[10]

Just as Rodrigo Niño had been intercepting Giambattista's correspondence from Venice, so the Imperial spies were working in England too. Queen Catherine of Aragon still presided over her side of the English court, and would be there for a few months yet: it was not until the summer of 1531 that Henry decisively broke off relations with her. That gave her ample opportunity for contact with more or less indiscreet courtiers, and sometimes they passed on letters from Rome. On 27 November, Eustace Chapuys, Imperial ambassador in London, reported that the Duchess of Norfolk had sent to the queen 'a present of poultry and an orange, enclosing a letter from Gregory Cassal, which I send'. Although the duchess, Elizabeth Howard, was married to Anne Boleyn's uncle, she was no great friend of her niece's cause. Catherine thought she was moved by genuine friendship, but Chapuys suspected that it was a ploy by the duke to establish a line of communication with the queen. Either way, the incident offers a rare glimpse into the ways in which the women of Henry's court might conceal secretive political trans-actions amid the daily exchange of domestic gifts.[11]

In Venice, Giambattista Casali was still trying to gather opinions favourable to the divorce. Indeed, he went to some lengths to do so, more evidence that Croke's criticism was somewhat unfair. With the Italian princes now extremely reluctant to upset the emperor, discretion was vital. So Giambattista passed on to his Imperial counterpart a rather neat piece of disinformation. He was, he told Rodrigo Niño, going to England to discuss a possible marriage between Princess Mary and the Duke of Milan. This was a tale guaranteed to arouse Niño's interest, for Milan had huge strategic importance, and Sforza held his duchy thanks to an agreement between the emperor and Venice. If there was any prospect of coming to a deal over Henry's divorce, a good marriage for Mary would have to be part of it. To add colour to his account, Giambattista claimed that Sforza had promised the Casali a substan-tial feudal property in the duchy if they could successfully complete the arrangements. The detail of the proffered reward made the story all the more plausible, although the Mantuan ambassador in Rome was sceptical about Giambattista's claim of marital dealing, describing it as 'a fairytale' – and not in the sense of 'fairytale wedding'. He was right to be suspicious, for in fact Giambattista had headed off on a quest for further opinions – this time, in semi-disguise, to Mantua.[12]

Unfortunately for the English, the rulers of Mantua were no longer the friends they had once been. Just like the Venetians, they had come to terms with Charles V. When Giambattista Casali trekked off to Mantua to convince the learned men of the city to back the English cause, he was promptly discovered and forbidden from doing so. Moreover, the Mantuan ambassador in Rome – once Gregorio's ally – shopped him to the Pope, who was delighted to hear of Duke Federico's 'most prudent' government. Miguel Mai was sure the emperor would be 'most satisfied' too.[13]

On 6 December 1530, Henry wrote to the Pope declaring that he would not 'brook denial'. On the same day he sent a peremptory letter to Benet and Edward Carne, the latter newly dispatched to Rome, which was striking for its uncompromising tone. Although Henry was prepared to play along with strategies for delay, he was reluctant to acknowledge the Pope's 'jurisdiction, power, authority and laws' if they precluded settling the question of his marriage in England. Only in extreme circumstances, therefore, should the ambassadors engage with the process in Rome, and if they must, only in such a way as to avoid acknowledging the Pope's jurisdiction. The matter was couched as a dispute over spheres of jurisdiction rather than an all-out attack on papal authority. Nonetheless, insofar as there was 'question or contention' between that authority and Henry's 'dignities and prerogative royal', the king was sure that his ambassadors would rather be reputed 'entire Englishmen than Englishmen papisticate'.[14] Once again Henry turned to the English trope, defining the papacy as foreign, alien to England, and Englishness in terms of religious loyalty to the king. On his Italian servants, Henry stayed silent. But if the most desirable ambassadors were now 'entire Englishmen', then surely the untrustworthy Italians of Croke's letters, who used 'cloak and colour' to hinder the king's cause, stood in contrast. It was a far cry from Wolsey's praise of Italian skill in gaining access to Clement, or Gardiner's tributes to Casali's credit and reputation.

On 9 December, the College of Cardinals met in Consistory to consider Henry's latest request, in a letter dated 24 November, for the creation of two cardinals: Girolamo Ghinucci and Giambattista Casali. Having failed in his attempts to lobby Clement alone, Henry had clearly decided that writing to the College as a whole might yield more results, and the Imperial ambassador was certainly suspicious that the English might succeed. Indeed, following Wolsey's death, it is rather surprising that they did not. It was customary to have a spread of nationalities in the College: Wolsey had succeeded another English cardinal, Christopher Bainbridge. But Henry's choice of Italians as his preferred candidates gave his opponents an excuse to refuse him. Fray Garcia Laoysa, a Spanish cardinal, wrote to the emperor that he had not been at Consistory, but had heard that the Pope was sympathetic to Ghinucci's promotion. Ghinucci, he wrote, 'is a very bad man, and behaves as an enemy of the Emperor in the divorce case of the Queen of England [. . .] If the King of England had asked to make one of his subjects a Cardinal, a man of good conduct and a scholar, His Holiness would be right in doing his will, but as this demand is made in favour of an Italian, the King of England has no reason to be offended, if it is not granted'. On 6 January, Henry wrote to Clement complaining that Ghinucci had not been promoted to the cardinalate. To deny England a cardinal was an insult. He added, somewhat inconsistently given his recent comments on Englishmen, that to object on grounds of nationality was specious.[15]

The Imperialists were increasingly disturbed by the delay in hearing the divorce case – now almost eighteen months on from the initial advocation to Rome. On 17 December, Catherine of Aragon herself wrote to Clement protesting at the delay. The 'salvation of her soul', she declared, depended on Clement's help. She hoped the Pope would see that it was God's will that justice be done in her cause. She could not but complain of his neglect of her petitions. She endured her tribulations with the thought that this might be God's punishment for her sins; indeed, she endured them only with God's strength, 'God, in whom all my hopes are concentrated, sure as I am that He will not abandon me in this cause, in which justice is so clearly with me'. The pious language of her letter represented genuine religious belief and not merely an effort to win friends. It stands in contrast to the secular tone that prevails in the correspondence of her husband's ambassadors.[16]

As the diplomacy continued, there were also moves afoot in the Pallavicino family. The marital alliances between the Pallavicino women and the noble families of Italy were so complex that every birth or death provoked further manoeuvring. In November 1530, Livia's stepmother, Lucrezia Borasca, died. Rumours reached the papal court that she had been pregnant. Such were the tensions surrounding the Pallavicino inheritance that the Pope immediately dispatched an official to inspect her corpse and check whether her child had survived. The last thing anyone wanted was for a baby to be hidden away only to be produced later as the true heir to the contested fortune. The absence of a child had to be confirmed and documented. Lucrezia's case also sheds light on a very murky allegation apparently made by Gregorio's secretary, Giambernardino di Ferrara, some time in late 1530 or 1531, by which time Livia had given birth to a son, Michele. Just like the tale that Giambernardino had never been more than a pimp in the Casali household, the story was told by his subsequent employer, Cardinal Benedetto Accolti, not the most reliable of witnesses. It is nonetheless intriguing. The cardinal wrote that Giambernardino, suborned by Casali's enemies, had falsely testified that Livia's child was not her husband's. Casali acted decisively. On discovering the 'nefarious lie' about his heir, he had his secretary thrown into the infamous prison of Corte Savella, located conveniently on the same street as the family house. But for his master's mercy, Giambernardino would have faced the public pillory, made to wear a paper mitre listing his crimes.[17] Who were these enemies? Rivals from the Pallavicino family trying to discredit the legitimacy of a male heir, or to suggest that someone else's child was now being passed off as Livia's? It is certainly possible, and all the more reason for Gregorio to silence his garrulous secretary.

Following confirmation that Lucrezia had not been expecting, legal moves could proceed in favour of Gregorio and Livia. On 17 December 1530, Gregorio Casali was given part of his wife's contested property in trust, a half-share of the countship of Castro Zibello that had reverted to the Camera Apostolica (the papal treasury). The letters patent from the treasury cited 'the faith and nobility of mind which your Magnificence has shown on many occasions in recent years towards the Pope and Holy See, in all the most troublesome and difficult matters', an evident reference to Henry's divorce. Even the papal bureaucracy had sympathy for the English ambassadors. Six months later, on 19 July 1531, Clement issued a brief assigning one third of Zibello and all of Tizzano and Ballone to Livia. It was a positive result for Gregorio, who could now move to extract rents from these properties. Was his reliance on papal support to assert this claim a conflict of interest? At the courts of the sixteenth century such matters were not understood in the same way as we might see them today. Multiple allegiances were not quite so suspect; switching sides not quite so exceptional. Yet it would be easy to suspect that Clement, with these grants, was hoping to buy influence with Henry's ambassador. A rather garbled rumour around the same time claimed that Francesco Casali had been appointed governor of the papal town of Rimini.[18] Whether that was true or not, the perception among the diplomatic corps of Rome was certainly that the Casali were in the Pope's favour. Given the state of Henry's great matter, that was quite remarkable.

Nor was Gregorio entirely lacking friends at the English court. Among them was Sir Francis Bryan. Now posted to Paris, and in no position to lobby in person for his friend, Bryan could nonetheless offer his support to his erstwhile colleague. He must have known that Gregorio was under fire. On 20 December, he wrote to his counterpart in Rome, William Benet, 'farther desiring you to show Master Gregory that what shall lie in my power to do for him he shall be sure on', and asking him to ensure that Gregorio remembered to send on some black silk hose and 'two pairs of the best perfumed gloves'. Bryan also asked to be recommended to a certain 'Signora Angela', whose identity, however, is unknown. In this letter arrived too the news of Wolsey's death. Should there have been any suspicion as to the cause, Bryan added that it came 'by God's hand'.[19]

Under pressure from the Imperial ambassadors, consideration of Henry's case was slowly progressing. On 23 December 1530, the cardinals met in a secret consistory to consider the king's great matter. Their conclusion was to forbid Henry's cohabitation with

Anne or his remarriage, an injunction confirmed in a papal brief
of 5 January. Henry, however, cared ever less for papal briefs. His
campaign for university opinions was more or less complete. They
were published in Latin in April and in English (as *The Determinations
of the Most Famous and Most Excellent Universities of Italy and France*)
in November of 1531. The Imperial ambassador believed that
Gregorio himself had taken the assembled documentation to
England, but he may have been wrong, for the dates are extremely
tight. But had Gregorio been in England in January 1531, he would
have seen the opening of the Reformation Parliament's second
session, and of Convocation, the assembly of the Church in
England, as lords, commons and clergy gathered to witness the
next act of Henry's campaign for royal supremacy. Although the
king's skirmish with his clergy saw both sides demand and win
concessions, the assembly was a portent of things to come. And
behind the scenes Henry had a new manager for his campaign:
Thomas Cromwell, former servant to Cardinal Wolsey and a man
fast rising in royal favour.[20]

13

Murder in Naples

In February 1531, as Henry's lieutenants led the charge against the English clergy, for our man in Rome it was business as usual. At the papal court, the ritual of the liturgical year continued, a semblance of timeless tradition in the face of change outside. On 2 February, Candlemas, Gregorio carried the Pope's train as Clement processed through the papal suite and into the Sistine Chapel, symbolising his master's allegiance, albeit increasingly tenuous, to the successor of St Peter. The processional route from the papal apartments, remodelled in the early years of the century under Pope Julius II, took him down a ramp stair from Raphael's loggia and into a series of three connecting halls leading to the chapel. The Sistine Chapel did not yet feature Michelangelo's *Last Judgement*, but the master's ceiling frescoes of scenes from Genesis soared above the heads of the papal court. As they sat in their allotted places, in strict order of precedence, they would have seen too the lives of Moses and Christ portrayed in frescos around the walls by artists including Botticelli and Ghirlandaio. The liturgical ceremonies of the papal court were splendid occasions, remarkable for their grandeur and magnificence. Clad in the appropriate colour – costly reds and purples, along with black, were favoured – the celebrant and his assistants would follow a detailed ritual, jealously guarded by the expert staff of the office of ceremonies. This occasion, Candlemas, marked the entry of Christ, light of the world, into the temple of Jerusalem, and the purification of the Virgin Mary. After a candlelit procession, Cardinal Santa Croce said Mass.[1]

Behind the ceremonial scenes, work for Henry's divorce continued. He and Anne Boleyn cannot have anticipated waiting four years, but although they might have wished to move quickly, there were difficulties to overcome. A radical approach risked losing the support of the nobility, not to mention the church hierarchy, whose sanction would be needed if the marriage were to be accepted in the land at large. It would take time to win them over, and to marginalise those who would not be convinced. Moreover, the French, keen to maintain amicable relations with the Pope and avoid Imperial hegemony, were apparently willing to broker a deal between Henry and Rome, and given the political problems inherent in a schism, that was one more reason to take things slowly.[2]

The opinions gathered from Europe's universities were now safely in England and would be read to Parliament at the end of March, all part of Henry's plan to establish his authority over that of Rome. Meanwhile, a new envoy joined Casali, Ghinucci and Benet at the papal court. Edward Carne was not an ambassador; he had no royal credential, and that was the point. For Carne came to Rome, he insisted, in the name of the kingdom, not of the king, to excuse Henry's non-appearance for trial (hence his title of 'excusator'). His arrival, as was the plan, provoked procedural chaos in the curia, a bureaucracy packed with lawyers who delighted in the sound of their own deliberations. It was a cunning tactic, which Carne, a member of London's College of Advocates, with an Oxford doctorate in law, was eminently qualified to put into action.[3]

The dilemma, as Carne posed it, was this: with Henry's conscience at the heart of the matter, the king could not reasonably appoint a proctor to act on his behalf, especially in a case of such importance. The people of England, however, would not stand for the absence of their monarch from the realm. Refused permission to appear before the Rota (the judicial arm of the curia), Carne went to Consistory (the assembly of the cardinals) to argue the point. The cardinals squabbled over whether to grant him entry, and eventually concluded no. That, however, did not matter. For precisely as was intended, Carne's mission had held up Henry's case while the English government carried on its work. And in the meantime the ambassadors – along with their French colleagues – could continue to lobby Clement in the hope of persuading him to compromise.[4]

In March 1531, a two-month suspension of the king's cause was agreed, in order to allow time for a royal mandate to be sent from England commissioning Carne to act on Henry's behalf. Without the proper paperwork, the ambassadors could do nothing, and getting it would take time, especially when the courier understood that there was no need to rush, and no one would mind if he dallied along the way. In fact the mandate was already in Rome, and the whole exercise was a feint to buy time. The Imperial ambassador, Miguel Mai, was infuriated. On 13 March, he wrote lamenting the Pope's decision to hear Carne again. There wasn't a man in Rome, he said, who wouldn't 'give his blood to prolong the case'. Thus the lines were drawn. The English tactics were even provoking dissent within the Imperial camp itself. The Cardinal of Trent, Bernhard von Cles, a long-standing Imperial counsellor, proposed that in the absence of agreement, a two-year delay in the English divorce might be in order. His suggestion received short shrift from Mai, who described it as 'a hole to let in a thousand inconveniences'.[5]

Gregorio still had family business to take care of. In a letter of 7 March to Cardinal Grammont, he continued to lobby for a French captaincy for his brother Francesco. Just as Paolo's connections with the Hungarian pretender John Szapolyai allowed the Casali to spread their risk, so a French job for Francesco would ensure an alternative sponsor should their ties to the English fray. Keeping up his lobbying in a second letter that month, he highlighted to the French the family's links with the Hungarians, pointing out the assistance they afforded to Szapolyai's secretaries in Rome. In the quest for new patrons, the Casali's ties to multiple European powers were an attractive commodity. He followed up early in April with a polite reminder to Montmorency that he was due a pension payment. No wonder Gregorio was worried about money: amid the complex negotiations over Livia's inheritance, in mid-April 1531 he had handed over an astonishing 2,500 ducats' worth of jewellery as security for the debts of a Pallavicino relative: a gold necklace adorned with ten rubies, a rosette of ten diamonds and another of eighty pearls; two gold bracelets with six rubies, six diamonds and twenty-two pearls; one pendant with a spinel and an emerald;

a string of forty-eight pearls; and a rosette of diamonds with another five diamonds around it.[6]

At the papal court, dramatic rumours of events in England were circulating once again. The Pope had been told by his nuncio and the Imperial ambassador that the English clergy had declared that they recognised only royal authority, and not papal. Casali insisted – correctly – that that was not true. Although the clergy had accepted Henry's new style as 'protector and only supreme head of the English church', they had insisted on the rider 'as far as the law of Christ allowed', a political fudge to accommodate wildly divergent opinions on just what that meant. Henry had yet to achieve a full acknowledgement of his royal supremacy, but the trajectory of the king's campaign was clear.[7]

Gregorio Casali now found himself increasingly isolated in Rome. He was excluded from the renewed diplomatic discussion around Henry's divorce. While the envoys awaited the return of the courier sent to England for Carne's mandate, William Benet and his French counterparts went back to Clement to argue that the cause should be heard in a neutral place. Casali and Ghinucci were not invited. The French negotiators were apparently proposing a secret deal with the Pope for an alliance against the emperor, for which Henry's support would be guaranteed with agreement to his divorce. Their embassy secretary, Nicolas Raince (he of the Sigismondo kidnapping), reported to his masters that Casali and Ghinucci knew nothing of these discussions, and emphasised the importance of their continuing exclusion.[8] Precisely why they were to be left out was never put in writing: perhaps it was for fear that they would leak news of the talks to the Imperial ambassadors. A more cynical explanation is that they were excluded on Clement's request because the Pope did not want too many witnesses to his stringing the French along. It is very unlikely that Clement seriously intended to come to a secret understanding with France against the emperor. Rather, he was playing one power off against the other. Having made his peace with Charles, he now planned to consolidate relations with King Francis by marrying his 'niece' Catherine de' Medici (technically, his first cousin twice-removed) to a French prince. The future Queen Mother of France was only twelve years of age, but that was quite old enough for a diplomatic marriage.

With hindsight, Raince's assessment of these discussions is implausibly positive. 'The English are most content,' he wrote to Montmorency on 4 May. And Benet, whose scepticism about Henry's plans for divorce had been apparent to Richard Croke, may have been happy enough. But Casali, also writing to Montmorency, took quite the opposite tone. 'All I will say,' he wrote, 'is that our king's cause is in a bad way, because these Imperialists . . . have managed to rebut everything that we've come up with to avoid getting to a sentence, so that we now find ourselves without defence or remedy.' Gregorio hoped that Cardinal Grammont might come up with something, but was increasingly doubtful.[9] He knew better than to trust papal promises.

On 23 April, Henry wrote to Benet alone – an indication of the mistrust that now surrounded the activities of his Italian representatives. Just as Pietro Vanni two years before had been instructed to plead 'as of himself' the destruction that would ensue in the event of Clement's refusing Henry, so Benet was to pretend to be acting on his own account. He was to tell the Pope that learned friends in England had advised him that insistence on calling Henry to Rome was 'the plainest entrée the Pope might make to the destruction of his whole authority here', and to request instead that Clement publicly offer a hearing of the case in an 'indifferent' (neutral) place and by 'indifferent judges'. But Henry made clear that this was simply a stalling tactic. 'We will,' he wrote, 'abuse them as they have abused us, for they have been to us always like [a] willow tree, showing fair buds and leaves without any fruit.' The Italian diplomats were to be marginalised. Benet could approach Casali or Ghinucci if necessary, but Henry thought it might be best to keep the matter secret.[10]

Benet, however, either missed or entirely ignored the suggestion that he should keep matters to himself. Having received Henry's letter on 7 May, he immediately told Casali of his commission, 'to the intent that he should advise those cardinals, which be his friends, to look upon the matter with a better deliberation and study, than they have done hitherto, and that they should counsel the Pope to excogitate some offer to be made to Your Highness that might be to your satisfaction'. Benet was still in the old operating mode, making the most of Casali's networks in Rome in an apparently genuine effort to win support for the diplomatic solution he yet hoped might be found. 'And indeed some of them at the first,' he wrote, 'of themselves thought good that it were well done that the Pope should offer unto Your Grace to commit the cause in some indifferent place.'[11] Benet resisted the conclusion that Henry had no intention of following this course. We are left to wonder whether he was disbelieving of English policy, disconnected from it as a product of his distance from court, or deliberately disingenuous in the face of an order he disliked.

On 10 May, the cardinals, meeting in Consistory, rejected Carne's latest arguments. The English – with French backing – continued to insist on a move of the case away from Rome, preferably to Cambrai, in northern France, and Clement began to consult with his advisers on the option. If the alternative was the withdrawal of English obedience to the Holy See, perhaps the emperor might be persuaded. As the curia wrangling continued and options for further delay diminished, on 31 May a delegation of Henry's advisers went to Catherine of Aragon to ask her to agree to the plan. She refused. There was now enough concern in Rome about Henry's activities for the men of the curia to worry. Having refused to lobby the Pope for the new strategy of a neutral place, Cardinal Campeggio was removed from the office of cardinal-protector of England some time before mid-May, and as part of the general attack on the clergy earlier in 1531 was constrained to pay a 'good sum' of his diocesan income over to the king. He 'feared worse'. Moreover, he blamed the Casali for the suggestion that he be stripped of the protectorate. Campeggio was not finally deprived of his English bishopric, the rich diocese of Salisbury, until March 1534. Later that year, Gregorio would acknowledge that he was now 'much hated' by his one-time patron.[12]

As preparations for the trial continued in Rome, Gregorio and his colleagues moved to secure the lawyers who would represent Henry. On 10 July, Girolamo Previdelli was formally authorised by the Bologna authorities to leave his duties at the city's university

and head to Rome. The same day, Henry dispatched new instructions to his ambassadors. Once again they came in two parts: one for
Benet alone, and one for all three of the diplomats. The differences
are instructive. Casali and Ghinucci were not privy to Henry's
instruction to Benet that he should try once again for a move of
the case to England. Nor were they given Henry's opinion on the
marriage of Catherine de' Medici. Why were they excluded? To
make a point about their reduced status? At papal or French request?
There is a less conspiratorial explanation. It was common practice
for ambassadors to receive two sets of instructions: one that could
be read openly at the court to which they were posted and another
making those points their master would rather keep secret. If Benet
was, in any case, discussing his tactics with Casali and had explicitly
told the king so, then Henry's separate communication seems
superfluous. For Henry, negotiations in Rome were increasingly
uninteresting. In July, the Imperial ambassador heard that Henry
had said the Pope 'did not understand that if he pleased he could
play a fine game'.[13] Whether or not the tale was true, it gave a
good assessment of the king's disdain for Clement.

Late in August 1531, the diplomats in Rome were briefly distracted
when the phenomenon now known as Halley's Comet appeared
in the skies over Europe. To the viewers of the sixteenth century,
comets were objects of mystery. Only in 1577 were they definitively
proved to be astronomical rather than meteorological phenomena,
and it was not until the eighteenth century that Edmond Halley
identified this one's recurrent pattern. To our men in Rome, the
appearance of a comet was a portentous event, often interpreted
as a heavenly omen. Francesco Gonzaga, the Mantuan ambassador,
reported divergent opinions on its significance. Some said it foretold
the loss of one of the great Christian princes; others that it presaged the ruin of the Turk. 'We will see what happens,' he added.
For three or four hours every night the comet had appeared in the
sky over Rome, and reports from Puglia were even more intriguing.
There, on 12 August, three 'celestial arcs' had been seen, and
between two of them were three suns. It was really quite notable,
wrote a Bolognese ambassador to his masters, 'because such things
have only rarely been seen before, except in our age'. When a

comet appeared the following year, Thomas Cranmer would write, 'What strange things these tokens do signify to come hereafter, God knoweth, for they do not lightly appear, but against some great mutation; and it hath not be seen (as I suppose) that so many comets have appeared in so short time.' Theirs were typical identifications of celestial disturbance with a period of political turmoil and religious divide.[14]

As meetings continued between the English and French ambassadors and Clement early in September 1531, Imperial suspicions were aroused, and Henry's next move only exacerbated them. With Wolsey's death, the archbishopric of York and the bishopric of Winchester had fallen vacant. Under normal circumstances, his replacements would be agreed at Consistory, although it was usual to accept the king's nominations. But would Henry, given all his moves against the English clergy, stick to the customary process? The answer – to the Imperialists' surprise and suspicion – was yes. Henry thus ensured that the nominations would have papal approval, and therefore that they would be legally watertight. Catherine of Aragon, wrote Eustace Chapuys, feared that this indicated 'some new understanding between the Pope and the King to her disadvantage'. On 20 October, the appointments were processed in Consistory, and on 24 October, the new Archbishop of York duly received his pallium. Henry was not yet fully prepared to make his break with the papacy, and the manoeuvre kept his options open, just in case a settlement might be forthcoming. But the men promoted were Edward Lee and Stephen Gardiner, both significant participants in his campaign for divorce, who would swell the numbers of his supporters in Convocation.[15]

In the meantime, Pietro Accolti, Cardinal of Ancona and perhaps the most outstanding canon lawyer of the College of Cardinals, had been in discussions with Gregorio Casali, following the papal line that the process could easily be strung out for a year or two. Casali was sceptical. 'I said that this did not seem likely,' he wrote, 'since the Pope was so keen to comply with the Emperor that the progress of the cause would not be stopped for even a single day. "It's not like that," said Accolti, "because however quickly the process happens, nevertheless the proposing of the sentence will be dragged out for a long time; and then pretexts will be found, by which means the Imperialists will agree that the sentence should not be given yet."' He added, with the phrasing of a true politician, 'I want you to trust me on this one.' Besides, he told Casali, he had 'never seen the Holy See act rashly or hastily in a cause which pertained to some prince but rather prudently, and at the appropriate time'.[16]

Why was Clement so content to delay? In the first place, because the alternative – a quick sentence against Henry – would undoubtedly alienate England from the Holy See. Perhaps also because he genuinely thought Henry's infatuation with Anne Boleyn might be waning. On 23 October 1531, he wrote to Cardinal Campeggio that 'the real cure for this evil will come from time – especially if it's true what we hear from some sources, though I don't know how reliable they are, that that Signora Anna has begun to decline in the king's favour'. Not so: it was precisely at this time that Catherine of Aragon was finally excluded from court life and retired to Wolsey's manor house at The More in Hertfordshire. Had the English diplomats been hinting, nonetheless, that Anne was on her way out? Did they truly believe it? Was it wishful thinking, or simply another delaying tactic? By now, they had thoroughly honed their collective skills in hindering the progress of Henry's case. Even the king collaborated: under final pressure to accredit a proctor for the trial in Rome, instead of a formal credential and powers Henry sent an insulting letter full of what Imperial agents called 'invectives against the Holy Father'.[17]

Matters could not be delayed for ever, however, and the English decided to campaign for more explicit support from Cardinal Accolti. They made little progress, and in October 1531 William Benet, in a letter to the king, described the cardinal as 'very obstinate'. But obstinacy could surely be overcome if enough cash was on offer, despite the papal mandate that prohibited the acceptance of gifts for advising on Henry's divorce against one's conscience. So when Henry VIII wrote to Benet with instructions concerning a 'princely reward' for Accolti, he covered his back with one of the most outrageous pieces of dissimulation in the thousands of letters concerning his divorce. Benet was to explain that 'This offer the king's highness maketh unto him, not to corrupt him, whose integrity, his grace knoweth well, neither would admit it, nor his highness' honour, most addicted to truth and justice, would be persuaded so to do; but only to animate and encourage him to defend and sustain the truth, and to let and empech [prevent] such injury and wrong, as is enterprised against his highness, in this his grace's matter.' The honour and integrity of the whole affair was rather belied by the fact that when Benet left for London to retrieve the paperwork, his trip had to be described as 'private business'. He arrived in London on 23 December. He would tell his master, said Miguel Mai, that 'his case is very differently thought of in Italy than in England or by his Council'.[18]

In London, Benet duly obtained authorisation to offer benefices to Accolti. But more intriguing tales of his sojourn in England come from Eustace Chapuys, the Imperial ambassador at Henry's court. Benet, wrote Chapuys, was 'very friendly'. Moreover, on his departure he had 'sent word to Queen Catherine that he begged her to pardon him for what he had solicited against her, to which he had been constrained, and was still constrained'. Furthermore, the Pope told Chapuys' counterpart in Rome, Miguel Mai, that before Benet's departure the ambassador had spoken in Catherine's praise, saying that as a doctor of law he could see the quality of the queen's case, and concluding that the Pope, in such circumstances, could not but do justice. Most tellingly, Benet regretted that the king sought to throw the world into confusion for such a fantasy.[19] Yet it seemed less likely than ever that Catherine would be restored to her former position. She and Henry were now living firmly apart.

In a letter of 2 October to Ghinucci, Benet and Casali, Henry declared that if the trial proceeded in Rome, all three were to up and leave. Clement had asked him for aid against the Turks, who had invaded Dalmatia (the area on the eastern shore of the Adriatic, now mostly part of Croatia but then ruled by Venice), but Henry described the reports of Turkish danger in scathing terms as baseless, resting on nothing better than 'idle rumour'. His ambassadors, reported the Spanish, spoke 'very cold words' on the matter. Henry had no interest now in subsidising campaigns that could only favour the Habsburgs. Although the following year the sultan would once again launch an invasion of Austria, that was Charles V's problem. The Casali family were in a position to know much more about the Turkish threat. For some time now Paolo Casali had been facilitating communication between John Szapolyai and the papacy. In the aftermath of the 1529 siege of Vienna, as Clement and Charles negotiated in Bologna, Szapolyai, who had been left in control of Hungary, had been excommunicated over his alliance with the sultan. On 9 October 1531, he wrote to Paolo again, with messages from Sultan Suleiman and the Grand Vizier Ibrahim Pasha. Under attack for his alliance with the Turks, Szapolyai – whose rule depended on the sultan's backing against his Imperial rival – was in a tough diplomatic position when it came to Rome. Nonetheless, he protested his loyalty to the papacy, and said he would be grateful to both Paolo and Gregorio if their efforts on his behalf bore fruit.²⁰ Thanks to their multiple diplomatic associations, the Casali now found themselves at the heart of a network of opposition to the Holy Roman Empire, linking the English, French, Hungarians and, indirectly, the Turks.

On 30 November, Carne was finally, definitively, refused admission to Consistory. The dramatic scenes were recorded by the Mantuan ambassador. The English and French 'bemoaned, lamented, protested, bullied and threatened'. The Imperialists demanded an immediate sentence against Henry. The English opposed it, else their king 'would cry to heaven, withdraw obedience from the Church, protest that justice had been denied, and appeal to a future Council'. Nor, if Clement proceeded, 'can the Holy See think ever again to have England a friendly or obedient subject; moreover they are hinting that they'll become Lutherans: beyond heretics'. It was, said the ambassador, 'the most scabrous matter'. Not hesitating to mix his metaphors, he added that it was a dish to provoke the worst indigestion.²¹

The English then demanded public audiences, in which the issue of Carne's admission could be debated. By this time, the question of the excusator had successfully exhausted ten months of curia debate, and there was scope to procrastinate still. In a Consistory of 11 December, the process of public disputes was agreed, but the

English were given only until 6 January to bring lawyers to Rome. There was, ruled the cardinals firmly, 'no hope of further delays'. Lawyers cost money. Just as he had pawned the family silver to fund troops during the Sack of Rome, and put up his own money as security for Andrea Doria's continued service to the papacy, now Gregorio Casali drew again on his own resources, this time to fund Henry's advocates in Rome. In the space of less than two months, from 8 November to 30 December 1531, he liquidated landholdings and other property to the value of at least 4,353 Bolognese lire (plus a further 70 gold scudi) – about 1,100 gold crowns. As Carne explained in a letter to Benet, describing their lack of funds, 'Master Gregory is glad to sell his lands, to get money to pay learned men in the king's cause; and so likewise the Auditor [Ghinucci]. I ensure you, both did it at this time with so good a will, that methought they would have sold all that they ever had.' Even allowing for the fact that during the same period Gregorio purchased a house for 600 lire, the sums involved were significant, and in January 1532, Henry wrote to thank him and Ghinucci for being 'ready and willing' to pledge 'all your property'. But if Gregorio's control of Livia's Monticelli holdings afforded him the credit to advance such cash, his grip there remained tenuous. He had to expend considerable effort protecting his wife's land from encroachment, lobbying the Duke of Ferrara for assistance in November and December 1531 when one of the duke's vassals threatened to raise troops against a Pallavicino castle.[22]

In Venice, in contrast, Giambattista Casali was apparently doing very little. A charitable explanation is that he was exhausted by his wrangling with Croke; an uncharitable one that he was increasingly hostile to Henry's cause. Either way, in the period after Wolsey's fall, from the beginning of 1530 to the end of 1533, his surviving correspondence with England consists of just five letters. It is hard to avoid the conclusion that he was increasingly withdrawing from diplomatic activity. (It seems unlikely that other letters were lost: Gregorio's correspondence survives, and in one letter Giambattista himself admits that he is leaving it to his brother to send news.) In November 1531, however, he managed to dispatch two cases of oysters to Isabella d'Este Gonzaga. But if Giambattista was pretty well distracted from Henry's cause, his cousin Andrea was still putting in the hours: on 22 December, he was back to consult with the canon lawyers at Bologna University.[23]

As preparations for the disputes began, tragedy struck the Casali family. Travelling to the kingdom of Naples, thoroughly Imperial territory, Paolo Casali was attacked by six assassins. He and his servants managed to fight them off and put them to flight, but when another twelve appeared, they proved too much for Paolo and his men, who were tied up, robbed of their money and stripped of their belongings. Suffering a blow to the head, among other wounds, Paolo was taken to Naples for aid, but died on 27 November. The Mantuan diplomat Girolamo Gonzaga wrote that his death had brought 'incredible sadness, not only to his relatives, but to the whole court, for he was always young, virtuous and lovable, and not little esteemed by His Holiness'. Gregorio had suffered the greatest calamity, but, wrote Girolamo, 'he is coping, with his usual prudence'. Giambattista seemed to cope a little less well. On receiving the news, he abandoned Venice and left for Padua, not returning for several weeks.[24]

Exactly what Paolo was doing in the realm of Naples is a murky business. Much later, Gregorio would tell the English that his brother had gone to obtain counsel in the king's favour.[25] At the time, though, others in the diplomatic corps believed that he had been on his way to the bishopric of Bovino, which he was due to take over from Cardinal Benedetto Accolti, its current administrator. If Paolo was indeed on an undercover mission – and the timing would fit – the bishopric would have provided convenient cover as he did the rounds of Neapolitan scholars. But if that was his mission, was this really just a robbery, or was it something more sinister?

14

How to Bribe a Cardinal (Part Two)

In the aftermath of Paolo's death, a moment of poor judgement or perhaps carelessness was to cause trouble for Gregorio Casali. He was accused of exceeding his mandate, and it would not be the last time he was so criticised. The problems arose when Gregorio claimed falsely to the French ambassador that he was authorised to negotiate on the question of subsidies for a military campaign against the Turks – the very campaign that Henry thought the product of 'idle rumour'. Perhaps he thought it was reasonable to pretend. But while his old master Cardinal Wolsey might have given him such freedom to manoeuvre, Henry did not. The king was decidedly unimpressed. He was surprised, he wrote to the envoys, that Gregorio had said openly before Pope, cardinals and ambassadors that he had an express mandate from Henry to treat and conclude with the Pope on aid against the Turk. It was neither true nor, wrote the king, conducive to his affairs. It was perilous to so incur Henry's displeasure, particularly with Richard Croke back in England, no doubt gossiping about the unreliable Casali. Our man in Rome would have to tread carefully.[1]

Things were not progressing much better in the king's great matter, but the English bribery of the two most corrupt cardinals in the College, Pietro Accolti and his nephew Benedetto, went on apace. Any negotiations had, of course, to be discreet, and so when they went to see Cardinal Benedetto, Benet and Casali did so secretly, 'by the back door, just the two of them'. The source for this tale was the cardinal's secretary, who knew the English diplomats well. He was Giambernardino di Ferrara, the man whose allegations about Livia's son had once led Casali to throw him in jail, and whom the cardinal had poached from the ambassador's service with the promise of 'rich reward'.[2]

When, three years on, Giambernardino was interrogated about his master's dealings with the English, he had plenty of beans to spill. He may have been telling his questioners what they wanted to hear, for he had a grudge against the younger Cardinal Accolti, who had threatened to throw him out of a window (Accolti admitted as much). Through the tales of Giambernardino and his fellow agents, a grimy story of English bribes and Accolti duplicity unfolds. Benedetto Accolti himself called it a game of 'capra e cavoli', a logic puzzle in which a peasant must cross a river with his wolf, his goat and his cabbages. He can only fit two of them in his boat, but left alone the wolf will eat the goat and the goat the cabbages. It can be done, but only with some clever manoeuvring. In the cardinal's metaphor, the goat and the cabbages were the Holy Roman Emperor, Charles V, and the King of England, Henry VIII, with whose respective ambassadors he was playing a cynical double game.[3]

We know about this game because tolerance of the cardinal's degenerate doings eventually wore thin, and in 1535 he was put on trial for abuse of power in his role as Legate to the Marches. An astonishing seventy-four accusations were made against him, ranging from murder to blasphemy and taking in most of the seven deadly sins along the way. Of by far the greatest import was the claim that he had conspired to put to death five members of the Ancona nobility on trumped-up charges. Relationships between the papacy and local ruling families were often tense, and inflammatory behaviour like Accolti's could create serious political problems. The accusation that he had been corrupted by the King of England was of relatively minor interest; by 1535, probably no one in Rome was very surprised. Nonetheless, the rich collection of surviving documents gives a striking picture of back-door diplomacy.[4]

With the patronage of his uncle Pietro, Cardinal of Ancona, Benedetto Accolti had accumulated church benefices from an early age. Born in 1497, and thus of an age with Gregorio Casali, he had his first bishopric, a hand-me-down from his uncle, in 1521, and became a cardinal in May 1527 on the strength of a promise of funds for the defence of Rome in the months before the Sack. In July 1532, another generous disbursement – nineteen thousand ducats – would buy him the office of Legate to the Marches for life. The six thousand ducats he was accused of receiving from Henry that year would surely have come in handy. The cardinal admitted in a note to his lawyer 'that the king sought in every way to have my uncle and me at his devotion', and that Gregorio Casali 'tempted me many times with the greatest of offers'. But he insisted he had turned them all down.[5]

By January 1532, it was becoming increasingly difficult for the English to sustain a strategy of delay. Despite Pietro Accolti's assurances of the previous September, Ghinucci and Casali had to report that neither he nor the Pope was now holding out any firm hope of an adjournment. On 8 January, the Consistory hearings opened, but a week later, following the umpteenth English stalling tactic (this time they claimed that their advocates had been delayed in getting to Rome), they were suspended until the end of the month. On 21 January, another English diplomat was dispatched to Rome to join Casali, Ghinucci, Benet and the excusator Edward Carne. Edmund Bonner was qualified in both civil and canon law and had previously served on diplomatic missions to France and the Netherlands; his mission was to protest the citation of Henry to Rome, thus further delaying affairs.[6]

The suspension of the hearings did not stop Clement writing to Henry on 25 January 1532 that his cohabitation with Anne was a scandal, and hoping he would take Catherine back. (The word cohabitation here should not be taken to imply that they were having sex: Clement was referring to Catherine's effective expulsion from court, and Anne's constant presence.) At New Year, Henry had pointedly refused to send the customary gifts to the queen and her ladies, favouring Anne instead with a lavish set of bedroom hangings in cloth of gold, cloth of silver and crimson satin.[7] It was increasingly clear that Henry had rejected his wife.

On 3 February, William Benet returned to Rome from England. On 7 February, he duly wrote to Benedetto Accolti, Cardinal of Ravenna, offering French benefices to the value of six thousand ducats a year, and a nomination to the first vacant cathedral church in England. If the bishopric in question was not Ely, then the cardinal would be transferred to Ely at the first subsequent vacancy. Ely was the fourth most lucrative bishopric in England, providing an income of over £2,000 a year, and perhaps a vacancy was anticipated: the incumbent, Nicholas West, was a supporter of Catherine. But later in the month, as the Consistory disputes resumed, the younger Accolti had still failed to convince his uncle Pietro, the Cardinal of Ancona, to back Henry, and Benet and Casali wrote to the king detailing their difficulties in winning over the elder cardinal. After fretting that the business might 'savour of corruption', Pietro Accolti had got down to serious negotiations. He demanded a set of promotions in the Church worth an annual six or seven thousand crowns, and not just promises thereof. He wanted a bishopric in England; he wanted part of the income to be derived from France; and he wanted the Abbey of Ferres, nine leagues from Paris, said to be worth three thousand crowns a year. Furthermore, he would like 'some jewel of great estimation' as security. Adding drily that Henry would marvel at the 'great desire' of Accolti's nephew, the Cardinal of Ravenna, 'to get promotions', the ambassadors nonetheless wrote that it was 'very necessary' that Henry agree to all the demands. They dispatched an agent to the French court to keep an eye out for appropriate church vacancies, pretending they were for Giambattista Casali. This new strategy found favour back in England: the king, wrote the Duke of Norfolk, could be 'no better pleased'. Henry sent letters enabling his envoys to obtain the requisite papal bulls for the bishopric. But to avoid the appearance of open bribery, he proposed to pay the cardinals in secret until such time as it was expedient to make the grant of the benefices public. Such a strategy conveniently ensured that the offer could be withdrawn at any time.[8]

In Consistory the formal disputes began on 28 February, and continued weekly. Sigismond Dondolus of Pistorio or Pistoia and Michael Conradis de Tuderto, two obscure lawyers about whose careers we know little, led for Henry. Carne kept up the delaying tactics, enabling the king to continue his complaints to Clement about the excusator's non-admission. In meeting after meeting with cardinals, the English blamed the delay on their opponents' 'chiding and scolding, and alleging laws and decisions that never were'. It is testimony to Carne's abilities that he had now held matters up for well over a year. On 29 February, Henry wrote instructing his ambassadors, once again, to urge Clement to allow the divorce to be determined in a neutral location. This was, however, still intended as a means to postpone the decision, much as Henry had envisaged it when he had written to Benet back in May 1531.[9]

Troubles with the divorce were matched by new problems for the Casali family. Gregorio's cousin Andrea held the title of Count of Mongiorgio, a small fief located eighteen miles south-west of Bologna near the family's country villa. He was now hit by Clement's decision, in a bull of 30 January 1532, to remove a number of countships that had been granted to Bolognese citizens back in the fifteenth century under the rule of Pope Sixtus IV. Gregorio would later blame this misfortune on the family's loyalty to England. Direct evidence to that effect is hard to come by, but in the aftermath of Paolo's death it is easy to imagine that the Casali might have believed themselves persecuted. However, a combination of a broad policy push for centralisation in the Papal States and simple bad luck on Andrea's part seems just as likely an explanation as papal vengefulness. What is true, though, is that despite vigorous lobbying, Gregorio was not sufficiently in favour to convince the papal vice-legate to Bologna, Francesco Guicciardini, that Andrea should be treated as a special case. He did his best: on 22 March, he and Benet composed a joint letter asking that Henry write to Clement in favour of Andrea Casali's claim to Mongiorgio. Several months later, Edward Fox wrote to William Benet that Gregorio was so troubled by 'the injuries the Pope doth to him' that had it not been for his diplomatic responsibilities, he would have quit Rome altogether. Henry was slow to respond: only on 18 May did he finally write to Clement requesting the return of Andrea's countship and favour for Casali in the dispute over Livia's property. One must wonder, given Giambattista Casali's apparent doubt over the whole matter of the divorce, how this might have affected him too. But whatever his inner opinion, and despite his apparent withdrawal from correspondence with England, in February 1532 he was to be found dutifully lobbying the Venetian authorities to allow lecturers from Padua University to travel to Rome and testify in Henry's favour.[10]

While Henry dismissed the Turkish threat, Giambattista was sufficiently worried by reports from Venice about the likelihood of Turkish invasion that in January 1532 he wrote to his cousin Andrea, urging that the women of the family should leave Rome and retreat to Bologna. Evidently they did not – or at least not immediately – for on Shrove Tuesday 1532, Livia Pallavicino attended a lavish carnival party in Rome for the ladies of the city, hosted by Felice della Rovere, widow of Gian Giordano Orsini and illegitimate daughter of the late Pope Julius II.[11] Perhaps she took the opportunity to lobby for the restitution of the Casali family property, for the guests included influential matriarchs of the Roman nobility.

With the loss of Andrea's countship, and English affairs looking increasingly shaky, the Casali now needed to ensure that Paolo's passing did not compromise their Hungarian connection, for as well as useful patronage, it brought the family information, a valuable commodity that could be exchanged with others in the diplomatic corps. On 6 January, Gregorio wrote an elegant letter to John Szapolyai's privy councillor István Broderics proffering the services of his brother Francesco as a substitute for Paolo. Francesco, he emphasised, was 'no less desirous' of serving King John than had been his brother. On this front at least, circumstances conspired in the family's favour. In January 1532, Antál Verancsics arrived in Venice as ambassador from Szapolyai, on a mission to make his master's peace with the rival claimant to Hungary, Ferdinand, King of the Romans and brother to Charles V. Verancsics had been directed to meet Paolo Casali, but on learning from Giambattista of Paolo's death, he went instead to stay with Gregorio in Rome. Gregorio announced the envoy's arrival – and his peace mission – to Ferdinand's ambassador in Rome, Andrea Burgo, whose response was far from encouraging (Verancsics, he wrote, would have done well to stay at home). In the company of Francesco Marsuppini, a Florentine diplomat in the Hungarian service, Gregorio presented Verancsics to the Pope. Unfortunately for the Casali, though, their Hungarian correspondence was being systematically intercepted in transit. Rodrigo Niño, Imperial ambassador in Venice, knew exactly what they were up to.[12]

Easter fell at the end of March, and on the 28th, Holy Thursday, Gregorio Casali processed to chapel, once again carrying the papal train, in an increasingly ironic demonstration of Henry's loyalty to Rome. On Easter Sunday, he joined the Imperial ambassador, the Venetian ambassador and the governor of Rome in bringing water for the papal ablutions during Mass. After Easter, the Consistory debates resumed: on 3, 10 and 17 April. Girolamo Previdelli, professor of law and one-time tutor to the Casali children, made his first appearance on the 10th. His performance was a credit to his home city, wrote the Bolognese ambassador Vianesio Albergato. Though he had little to add to the content of the English argument, his elegant Latin style played to a curia attuned to oratory; his speeches were quickly printed up by Asulano Blado, a leading Roman publisher, and rushed out within the month for the edification of interested parties.[13]

The English efforts at bribery, however, were not going so well. By the end of April, Benet and Casali had serious problems with the Cardinal of Ancona, who told them disingenuously that as he had initially declared himself in Catherine's favour, he could not, 'saving his honour, truth and conscience', change his mind without very good grounds indeed. If he were to suggest to any other cardinal that he favoured the king's case, his about-turn would be bound to incur suspicion, leading to the disclosure of their plotting and the 'utter loss of reputation and opinion'. Henry's ambassadors found themselves in a double-bind. Without revealing their own attempt at bribery, they could not push the cardinal to act. It was a perpetual hazard in the world of Renaissance reward.[14]

Henry, however, was moving ahead with the next step in a strategy that would dispense with any need for the backing of awkward cardinals. His attempt to assert supremacy over the Church a year earlier might have ended in a sticky compromise, but this time round things would be different. He now called the third session of the Reformation Parliament. In March 1532, he dispatched to his ambassadors news that Parliament had passed the Act in Conditional Restraint of Annates, which slashed the fees paid to Rome by English bishops on taking up their offices. In May this was followed up with demands for the outright submission of the clergy to royal authority. The ploy is often credited to Henry's new chief minister, Thomas Cromwell, but it was hardly unwelcome to a House of Commons that had shown considerable enthusiasm for anti-clerical measures over the past two and a half years, drawing up their own petitions on the subject with no need for government encouragement. The Church was another matter. There, Henry won the day not by convincing but by coercing both Northern and Southern Convocations. (Convocation was the formal assembly of the English Church, which met in separate synods for the archdioceses of Canterbury and York.) The lower house of Southern Convocation did not even vote on the proposition that future church legislation would require royal assent. For his pains, Henry's chancellor, Thomas More, resigned his office.[15]

Amid his accelerating campaign for the royal supremacy, Henry had not forgotten how to enjoy himself. As May wore on into June, he dispatched a request that prompted Casali to write to the Duke of Mantua in a tone of ironic resignation at the state of the king's great matter: 'The Most Serene King of England, having at present no other solace but to amuse himself with racehorses, wrote to me in days past, and now writes to me again . . . that he would like to have some Barbary horse.' It was almost three years since the advocation of the case to Rome, yet on 8 July, Clement ordered a further adjournment of the cause, until October, to give Henry another opportunity to produce a mandate for a proctor to represent him at the forthcoming trial. Apparently not realising the significance of Henry's move against the clergy, he still resisted the temptation to rush, making his attitude clear in a letter to Cardinal Campeggio of 19 June. 'The English cause,' he wrote, 'as Your Most Reverend Lordship knows, must not be handled precipitously, and is best dealt with step by step; and God knows that if it had not been so dealt with, perhaps some great scandal might have followed, whereas up until now nothing bad has occurred, except that the King has kept the Most Serene Queen at a distance from him, which he could have done with any number of sentences against him.'[16]

As Henry prepared the ground for a marriage to Anne Boleyn, English interest in the activities of our men in Rome all but evaporated. *A Glass of the Truth*, a justification of Henry's divorce, was published in England and rapidly translated into French.[17] Benet and Casali continued their project of bribery, but by mid-September were in a quandary as to how to continue, for no money had come from England and no paperwork for benefices from France. For a while, Casali had managed to string the Cardinal of Ravenna along, first promising that by the beginning of August he would be on his way to London and then using personal business to excuse the delay in his departure. But that bought only a temporary respite. In a panic, Benet wrote to the Duke of Norfolk: 'We here be in a great anxiety of mind, because we have had no letters from the King's Highness these four months, and also in a perplexity, as we cannot tell what to do.' The absence of correspondence can be dated exactly to the submission of the clergy, the point at which further dealings with Rome were rendered formally unnecessary. The lack of news had put the Accolti cardinals in 'such a suspicion, as it is not possible as yet to remove it out of their heads'. Benet was worried that Pietro Accolti's failing health would leave the matter in the hands of his nephew, and further, that if the promised benefices did not turn up, the cardinals might throw in their hand and 'bring the practice to light'. There was only one thing to do: send a messenger to the king. This time, Gregorio Casali would go in person.[18]

Casali finally left Rome at the very end of September 1532, taking the long post road to Calais, where Henry was due to meet Francis I, King of France. The Imperial ambassadors were suspicious of his trip on more than one account. No one was quite sure what he was going for. A Venetian ambassador in Rome reported that he took with him a papal brief asking Henry to send a mandate so that he would be formally represented in the divorce trial. The Imperial ambassador Ortiz wrote that he was conveying an order from the Pope for the king to leave Anne and restore Catherine (perhaps Clement had told him this). In a reference to Charles's continuing military campaign against the Turkish sultan, Ortiz commented that he expected the Pope to wait for 'the Emperor's victory as well as Casali's answer' before proceeding in Henry's cause. His colleague Miguel Mai wrote to the emperor that he feared that Casali, 'who had been much favoured by the Pope', had taken with him a secret commission. Moreover, he had heard that just before Casali's departure from Rome, Clement had dismissed a lawsuit from a rival in the thorny dispute over Livia's property. But in a subsequent letter to his counterpart Niño in Venice, Mai declared that no one should be deceived by Casali's claim that he was going to 'do good'. As usual, the English would all 'follow the king's madness'.[19] It was a telling observation, for even when they disagreed, like Benet or Giambattista Casali, follow is precisely what Henry's ambassadors did.

On 20 October, Henry and Francis began their summit, travelling first to Boulogne and then Calais. If it was not quite the lavish occasion that their 1520 Field of Cloth of Gold meeting had been, it was nonetheless magnificent. A propaganda account rushed out in the subsequent weeks described the yellow, blue and crimson velvet worn by Francis's guards as they arrived, the exchange of costly gifts and the entertainments, including banquets, bear-baiting and bull-baiting. And this was the first state occasion to feature an official appearance, albeit a brief one, by Anne Boleyn. On 1 September, she had been created Marquis of Pembroke in a ceremony at Windsor Castle. Her rank and condition thus established, it was even rumoured that she might marry Henry at the Calais meeting. Although her participation in the summit was limited to a single appearance at an official dinner (one featuring no fewer than a hundred and seventy dishes), her formal presentation before a foreign monarch was no small matter. Meanwhile, she had plenty of opportunity while Henry spent time with Francis to deal with her own business, and that gave her the chance to lambast Casali for his failures. A Captain Thouard passed on reports (albeit at second or third hand) that Casali had been 'ill-treated by the Lady for not managing her affair better, for she had hoped to be married in the middle of September'. He believed that Henry had intended to marry Anne in Calais, but for some reason the ceremony had been delayed, 'to the advantage of the Emperor'. One can only speculate what wrath the newly promoted Anne might have vented on an agent who had let her down. She had not got where she was without an assertive personality, and after five years to be so close, but not yet close enough, to marriage must have been extraordinarily frustrating. Casali's reported response – that fear of the emperor was behind the Pope's actions – cannot have been much consolation.[20]

Despite Anne's displeasure, Gregorio Casali left the summit with the substantial sum of three thousand ducats for the purpose of bribing the cardinals Accolti, and the grant for the bishopric of Ely that Pietro Accolti had demanded eight months earlier. By this time, however, it was of little use. The Imperial ambassador, Miguel Mai, who had simultaneously been courting the Accolti pair, reported to Charles V on 27 September that 'the cardinal of Ancona is very resolute'.[21]

On 4 November 1532, the Cardinal of Ravenna wrote to his uncle, who was now seriously ill, reporting the arrival of just two thousand ducats from England on 17 October (with another two thousand still to come). He proposed that they should hold out to see what both the English and the Imperialists were prepared to offer before deciding which would be the more 'expedient' way to lean. Two and a half years on, as the Cardinal of Ravenna faced trial, accusations and recriminations about the discrepancy in these sums flew between his one-time servants. The cardinal and his agent Flavio Crisolino both claimed that a second agent, Sisto Zucchelli, had helped himself to five hundred ducats. Accolti did not trust Zucchelli, whom he believed had been bribed by William Benet. His secretary Giambernardino had heard tell that the cardinal blamed Casali for keeping back some of the money. As Étienne Dolet had pointedly asked in his treatise on diplomacy, 'What involves more risk than the disclosure of your aims through disloyal servants, bribed by the enemy of your prince?' There was no honour among the Accolti household's thieves.[22]

But back in 1532, as the cardinal's servants skimmed off their personal premiums from the English bribes, events in the divorce were moving rapidly. On 15 November, Clement issued a warning to Henry to leave Anne and take back Catherine within one month, on pain of excommunication. Three days later, the Pope left Rome to meet Charles V in Bologna. Gregorio Casali headed there too. On his way, he ran into Marin Giustinian, a Venetian diplomat, at an inn in the small town of Briare, south of Paris on the Loire. Casali 'spoke much against the Emperor', said Giustinian, and threatened that England would break with the Pope. Giustinian sent this account on to his masters in Venice. On 15 December, the Imperial ambassador there, Rodrigo Niño, forwarded it to Charles V.[23]

Pietro Accolti, Cardinal of Ancona, died on 12 December. To his nephew Benedetto, Cardinal of Ravenna, he left a document outlining his opinion on the subject of Henry's divorce. It came down firmly on Catherine's side. But Benedetto told the English ambassadors otherwise. His uncle would have supported Henry, he claimed, but for now the Pope had asked him to keep that quiet. Casali therefore gave Benedetto Accolti the promises of benefices originally intended for Pietro – and, according to Benet, would have given him the money too, but for his own insistence that they wait for news from the king. Henry wisely instructed that Benet take precautions to make sure he was not double-crossed. He was to get a copy of the late cardinal's opinion, check that it was indeed in the king's favour, and only then hand over the money with an apology for the delay. And he should ensure that Benedetto kept the original safe, so that no one might 'counterfeit and adulterate the same to serve and make against us'. The king's caution was well-judged. For, as Flavio Crisolino told his interrogators, Cardinal Benedetto Accolti was entirely capable of forgery. Indeed, following his uncle's death, he had commissioned Sisto Zucchelli, his agent, to 'study that cause and note what was in favour of the aforesaid king'. The English, Flavio explained, had been late with the cardinal's money, and Benedetto 'was thinking to persuade the said agents of the king that the writings of messer Sisto were by the cardinal'. Sisto Zucchelli himself admitted that the cardinal had commissioned him to study in favour of the king – though not for what purpose. He added the politic observation that he had found the queen's case to have a better foundation.[24]

The Venetian ambassador to Rome, Marco Venier, would have been surprised by none of this. The Cardinal of Ancona, he noted, had advised the Pope on the brief he wrote to Henry desiring him to return to live with Queen Catherine. Benedetto Accolti himself would later admit as much. Pietro, after all, had been secretary to Julius II when the original dispensation for the Aragon marriage was issued.[25] But as Clement and Charles met for the second time in three years, Benedetto Accolti could reflect that his game of *capra e cavoli* had worked a treat. He had kept the Imperialists happy, and in the meantime had pocketed a good fifteen hundred ducats from the English, for which he had done absolutely nothing of use.

Did Henry care? Probably not very much. If he was not yet married to Anne Boleyn, it is a safe bet that they had begun sleeping together. By now, Rome was barely relevant to his plans.

15

The Break with Rome

Although Clement had agreed to keep the divorce case suspended until Gregorio Casali arrived back in Italy, our man's efforts at the Bologna meeting of Pope and emperor were no more successful than his attempt to bribe Benedetto Accolti. That was not entirely his fault. Perhaps stung by Anne's criticism at Calais, early in January Casali made a rash final attempt to broker a deal that would deliver the divorce. He took the long-standing English proposal for a trial in a neutral place, perhaps Cambrai, and floated it again. In the past – as Henry had made clear to Benet – this idea had been a delaying tactic. But now delay was no part of Henry's plan. The initiative would badly damage Casali's standing in England. Although the ambassadors in Italy did not yet know it, these were the last days of the campaign for the king's divorce. With Henry and Anne now lovers, there was every possibility of a pregnancy. It was of utmost importance that any child be born legitimate, for this could be the heir to the English throne. Anne and Henry married in secret, probably on 25 January 1533. Chapuys reported news of the ceremony on 23 February. Unaware of developments in England, and in the shadow of Henry's threat to abandon Rome, Clement, lacking alternatives, was finally prepared to support Casali's plan for a trial in a neutral place. Under very stringent (and quite unrealistic) conditions – notably Catherine's consent and the reversal of English reforms to the Church – Charles was ready to entertain the possibility too.[1]

Rumours flew round the English court that Henry had pulled off some sort of deal with Clement. On 24 January 1533, Carlo Capello, Venetian ambassador to England, wrote that the king had told him he had letters dated 2 January 1533 at Bologna from Casali, 'who writes that the Pope is inclined to satisfy His Majesty'. Whatever Casali's promising spin, the actual letter of 2 January was rather more ambiguous. Clement told Henry that following his meeting with the emperor, he now believed it right to summon a Council against the Lutherans. He did not, explicitly, promise that the divorce could be settled at the Council, but the more desperately optimistic of Henry's counsellors might have thought along those lines.[2]

Just as eighteen months earlier the appearance of a comet in the sky had occasioned portentous interpretations, so now did another heavenly event in London. Capello reported that 'on the eighteenth of this month, around sunset, there fell from the sky at Greenwich, to the south, a ball of fire as large as a human head, which is reckoned a prodigious thing, and has given them something to talk about'. The 1531 comet had been thought to presage the loss of a Christian prince, or the ruin of the Turk. We can only imagine what Henry's courtiers made of the meteor.[3]

Yet if Capello thought Clement was close to compromising, the Imperial ambassador Eustace Chapuys knew better. 'I do not know,' he wrote, 'whether he [Henry] makes up such stories to please the Lady, or whether his ambassadors feed him with such sweetmeats.' The arrival of Edmund Bonner from Bologna on 24 January can only have fuelled the rumours that something was afoot. On 29 January, Capello wrote that 'the king has large offers for the divorce'. The only sticking point was that the emperor wanted Henry to marry his sister Mary of Habsburg, widow of King Louis II of Hungary and governor of the Netherlands. The excitable Capello followed this up on 10 February with a report that a deal might be done by means of Princess Mary Tudor's marriage to the Duke of Milan, an Imperial ally, the problem now being that this would involve Henry breaking with the French. Others still believed that Princess Mary had secretly married the King of Scotland.[4]

Casali's proposed compromise, however, was about to get him into trouble. Just as he had been accused of negotiating beyond his authority in a discussion of aid for the Turkish campaign, he was now accused of negotiating beyond his powers in his proposal to move the case to a neutral location. In a letter presumably to William Benet (it survives only in drafts), Henry wrote that the papal nuncio in England had put to him a new deal from the Pope to resolve the divorce that had, apparently, been proposed by Casali in the king's name. 'Whereof,' wrote the king, 'we do not a little marvel, considering that we of late never gave unto the said Sir Gregory or any other any such commission or instructions for the same.' Involving the move of the divorce case to the much-discussed 'indifferent place', a general truce with the King of France and the conclusion of the divorce at a General Council of the Church, the deal was not much different to that proffered by the ambassadors to hold up proceedings over the past years. But that was no longer good enough for Henry, who insisted instead on employing 'the prerogative and privileges of our realm' to determine all such matters, without reference to any foreign jurisdiction. Gregorio Casali had had no commission to speak of such a deal, 'but rather to the contrary'.[5]

Henry's attitude – now that there was no choice but to ensure a quick divorce – was hardening. His instructions to Benet for his next audience with the Pope sum up the change of line. Once again, Benet was to speak 'as of himself', and once again, he had a script from Henry. It was an elegant one. 'Whatsoever your authority be,' Benet was to tell the Pope, 'which I will not dispute, You be Saint Peter's successor, a fisher, who when he draweth his net too fast and too hard, then he breaketh it, and pulling it softly taketh fish good plenty.' Referring to Cardinal Cajetan's failure to persuade the German princes against protecting Martin Luther, Henry went on: 'Remember how the net broke in Pope Leo's days by the foolish handling of a cardinal, who pulled and haled and so rent the net, that it is not yet made whole again, but rather rendeth more and more. Princes be great fishes, and must be with policy handled, and with evident and manifest right entertained, and neither can they, nor will, abide wrong, nor the shadow or visage of wrong.'[6]

There had, in these past months, been a gradual change in Casali's status. Previously, on his own account (and as he would say in his defence), he had been free to judge himself what would be necessary for the 'victory'. That was no longer the case. He was constrained to stick to orders, subordinate to Benet, to whose instructions he was not officially privy. Antoine des Prex, French ambassador to England, wrote on 3 February to King Francis that Henry was 'discontented' with Gregorio, and so was the Duke of Norfolk. 'He has barely any credit left here,' he wrote. 'All the same, the said lord of Norfolk told me that there are still some men on the Council who support him.' Norfolk expected that the king would keep Gregorio on until Clement made a final decision on the divorce.[7]

By February 1533, within weeks of Capello's overheated reports, the Imperial ambassadors had begun to suspect the marriage of Henry and Anne, and on 27 February – despite the fantasies that may have been spun around Clement's promises for a Council – a treaty was concluded between Pope, emperor, the dukes of Milan, Ferrara and Mantua and the republics of Genoa, Siena and Lucca to establish a defensive league of Italy. It included a provision that Henry's marriage would be tried only in Rome.[8]

The English countermove was decisive. Following the convenient though entirely natural death of William Warham, Archbishop of Canterbury, in August 1532, Henry had the opportunity to replace him with a candidate who – unlike Warham – would be prepared to rule the king's marriage invalid. That was Thomas Cranmer, architect of the opinion-gathering strategy. On 21 February, Cranmer's promotion, like the appointments of Gardiner and Lee, was approved by the cardinals in Consistory. It was proposed by none other than Lorenzo Campeggio, in return for a sum of about fifteen hundred ducats, only one of the many tips that had to be paid in such proceedings. On 3 March, at a subsequent meeting of Consistory, Cranmer's agents received the pallium – the long white lambswool cloth blessed above the tomb of St Peter and signifying his papal authority – and the appointment was complete. Cranmer was consecrated at the end of the month, and the principal arch-diocese of England was now held by a wholehearted supporter of the divorce. It may seem strange that Henry was so keen to ensure that the man who would approve his second marriage enjoyed the papal authority he purported to hold in contempt. But the king was not yet legally head of the Church, and if Cranmer was to rule on Henry's marriage, with all that that entailed, his authority to do so had to be unassailable.[9]

The news of Henry's displeasure with Gregorio filtered through slowly to Rome. On 10 March, Gregorio wrote to the king in his own defence. His tone was strikingly, and unusually, personal. 'Nothing could torment my soul more,' he wrote, 'than to know that Your Majesty has faith in those who have given false reports of me.' His loyalty and diligence had been proved over years of negotiating for Henry, but 'nonetheless, now you consider me stupid and lacking in reason'. He fiercely denied that he lacked diligence or was loose-lipped. On the specific charge of contravening his commission, he responded: 'I in no way deviated from the prescribed mandate, but in carrying out that which was itself in the mandate, brought to bear all my care, study and vigilance, and moreover contrived on my own account many supports for the completion of the negotiation, trying in all ways to lead the Pope to that which I sought.' Clement could testify to that. Casali did not wish to call the tales of him spiteful, but 'inaccurately written and related', as his colleagues very well knew.[10]

The said colleagues, among them Ghinucci and Bonner, were half-hearted in Casali's defence. Gregorio had indeed proposed that the cause should be committed to a neutral place, and had implied to Clement that he did so with the king's approval, but according to one account, he had only done so after the Pope had told him that insistence on hearings in England would 'destroy all'. 'It may stand well,' wrote the ambassadors, 'that Sir Gregory, labouring to have the matter committed into your realm, in conclusion descended to this, to have the matter committed to a place indifferent. And to say that he did this of malice, we cannot say, but peradventure he did it, thinking thereby better to serve Your Highness.' It was hardly the most enthusiastic of testimonials.[11]

Yet precisely what Gregorio had or had not done now mattered little in England. Within a few days of his letter, on 14 March 1533, a Bill in Restraint of Appeals was presented to the fourth session of the Reformation Parliament; at the end of the month the university determinations were read in Convocation, and within weeks any appeal to Rome against decisions taken in the realm had been outlawed. Henry was, as the famous preamble to the Act put it, 'furnished by the goodness and sufferance of Almighty God with plenary jurisdiction, to render and yield justice and final determination to all manner of folk, residents or subjects within his realm, in all causes, matters, debates and contentions happening to occur, insurge or begin within the limits thereof, without restraint or provocation to any foreign princes or potentates of the world'. No Vicar of Christ on Earth – or, as he would now be known, 'Bishop of Rome' – was to come between the king and his people.

On Palm Sunday, 6 April 1533, John Fisher, Bishop of Rochester and Catherine of Aragon's leading supporter among the English clergy, was arrested and held in the custody of Stephen Gardiner until Queen Anne could be safely crowned. On 4 May 1533, Anne and Henry were officially married. Less than a week later, the trial that would determine the validity of the king's marriage began. Thomas Cranmer presided, and on 23 May 1533, the new archbishop declared Henry's marriage to Catherine null and void. The king had been free to marry all along.[12]

In Rome, the mood veered between uncertainty and nervousness: uncertainty as to what the Pope might do in response to Henry's marriage and the Act in Restraint of Appeals; nervousness at continuing Imperial pressure to push the case forward. If Henry were to be excommunicated, that would offer his enemies religious justification for war with England. On 8 May, Casali wrote to the Duke of Norfolk, saying that he had heard that the duke had accepted his defence of his actions and, moreover, was trying to convince others to accept it too. Gregorio would be eternally grateful. He was anxious indeed that his innocence 'should be known to all'. His pleas appear to have worked. At the end of the month, Gurone returned to Rome bearing the sum of five hundred crowns, granted to Casali by the king in addition to his ordinary stipend. Precisely what debt this sum was meant to cover remains unclear – but it was evidently urgently needed. If Norfolk and, perhaps, others at court had not yet entirely salvaged Gregorio's reputation, they had at least convinced Henry that he should not dispense altogether with his ambassador's service.[13]

On 1 June, Anne Boleyn was crowned queen. The ceremony was lavish, but reports of it differed widely. An account unfavourable to Anne – probably by the Imperial ambassador, who declined to attend the coronation – described the refusal of the people to exclaim the requisite 'God Save the Queen' as she passed, and observed her disfigurement by a wart and a swelling on her neck. A description friendlier to the new queen portrayed the beauty of the flotilla in which she sailed from Greenwich, and the array of satin, cloth of gold, velvet, ermine and taffeta on display. As she processed to Westminster, tableaux were staged along the route, and fountains filled with wine. The French and Venetian ambassadors attended, though the former, according to Chapuys, had to endure the insults of the populace along the way; they called him a 'whoreson knave' and a 'French dog'. He probably found consolation in the extensive participation of French merchants in the procession: the English were concerned to curry favour with his countrymen, for they could not afford to lose King Francis's support for Henry's new match. Some courtiers, among them the Duchess of Norfolk – she of the secret messages to Catherine – did not attend at all. Nor did Gurone Bertani, whose courtesy letter from Henry dates his departure to 27 May.[14]

In response to this insult to Queen Catherine and her daughter Princess Mary, the Imperial ambassadors in Rome sought to push on with a public excommunication of Henry VIII. At first, many at the curia demurred. As Fabrizio Peregrino, a Mantuan agent, explained: 'Neither His Holiness, nor the Sacred College assent, so as not to multiply the scandal, and it would be a scandal to push him into withdrawing obedience from the Church entirely and falling into Lutheranism.' Carne and the English ambassadors continued to protest. Casali – who must have been at a loss to know where to turn next – insisted that he was doing 'all he could'. As the discussions of Henry's marriage proceeded in Consistory, some cardinals, notably Antonio Maria Ciocchi del Monte, were convinced to speak on the English side. By the end of the month, however, Peregrino could see no way for the Pope to avoid excommunication. Henry's 'great error' could not be excused: one could truly call him a Lutheran and an infidel. To sentence the king would be bad, he wrote, but to leave him unpunished worse.[15]

Gurone's journey back to Rome was not going well – after a fall in Savoy, he was 'very sick'. Even so, he managed to arrange for another courier to take on the letters he had been bringing from the king. Casali – unaware as yet that his agent had indeed secured the promised five hundred crowns – was still worrying for his position. On 18 June 1533, he wrote to Cromwell begging the minister to intercede for him with Anne Boleyn, thanking him wholeheartedly for his assistance, and stressing that if Gurone were to return without the grant in question, the scandal and damage would be incredible.[16]

On Sunday 29 June 1533, the Feast of Saints Peter and Paul, Gregorio Casali carried out his last ceremonial duty as English ambassador to the papal court. Once again, in his best silks and velvets, he walked the route through the papal apartments to the Sistine Chapel. As the senior diplomat present in the chapel, he brought water for the Pope's ablutions during Mass; this time, he held the basin of water for the pontiff's final ablution, the most prestigious diplomatic role in the ceremony. Perhaps, amid growing realisation that Henry was not long for this Church, it was a deliberate honour for our man in Rome. On the same day, Henry made his appeal to a future General Council in the event of his excommunication. The explicit defiance of papal authority that his ambassadors had resisted two and a half years earlier was now a reality.[17]

On 9 July 1533, Consistory finally moved to debate the sentence against Henry. On 11 July, it was duly given, and Clement formally condemned Henry's separation, declaring his marriage to Anne null and void. A bull was prepared commanding the king to restore Catherine and put away Anne, on pain of excommunication. It endorsed military force against him should he fail to do so. But still the Pope evaded a final decision. The censure would not be enforced until the end of September.[18]

On 12 August, Henry's envoys received their orders to leave Rome. The king had broken off diplomatic relations. Benet was withdrawn. Casali and Ghinucci were to stay, but no longer enjoyed the title of ambassador. Fabrizio Peregrino described how Ghinucci's nephew, a lad twenty-one or twenty-two years old, rode desperately across the continent bearing this news. Having tried to make the journey in four days, he died of heat exhaustion, the fourth traveller involved in Henry's great matter to succumb to the perils of the road. Summer sun could be as dangerous as Alpine snow. Peregrino reported the rumours too: Henry, it was said, had sent to Philip of Hesse, chief among the Lutheran princes, offering him 'accord, and good friendship against priests and the Roman Church'. He admitted that he couldn't confirm it, but such were the whispers. The Spanish Cardinal Merino of Jaen also reported the arrival of the courier, and the news that Henry wanted a divorce not only from his wife, but also from the Church of God. The Pope, he said, had taken it badly: the emperor should send letters of encouragement and comfort. Yet his letter betrays a belief shared by many at the curia that this was a temporary matter. 'If,' he observed, 'for some short while, the Holy See should lose the obedience of one unfruitful isle, it will win it from many other realms of far greater importance.'[19]

William Benet left Rome late that summer, but he never reached England, dying in the town of Susa on his way home. His demise prompted a confrontation between his companions Edward Carne and Edmund Bonner, and local officials about the diplomatic privilege appertaining to his person and possessions, which culminated in one official breaking down doors. Only after some legal argument from Carne and Bonner (well-equipped to deal with this little local difficulty after their years at the curia) did the Duke of Savoy eventually apologise for his lackey's 'misorder' and lack of discretion.[20]

On 7 September 1533, Anne Boleyn gave birth to Elizabeth Tudor, princess of England. A second daughter in place of the long-desired son can only have disappointed Henry, but at least England's new queen had proved her fertility. She had not, though, won for herself the security that a son might have brought. Around the same time, Clement left Rome for Marseilles and a summit with the King of France. The prospect of their meeting was most unwelcome to Henry, who was wary of any move that might jeopardise Francis's support for his marriage to Anne.

Like Charles's coronation at Bologna, this was another grand occasion, all the more splendid because Clement's niece Catherine de' Medici was to marry Henry, Duke of Orléans, Francis's second son. Her trousseau was an astonishing treasury of gold, jewels, lace and fine cloths; King Francis gave her a chateau and ten thousand *livres* (pounds) a year; Clement bought her out of the Medici inheritance with a payment of a hundred thousand gold crowns. On 13 October, the Pope made his solemn entry to Marseilles, seated on the papal litter and followed by a grand procession of cardinals and prelates. Two sumptuously dressed men led a white horse bearing the holy sacrament before him. Behind, two by two, came fourteen cardinals, all dressed in red, on horseback; then at least sixty prelates. The young Catherine arrived ten days later, dressed from head to toe in cloth of gold; she had her own entourage of pages and demoiselles, richly dressed in the Italian fashion. For the ceremony itself, on the 28th, she wore diamonds, lace, red velvet and ermine, and her gold crown bore a ruby so great it was said to be worth a kingdom. Henry was decidedly unimpressed at this development. He had hoped that Francis – supposedly his ally – would delay the wedding until Clement agreed to the English king's divorce.[21]

This great festival was attended not by Gregorio Casali but by his younger brother Francesco, who, on the strength of his kinship with the late Paolo, had been accredited as John Szapolyai's ambassador to the Pope on 29 July 1533. As swiftly as the Casali had lost one ambassadorship, they had gained another. Their difficult balancing act maintaining multiple patrons now paid off. Szapolyai was – like Henry – currently excommunicated, due to his dealings with the infidel Sultan Suleiman against a Christian prince (King Ferdinand, his rival for the throne of Hungary), and Francesco was tasked with attending the meeting of Clement and Francis to complain that the sentence had been carried out without a hearing. The Imperial ambassadors – noting that Francesco was brother to an English diplomat – suspected some intrigue between Henry VIII and the Hungarian pretender.[22]

To Marseilles, with Francesco, went Gregorio's long-serving secretary Guido Giannetti, who was already acquainted with the present English ambassadors to France, Stephen Gardiner and Sir

Francis Bryan. He would be a useful guide for the newly appointed ambassador. Gianetti had prepared himself for the break with Rome well: on 7 December 1532, he had been naturalised as an Englishman, and shortly afterwards he became a cathedral canon in the diocese of Salisbury, thereby ensuring himself an income. Francesco Casali duly met the King of France, and sent on to Szapolyai letters of greeting from cardinals Pisani and Trivulzio. He also met the Pope alongside King Francis and prominent French and papal courtiers, whereupon, having presented his commission, he expressed his new master's goodwill towards the Holy See, his sadness at the censures, and his desire for peace with Ferdinand. The King of France begged absolution for his fellow prince, but the Pope declared that without an explicit mandate from Szapolyai, he could do nothing.[23]

The endeavours of Gardiner and Bryan, meanwhile, were entirely frustrated. Francis I proved a fair-weather friend to Henry; he had no intention of holding out for a deal on the English king's marriage before concluding an alliance with Clement. If the Imperial ambassador in London is to be believed, letters from Marseilles in late October 'brought the King no very agreeable news, for I am informed by those who were present that as soon as he began to read he changed colour, and crushed up one of the letters in his hand for spite, saying he was betrayed, and that neither the French king nor he was such as he thought'. All that remained was to protest. On 7 November 1533, Edmund Bonner dramatically forced his way into the Pope's presence to present Henry's appeal against excommunication. To no avail.[24]

On 12 November, Clement left for Italy. On his own way back, Francesco Casali came down with a fever. Too ill to ride, he had to be carried the five leagues to the city of Avignon on a cart. Bertani and Gianetti tended him, but although the fever was not serious, Francesco had 'such a delicate complexion' that even the smallest thing left him exhausted. It is an image hard to reconcile with that of the mercenary captain leading troops and escaping his captors in Puglia, but several years on, his health may well have deteriorated. And there were more troubles brewing. Just as back in the summer of 1530 Rodrigo Niño had succeeded in having English correspondence out of Venice copied, now, once again, Imperial spies in the lagoon city were busily intercepting Casali's letters to Hungary: one from Francesco to Szapolyai dated 18 November at Avignon; others to his counsellors Antál Verancsics and István Brodarics of the same date; a letter to Hieronym Laski, Paolo's old Constantinople contact, three days later. A reply from Verancics to Giambattista Casali, dated 10 December, was copied too.[25]

In Venice, Giambattista Casali's position was formally unchanged. He was still Henry VIII's ambassador to the Most Serene Republic. He still had troubles with his bishopric: even in June 1533, more than five years on from his appointment, he was denied the full possession. He went back to the Venetian College to discuss the matter on 12 September. For now, an uneasy compromise gave him formal spiritual power, but his rival Barozzi controlled the temporal authority, and with it the income from church property that Giambattista so desperately needed.[26]

As for Gregorio, some time late in 1533, he went to England.

16

The Ingratitude of Princes

Gregorio Casali arrived in England by mid-December 1533. He would stay for more than six months.[1] He had three objectives: to mend his battered reputation at Henry's court, to ensure a continuing income from England, and to obtain for his brother Giambattista the post of English ambassador to Hungary. If all went to plan, the Casali brothers would have in their grasp three dovetailing embassies: Giambattista representing England in Hungary, Francesco representing Hungary in Rome, and Gregorio taking over English affairs in Venice. Considering all that had passed, that would not be a bad result for our man in Rome.

Gregorio's last long sojourn in London had been ten years earlier, when as a young man he had lodged with Gabriele Cexano, secretary to Pope Clement VII, in a house belonging to the Italian merchants Bardi and Cavalcanti, dealers in arms and luxury goods and friends of the Medici. He had not had the grandest apartments, but his room had been decorated with green and yellow hangings, which covered the walls and enclosed a bed with a little mattress and a luxurious feather quilt. An arras decorated with clusters of flowers and animals on a green background had adorned one wall, and a rather worn multicoloured carpet, perhaps Turkish, had covered a round table. He had had one small square box, a reinforced chest and an old stool; further hangings had served as curtains for the window, and the fireplace had been supplied with a basket of coal, fire-dogs and a pair of tongs. There had been no pillow or cushions, and no paintings hung on the walls, but it would have been comfortable enough by the standards of the day, and the fireplace would have helped keep off the chill of the English spring.[2]

Perhaps Gregorio now went back to this or another Italian household in the city. But ten years on, he found himself in very different circumstances. Then, he had been an up-and-coming young soldier-diplomat, favourite of kings; now, his reputation was badly tarnished by the failure of the divorce. Anne Boleyn was no longer the king's inamorata, as she had been when Casali had seen her in Calais a few months earlier. She was now Queen of England, establishing herself as Henry's consort, having new palace accommodation constructed, replacing the heraldic devices of her predecessor with her own and taking advantage of the property settled on her to live in truly royal style. If she wanted someone to blame for the years of delay in achieving that status, then Henry's man in Rome was a good candidate. She 'held him in suspicion', it was said.[3] Casali would have to work hard to persuade her that over the past six years he had had her interests at heart.

The king's campaign for royal supremacy continued. To date, Henry had mounted several attacks on the clergy; he had barred any appeal to Rome against an English judicial decision. Now, he put to Parliament legislation to confirm his authority. In November 1534, the Act of Supremacy and the Act Respecting the Oath to the Succession became law. The former established crown authority over the laws of the Church; the latter required all those asked to swear that they recognised Anne Boleyn as queen and her children as the legitimate heirs to the throne. The Treason Act established that denial of the royal supremacy was treasonable and therefore could be punished by death.

Against this backdrop Gregorio Casali mounted an indignant defence of his own actions as ambassador. Much of it responded directly to Croke's claims of sabotage, which, despite the scepticism of many diplomats, clearly had some currency at the English court. For once, we can hear directly from Gregorio – more or less. His twenty-one pages of self-justification, addressed to the Duke of Norfolk, are somewhat clumsily translated from Italian into English, but enough of his style survives to give a good sense of his intentions.[4]

He began with a caustic response to the accusations of Richard Croke, who he described as malicious. John Stokesley, now Bishop

of London, had been in Ferrara and Bologna and could testify to
the truth of Casali's account. It was not Gregorio, nor yet his
brother Giambattista, who had divulged details of the king's cause,
but rather Croke, who had revealed it to 'abject and babbling friars'.
Giambattista Casali had written to Stokesley to inform him 'that
the king's business and affairs were evil governed and handled',
said Gregorio. He had invited Stokesley and Benet to go to Venice
and see for themselves 'how lightly and foolishly the king's affairs
were ordered, treated, handled and governed by Croke'. The charge
of lightness, so often used against Gregorio himself, was now turned
on his opponent. Had it not been for the criticisms levelled by the
Duke of Norfolk and Cromwell, Casali wrote, he would not have
dignified Croke's allegations with such a detailed reply. It would
take 'so long a book' to detail his service under Wolsey, but in
short, he had done entirely as the cardinal had instructed: he had
had the king's cause committed to Campeggio and Wolsey and
obtained both the decretal bull (given to Campeggio, as Wolsey
had 'in the king's name commanded') and the Pope's promise in
writing to confirm the legates' sentence. 'I spared not,' he added,
'also to show unto the Cardinal of York [Wolsey] that Campeggio
was neither profitable, nor yet to be trusted in this cause [. . .] I
declared also to the king's ambassadors (as Mr Bryan and Peter
Vannes being then at Rome know well enough) all such things as
Campeggio procured against the king's highness.'

Gregorio went on to list his achievements as ambassador. He had
secured written testimony of Pope Julius II's corruption from the
governor of the Sauli bank in Rome. He and his cousin Andrea had
won a favourable opinion from the University of Bologna; he
had found scholars in Parma and Piacenza to support the king,
and despite an interdict from the Duke of Ferrara, through his
prudent operation had obtained a favourable opinion from that city's
university also.

'Now would I require you to be judges in this cause,' he wrote.
'You know well that those men which brought those tales and
complaints of me to the king's majesty are now in great favour
with the Pope, and as for me (as it is openly known) and specially to
many of you, the Pope hath, most unjustly and not without his own

great shame, taken from me six thousand ducats which lawfully belonged and appertained unto me, given of my wife's patrimony. Also against all law and righteousness he hath taken from my brother a certain monastery which the Venetians had committed unto him; for which cause my said brother is now excommunicate. Furthermore my cousin is of the said Pope derobed and spoiled of such honour, dominion and authority as he greatly flourished with in Bologna; with all which things the Pope cannot yet satisfy himself but daily afflicteth and oppresseth us with diverse molestations and troubles.'

Casali's decision to tie his money troubles to his English service made for good rhetoric. But how accurate were his claims? The first, that Clement VII seized six thousand ducats from Livia Pallavicino's patrimony, is rather muddied by the legal dispute surrounding her inheritance. The loss of Giambattista's monastery was as much as anything a product of the dispute between Venice and the papacy over the right to nominate to benefices. The loss of Andrea's countship also involved broader issues. Gregorio may well have thought it useful, in maintaining his relationship with the English, to portray himself as the victim of papal wrath. But there was more than a little spin in his account.

Casali hoped that a 'just and sober man' could be sent to investigate the claims against him. He cited the testimony of a string of leading diplomats, many promoted since their early contact with him: John Clerk, Sir John Russell, William Knight, Stephen Gardiner, Edward Lee, Sir Francis Bryan, Pietro Vanni, Thomas Cranmer, John Stokesley, Edward Carne and Edmund Bonner. They could all testify to the 'industry, study, diligence, labour, carefulness and zeal' with which he had handled the king's affairs. And although Benet's death had deprived him of 'an ancient and grave witness of my labour, diligence and fidelity, who I would to Christ were now living', Gregorio 'feared not but he hath in his life time testified unto the king's majesty his servants and ministers what service I have done'.

'Of truth I will not deny,' he continued, 'that it is high wisdom sometime to have servants in suspicion but yet for a cause; but why ye should suspect me I cannot imagine any other cause but that ye take me for a fool and judge me to have played the fool in that I have preferred the king's service above my own profit.'

'I think there be no man in Christendom hath had more occasion to attain high honour and promotion than I. I saw the Pope both before and after his captivity in such calamity and misery that he had no man besides me that either would or could help him, such was the king's mind. If at that time I would have esteemed honour, dignities and promotions better than the king's service, who doubteth but I might have had a great many and of the best?' He gave an example. The Duke of Milan had offered him a lordship worth four thousand ducats a year – a vast improvement on the five hundred he had annually from the French – to circumvent English war policy and agree that French troops should stay in Lombardy. 'Yet because it pleased not the king's highness so,' he wrote, 'I resisted all their sentences and minds, and threatened that I would not deliver the money unless they would go further.'

Gregorio could have taken their offers, 'and done such things as did redound unto mine own profit'. All the more easily because he was left to act 'as I myself should judge to be most necessary for the victory to be obtained'. That was a convincing depiction of his early employment in the English service, when, under Wolsey, he had been trusted to devise his own tactics, whether those involved kidnapping enemy agents, intercepting the letters of supposed friends or managing the bribery of secretaries. Despite this latitude, though, he 'would ever keep myself sincere and faithful in all things'. No one would find him taking 'bribe or reward', as was evident from the 'poverty of my house'. Since he began to serve the king, he wrote, 'I have spent and consumed of my father's goods more than thirty thousand ducats, insomuch that if I had not had much substance come to me of my wife's dowry, I should now have been in an evil case. And yet the Pope doth daily so trouble and molest me that I think all that is left will shortly be brought to nought.'

'Ye shall find also,' he went on, 'that I and my kindred shall be an example to every man of the ingratitude of princes; and besides that, a common jesting stock to all men which for our service with great loss have no reward at all. Albeit I had daily so many promises that the purse wherein they be kept is now full. And now that I have thought the time of my reward to be at hand, I have perceived a right good one to be prepared for me, and precious one, and well coloured, that is to be released from the pains which servants taketh.'

Although his criticism of the French had lost him his pension and jeopardised the prospect of a command for his brother Francesco, he had no regrets. 'What I have done pleaseth me right well, and if it so required I would do it again, and I am glad that I have done it; for I think myself rich enough as long as I may save mine honour and fame without corruption.' Despite its obvious discrepancy with the string of pleas for financing he issued in previous years, Casali's emphasis on honour and fame above money has a fine rhetorical ring. He was far from the only courtier to feign indifference while pursuing a quest for lucrative offices. But it was also an ambassador's job to express his prince's honour through his chivalrous comportment and liberal lifestyle. He was expected to personify the monarch he represented, and his own reputation was far from irrelevant in his ability to do so. Gregorio's claim of papal persecution, meanwhile, would play well to the more anti-clerical cluster at Henry's court.

In these first months after Anne's coronation, Henry's attack on the clergy rolled on. For a while its focus was the notorious case of Elizabeth Barton, the holy maid of Kent, a nun whose prophetic visions of Henry's fall and death were exploited by the king's opponents. After months of imprisonment, she was executed in April 1534, and Henry took the opportunity to turn on her more prominent supporters too. Catherine of Aragon, now mere dowager princess, and her daughter Mary were marginalised and kept apart from one another. The former queen was moved from her lodgings at the bishop's palace in Buckden to the Cambridgeshire village of Kimbolton; Mary had been transferred from Beaulieu Palace in Essex to Hertford Castle in the autumn of 1533. At the end of March, the Act of Succession, definitively bastardising Mary in favour of her half-sister Elizabeth, received Royal Assent.[5] Those who refused to take the Oath of Succession, declaring their loyalty to the younger princess over her sister, faced grim consequences.

Among them was John Fisher, Bishop of Rochester – arrested once already over his support for Catherine of Aragon – who now went to the Tower.

A year on from Henry's marriage to Anne Boleyn, his divorce case was still not formally concluded in Rome. On 8 January 1534, Catherine's advocates appeared once again to demand its conclusion; it was agreed that it would be expedited as quickly as possible. Final sentence against Henry was given on 23 March, and the men who for more than six years had occupied themselves with the king's divorce began to drift on to new roles and new places. Around January 1534, Giambernardino di Ferrara, perhaps in England with Gregorio, declared his intention to establish himself permanently in the realm, and petitioned Henry VIII for assistance. Casali may have looked for alternatives too. The Imperial ambassador Eustace Chapuys knew that he was considering leaving the English service. Henry, meanwhile, was seeking new diplomatic alliances. In late January 1534, he proposed to the Venetians a secret understanding that would have emphasised the two nations' friendship but without any public statement to that effect. They turned him down, but the vote was close. Giambattista Casali was still there in Venice, facilitating – if perhaps half-heartedly – his master's business.[6]

In the meantime, Gregorio had gone some way towards mending his relationships at court. Perhaps Henry, buoyed up by news of Queen Anne's second pregnancy and the renewed expectation of an heir for the English throne, was moved to look benignly on his agent. Casali was certainly managing to rehabilitate himself better than his erstwhile colleague in Rome, Girolamo Ghinucci, who lost his bishopric of Worcester in March 1534, victim of Parliament's move against foreign holders of English benefices. Gregorio, in contrast, moved on with his plan to get Giambattista into Hungary. On 23 March 1534, he wrote to Andrea Corsini, an agent and secretary of John Szapolyai who was currently at the French court, asking him to come to England and telling him of Henry's enthusiasm for such a visit. There was probably some exaggeration there, but Gregorio had every interest in pulling together his English and Hungarian patrons, and the English had little to lose, if Corsini came, by dispatching a small-scale reciprocal mission to Szapolyai.

On Corsini's arrival in England, Gregorio briefed him on matters of etiquette and how to proceed with Henry, just as he had done on myriad occasions for visiting English diplomats in Rome, and accompanied his Hungarian colleague round a series of meetings with Henry, Cromwell and the French ambassador. His scheme clearly worked, for by the end of the month Chapuys was reporting the proposal that Gregorio might go to Venice on behalf of the English, while Giambattista went to Hungary.[7] Chapuys, however, was not the Imperialists' only source of information on Gregorio's activities, for in Venice, his counterpart Rodrigo Niño's spies were as active as ever.

In June 1533, the Holy Roman Empire had made peace with the Turks, but there were outstanding issues, not least the fate of Hungary, where domestic divisions in the nobility complicated matters. In the summer of 1534, Lodovico Gritti, now entrusted with Turkish affairs in Hungary, went to Vienna with a commission to treat with Ferdinand on the sultan's behalf. But his ambitions to install himself as ruler of Hungary led to his assassination in September of that year, and the future of the kingdom seemed ever less certain. In the circumstances, it is no surprise that Niño stepped up his activities from intercepting letters to kidnapping their bearers. The tactic that Gregorio had once used so effectively against Sigismondo di Ferrara was now turned on a courier taking Giambattista's letters to Hungary. In early June, it was discovered that this messenger had been captured near Vienna. 'He was held in jail for almost three months,' reported Giambattista, 'and during this time was often interrogated, and also brought to the torturers, so that they might terrify him.' It was common practice to frighten suspects into confessing by means of a display of torture instruments. But there was worse to come. Letters with news of the capture from both Giambattista in Venice and Francesco in Rome were intercepted too.[8] The much-hoped-for Hungarian connection was proving a poisoned chalice.

Unaware of all this, on 10 July 1534, in the small town of Chertsey on the river Thames, where Henry VIII had gone on summer progress, Gregorio Casali obtained for his brother the coveted English credential to Hungary. Shortly after he did so, Anne's second pregnancy ended: perhaps in miscarriage, perhaps in stillbirth.[9]

On 11 July, Gregorio left for Rome. Clement VII was again
seriously ill, but this time he was not expected to survive. Gregorio
was to assist at the conclave. Clement died on 25 September 1534,
and Gregorio reported the 'great rejoicing' of the populace at
the death of 'the saddest prince in the world'. The demise of the
man who had presided over the Sack and humiliation of their
city was no cause for mourning. Such was their gruesome glee
that one night his tomb was broken open and his corpse stabbed.
Like the desecration of Julius II's tomb during the Sack or Lautrec's
body after the siege of Naples, this was a gesture of unqualified
contempt. The epitaph 'Clement VII, Pontifex Maximus, whose
unconquerable virtue was surpassed only by his clemency' was
rudely amended to 'Inclement VII, Pontifex Minimus, whose
conquerable virtue was surpassed only by his avarice' and had
to be recarved. Henry celebrated too; according to Chapuys, he
took the 'greatest pleasure in the world' in Clement's death.
'Cromwell,' the ambassador went on, 'has been unable to refrain
from saying several times in public that this great devil was dead,
and it seemed as if he was very sorry he could find no worse
name for him than devil.'[10]

The conclave began on 11 October. For the purpose of lobbying
the cardinals whose votes would decide the election, Casali was
supplied with blank letters of credence from Henry VIII. These
came with a space to insert the name of the desired candidate,
once votes were counted and the diplomats could establish which
of the leaders in the race was most favourable to the English. (This
was standard practice: such diplomatic 'blanks' had a venerable
history.) Even having broken with Rome, the King of England was
still concerned with the outcome of the election, for the political
stripe of the papacy was important on the European diplomatic
scene. Gregorio too had his own interest in the result. It would be
bad news, he wrote to the French diplomat Jean du Bellay, if
Campeggio were to be elected, both for Anglo-French concerns
but also in personal terms, because Campeggio 'much hated' Casali.
He lobbied the cardinals of Lorraine, Bourbon and Tournon against
Campeggio, and arranged for Giambattista to travel to the conclave
with Cardinal Ercole Gonzaga in an effort to convince him too.

That meant Giambattista could not, for now, pursue his planned mission to Szapolyai's court at Buda. However, he had every reason to go to Hungary, for on 23 September the Council of Ten in Venice ruled once again against his entitlement to the bishopric of Belluno, and Giambattista found himself more than ever in need of alternative patrons.[11]

The conclave was brief, and Campeggio did not triumph. The ailing sixty-six-year-old Roman cardinal Alessandro Farnese proved an ideal interim choice for those who preferred to put off a longer-term decision, though it was an unwelcome surprise to some when he lived another fifteen years. Once Farnese's prospects for victory became clear, Casali took his blank letters, filled them in and handed them out. On 12 October, after only one day of conclave, Farnese was elected. He took the name Paul III. In the early days of the new papacy, Casali told Cromwell, he was approached by the Pope and asked for his opinion on the best way to achieve a reconciliation between England and the Holy See. He replied that having no commission to speak on the matter, he was unwilling to offer advice. His comment acknowledged the change in his freedom to manoeuvre: whereas previously he had been free to judge for himself what would be necessary for the 'victory', that was no longer the case. After the painful experience of his freelance efforts in Bologna, he had learnt his lesson. Instead, he asked Farnese's long-serving secretary, Latino Giovenale de' Manetti, uncle of his wife Livia, to make discreet enquiries of the Pope as to the possibilities. Despite receiving no regular response, he continued to write to England with updates on the situation in Rome.[12]

In the autumn of 1534, rumours circulated that Henry and Anne had fallen out, and Casali repeated the story to the Pope, hoping to be the bearer of good news. The Imperial diplomats were more cautious. One of Charles V's agents in Rome, Fernando de Silva, Count of Cifuentes, even wrote that he had told the Pope to give no credit to Casali's report. True, Anne had miscarried in the late summer of 1534, and her second failure to produce the much-desired royal son put her under considerable strain, but it was not the disaster for the royal relationship that her opponents at court would have liked. Casali, however, may have worried that disappointment for Henry – whose favour he had struggled to recapture – would work against his interests with the English.[13]

For the moment, Casali's English dealings were rather limited. Shrewder than his brother Giambattista in these matters, he kept up correspondence with Cromwell despite receiving little in the way of reply until April 1535, when the minister finally wrote to acknowledge the letters he had sent since his departure from England and to thank him for his diligence in writing. For the first time in over six months, Gregorio also received some diplomatic instruction from England: Cromwell suggested that he should try to persuade the Pope to pronounce Henry's marriage to Anne valid. This was not a serious attempt at reconciliation with the Roman Church; rather, as with so many diplomatic tactics, it was a means of playing for time, on this occasion in order to stave off any attempt to use Henry's excommunication as an excuse for war. Still, it meant that Casali once again had a useful, albeit informal, function in Rome that proved worthwhile to the English. His importance, though, should not be overstated: Rome was no longer the English priority.[14]

Gregorio Casali, therefore, had every reason to focus his efforts on other patrons. Although the conclave had temporarily delayed Giambattista's Hungarian mission, the Casali family continued to facilitate John Szapolyai's diplomatic business. In early 1535, Gregorio assisted a visiting servant of Peter Crusics, Count of Klis (in modern-day Croatia), who had some business in Rome. He also had to deal with the consequences of the courier's kidnapping, informing the French that Andrea Corsini's credential to Hungary had been intercepted and advising that, given the approaching talks between Szapolyai and Ferdinand, they should send another. With papal assistance, he was also working to restore himself to French favour, probably with the aim of regaining his pension, though he may also have hoped to find Giambattista some role in the French service. Gregorio was increasingly conscious of the risks of a mission to Hungary at a time when peace negotiations were about to begin between Szapolyai and Ferdinand, and went so far as to try and persuade Giambattista against it, in both his own name and the Pope's. His brother, however, was convinced the plan could work.[15]

Gregorio was also ill again, and that delayed his travel to Venice to take over the role about to be vacated by his brother. Giambattista was in financial trouble. Unable to extract either the income from his Venetian bishopric or his English stipend, he owed three thousand florins to merchants, and could not pay. 'With the thought that he could acquire some good benefice', he decided to head for Hungary. Andrea Corsini, too, had a financial motive for his mission: he had run out of money and needed to settle his accounts with his master. On 17 March 1535, after almost ten years' service as English ambassador to Venice, Giambattista Casali left his post. He received the traditional leaving gift from the Venetian senate: 'silver, gold or money' to the value of five hundred ducats; his secretary was presented with fifty ducats' worth of cloths of silk or money. From Venice, Giambattista headed east – perhaps by sea, perhaps land – to Zagreb, the capital of modern-day Croatia, where he hoped to meet the city's bishop. Well aware of the dangers of his mission, and having failed to obtain a safe-conduct, he took the precaution of disguising himself as a cattle trader, as did Andrea Corsini, who accompanied him. A servant went ahead, separately, with his diplomatic credentials.[16]

On 4 April 1535, having found lodgings at the castle of Samobor, some fifteen miles west of Zagreb, some of Giambattista's attendants were apprehended by the castellan, Leonard Grüber. Suspicious of their mission, Grüber soon discovered their identities: Giambattista was a sufficiently well-known figure that he thought it pointless to pretend. He admitted his real name, and that he was travelling on a mission to Szapolyai. He contrived to ensure that a servant fled to his brother with news of his capture, but the confession sealed his fate, and Grüber handed him over to the Imperialists. Giambattista was now a prisoner of King Ferdinand. The long-running Casali financial troubles – and the systematic spying of Rodrigo Niño – had finally led to real grief.[17]

17

A Mother's Tears

From Samobor, Giambattista was transferred two hundred miles north to the forbidding castle of Wiener Neustadt, some thirty miles south of Vienna, where he was held in 'a dark and miserable room'. The castle, built in the thirteenth and fourteenth centuries, had once been the Imperial court's principal residence, but was now more of a short-term country retreat. In 1522, the town had been the site of the infamous 'Hanging Court of Wiener Neustadt', where rebel Viennese councillors had been tried and executed as the new King Ferdinand imposed his authority in the area. Its prisons were not propitious quarters for an ambassador of the heretic Henry VIII. Gregorio feared that since Ferdinand knew that Giambattista had opposed his interests when at Venice, he would treat his prisoner worse than usual. It is no surprise that by the time Giambattista came to make his statement to Ferdinand's interrogators, he was 'totally terrified, his hands and lips trembling, and barely able to speak'.[1]

At first, Giambattista was careful indeed with his story. Omitting any mention of his brother Paolo's long-standing connection with the Hungarians, he explained that for many years he himself had been English ambassador to Venice. When, the summer before, his brother Gregorio had found himself at Henry's court and had met Szapolyai's envoys, it had seemed 'a matter of civility' for Henry to reciprocate by sending an embassy to Szapolyai in return. Giambattista had wanted for some time to leave his post in Venice, and Henry had thought to replace him with Gregorio. Before he did so, however, the king had committed him to carry out one last mission: to Hungary. This, however, had been delayed, because Giambattista had had to travel to Rome for the conclave, and had subsequently stayed there for two or three months. During that time, Gregorio had given him the details of his commission. As soon as he had taken his leave from Venice, he was to go to Szapolyai with a general message of friendship from Henry and, in particular, encouragement to settle his differences with Ferdinand. It seemed, so Giambattista told his captors, a rather tough business, given that the voyage would be long and uncomfortable, and that he would be bound to fall under suspicion. He had tried, via Cardinal Salviati, to procure a safe-conduct; Salviati had discussed it with Bernhard von Cles, Cardinal of Trent and an Imperial counsellor, but von Cles said he could do nothing, and the papal nuncio with Ferdinand, Pier Paolo Vergerio, could not help either. Despite Giambattista's efforts he was left, on his departure from Venice, with no safe-conduct. However, he explained, 'it seemed to me discourteous not to obey my lord in what he had commanded me, or at least not to try to obey him'. So he set off, hoping to acquire a safe-conduct at Zagreb via the offices of the city's bishop, or else to find some impediment that would prevent him from taking the journey altogether but allow him to show that he had, at least, tried.[2]

That was his first confession. By the time he faced his interrogators in Wiener Neustadt, he was scared enough to add much more to that story, telling them of his brother Paolo's meeting with Hieronym Laski in Constantinople, of his subsequent service to Szapolyai in Rome, and of how, after Paolo's death, Gregorio had secured for Francesco a position in the Hungarian service. He also related how Gregorio had seen to it that he, Giambattista, was sent by Henry to Hungary, yet he still insisted he had nothing to do with the 'intrigues of these princes'.

As soon as the news of Giambattista's imprisonment reached Rome, early in May, the Casali family protested to Paul III of the injustice. To be precise, Antonina Casali, Giambattista's mother, protested, and her tears, wrote the frustrated Imperial ambassador, won over the Pope. Antonina's family, the Caffarelli, had long-standing ties to the Farnese clan, their fellow Romans; indeed, they had intermarried with 'all the best families' of the city. She could plead for the release of her son on those terms, just as Giambattista had once turned to his patron Isabella d'Este to seek Francesco's release. Antonina is not mentioned in any other letter over the ten years of her son's diplomatic service. But for this one, we would know nothing of her existence. Yet suddenly it changes our picture of the family. Where was she, all these years? She must have been thirty or younger when she was widowed in 1506. Bringing up her seven children as a single mother, even with help from family and her fellow guardians, perhaps she became something of a matriarch. Was she the *éminence grise* managing her sons' careers? Or did she retreat, as many widows did, from the lives of her children, once her sons were grown and her daughters married? It is impossible to know, but it is at least conceivable, that there was one more diplomat in the Casali family than we have accounted for.[3]

Prompted by the Casali complaints, Paul III dispatched his secretary Ambrogio Ricalcati to Ferdinand's ambassador Gabriel Sanchez. Sanchez did not mince his words: Giambattista 'thoroughly deserved to be caught and punished', he said, because he was going to Szapolyai in the name of the King of England, against Ferdinand's interests and 'much against' the Catholic faith. Ricalcati said the French had told him that Giambattista also went in the name of the King of France; moreover, because his mother was a Roman and an ally of the Farnese, and because Giambattista was a bishop and a papal subject, the Pope would be most grateful if he might be freed. But he did Giambattista no favours when he admitted to Sanchez that 'His Holiness would not have intervened had he not been won over by the tears of Casali's mother'. It was bad luck for the Casali that Paul had entrusted Ricalcati with this task, for the secretary's loyalties lay with the Imperialists, for whom he later became a spy. Moreover, the extensive evidence of intercepted letters to Hungary, combined with Andrea Corsini's confession (obtained under torture), exacerbated Giambattista's troubles.[4]

Giambattista's imprisonment also posed problems for his brother's efforts to re-establish himself in the English service. Having just rebuilt relationships at the Henrician court, Gregorio now had to plead with his patrons for assistance to free his brother. On 14 May, he wrote to Cromwell, protesting that the detention was contrary to *jus gentium* – the international law of the day – and asking that Henry intervene. Giambattista, however, was about to fall victim to the vicissitudes of

Reformation diplomacy, caught between England and the papacy as the two powers clashed over the fate of John Fisher.

Fisher, the Bishop of Rochester, had been in prison since his refusal in April 1534 to take the Oath of Succession naming Elizabeth as Henry's heir. In a misjudged attempt to protect him, in May 1535 Pope Paul III appointed him to the cardinalate. The move did nothing to mollify Henry. Gregorio worried that as the man on the spot in Rome, he would be blamed for Fisher's promotion, and wrote to Jean du Bellay asking that the French ambassador in England remedy any such impression. Otherwise, he said, the nomination would 'completely ruin him'. He also insisted to Cromwell that he had remonstrated with England's friends in the cardinalate and with the Pope. He must have known that the affair did not bode well for the prospects of English aid for his brother. On 1 June, there was a flicker of hope, when news came that Giambattista had escaped. But despite Gregorio's optimism, it proved false.[5]

On 22 June 1535, John Fisher was executed. Some in Rome welcomed the news: anticipating a backlash, they relished the prospect of an English martyr. A few weeks later, on 6 July, Thomas More (briefly Henry's lord chancellor) was executed too. The two men were the first Catholic martyrs of the English Reformation.[6]

In the aftermath of Fisher's execution, Thomas Cromwell proved no friend of the Casali family. Perhaps harbouring his own doubts about their involvement in Fisher's promotion, he cut Giambattista Casali loose, and effectively denied to the Imperial ambassador Eustace Chapuys that his activities in Hungary had had official sanction. Chapuys gave a lively account of their meeting in a letter to Charles V. When Cromwell enquired about Giambattista's detention, Chapuys replied that Ferdinand would have had ample reason to prevent his mission, given that he was in the middle of negotiations with Szapolyai, which the English ambassador might have interrupted. Cromwell seemed unconcerned. Giambattista's detention, he observed, would at least save Henry the cost of his maintenance. 'He never thought the said ambassador a wise man.' It had been foolish of Giambattista to enter Ferdinand's lands without permission. He had only been sent, in any case, to 'manage some little business', at Gregorio's request. Besides, the English had 'not written him three letters' in the years that Giambattista had been at Venice, so he would be no use to Ferdinand as a source of English news. Andrea Corsini, Giambattista's companion, was 'a fool, and for such the King had christened him from the first time he spoke with him'. After a subsequent meeting with Cromwell, Chapuys told his master that 'Had the king of the Romans ordered Casali to be hung, he [Cromwell] would not have cared a fig for it; the King, his master, would have saved by the Protonotary's death the yearly allowance that is paid to him.' Cromwell must have been regretting that the English had provided diplomatic cover for Giambattista's self-interested quest for patronage. Giambattista's interrogators certainly thought he was up to something more nefarious than acquisitive self-promotion. Unfortunately for Giambattista, his mission, now discovered, was an undoubted liability for the English strategy of maintaining temporary neutrality while Cromwell and his colleagues, playing off France and the Empire, focused on the domestic consequences of Henry's break with Rome. Cromwell was a smart politician. It is no surprise that he did everything possible to dispel Chapuys' suspicions that Giambattista was involved in an English plot to destabilise Ferdinand's realm.[7]

Unaware of the minister's dismissive attitude, Gregorio kept up a flurry of lobbying letters throughout July 1535. Many cardinals, he told Cromwell, had written in Giambattista's favour to Pier Paolo Vergerio, the papal nuncio with Ferdinand, so much so that Vergerio was complaining that they had put him in a bad light with Ferdinand's counsellors. And Casali had genuine reason to fear for his brother, for news had arrived from Vienna that Giambattista's companion Andrea Corsini had been tortured into confessing that he had gone to Hungary to disrupt the peace negotiations.[8]

As hopes for Giambattista's release faded, Gregorio all but withdrew from diplomatic activity. He headed to the baths at Lucca, retreating later to the family home in Bologna. There, in August 1535, he wrote to Cromwell that 'it does not seem opportune to go to Rome, nor to Venice or Hungary, without a response from you'. In September 1535, Gurone Bertani travelled once again to England, this time to seek aid for Giambattista in person. If Anne Boleyn was indeed suspicious of Gregorio, perhaps Gurone – less tainted by the years of failure at Rome – was a safer option. Francesco Casali, who as Szapolyai's ambassador remained at the curia, took over his brother's remaining duties as English correspondent. In December 1535, he wrote to Stephen Gardiner to report that the hardliners of the curia were trying to push through a bull threatening Henry with deprivation of his kingdom, for it was the custom that heretics would forfeit both property and lives. Once again the diplomats were working on a strategy of delay. (Gardiner, after a period out of favour, had re-established himself by writing a defence of the royal supremacy, and was now English ambassador to France.)[9]

Gregorio himself did not immediately return to Rome from Bologna. On 20 December 1535, he wrote a perplexed letter to Gardiner. He had received a letter from Gurone, telling him he should have gone to Rome, but he was reluctant to do so. He could not tell whether Henry would rather he obstruct the process of deprivation or leave it be, and, if he were to obstruct it, whether he should do so officially or in his own capacity. He was 'such a noted servant of the king' that he feared his presence might make matters worse. Could Gardiner shed some light on Henry's attitude? Gregorio did not want to be accused of negligence.

It is indicative of Gregorio's diminished status at the papal court, and Henry's diminished interest in affairs at Rome – except as they impacted on broader continental policy – that such a letter proved necessary. Yet the English had not entirely abandoned our man in Rome. The one bright note in Gregorio's message comes in his thanks to Gardiner for obtaining – finally – a letter from Henry to Ferdinand requesting Giambattista's liberation. 'We owe you for this,' wrote Gregorio. 'We will always be your most devoted, most loving servants.'[10]

As Giambattista endured incarceration, so too did another of the players in Henry's divorce, perhaps rather more deservedly. Benedetto Accolti, Cardinal of Ravenna, already removed from his post as Legate to the Marches, was put on trial for abuse of power. As his servants gave evidence against him, they revealed both Henry's attempt to buy Accolti's favour, and the cardinal's double-crossing. To the statue of Pasquino in Rome, then as now a site for the display of seditious flyers, one wag affixed a satirical verse comparing the cardinal to Christ, 'crucified for us'. It was a tale that greatly amused the Imperial courtiers.[11]

Giambattista's imprisonment wore on into November. His secretary Marcantonio Bentivoglio went with a Hungarian envoy to meet King Ferdinand, but was barred from travelling either back to Italy or to the fortress of Wiener Neustadt where Casali was held. Only at Christmas was Giambattista allowed a little more liberty, moved into a more pleasant room and permitted to walk freely around the castle. Before Marcantonio was permitted to speak to him and to bring him money, clothes and books, Giambattista had to pledge to forfeit property, possessions and liberty should he try to escape, and the Cardinal of Trent was required to stand surety.[12]

On 7 January 1536, Catherine of Aragon died. Banished from court to the Cambridgeshire village of Kimbolton, even in her last days she was not allowed to see the daughter from whom she had been separated for four years. She was buried in Peterborough Abbey. Three weeks later, Chapuys reported rumours that the queen had been poisoned – and by none other than Gurone Bertani, on behalf of his master Gregorio! Chapuys was sceptical. One would have to have a particularly conspiratorial mind to believe that Gregorio had poisoned Catherine (presumably to restore himself to Anne's favour), but the fact that such a tale might gain credence is indicative of the fevered atmosphere at court. Catherine's death changed the political situation. Imperial efforts could now focus on restoring Mary as Henry's rightful successor over her half-sister Elizabeth. There was no longer any particular reason to resist Henry's marriage to Anne Boleyn: insofar as it prevented an unfavourable alliance with a French princess, it might be as well to put up with it. But Anne's miscarriage of 29 January, Henry's growing interest in Jane Seymour, and a deterioration in the queen's relationship with Thomas Cromwell, once a key ally, put Henry's bride of three years at risk.[13]

In early 1536, Gregorio returned to Rome and recommenced regular correspondence with England, providing the military updates that had been a staple of his early diplomacy. Imperial victory in north Africa the previous summer had given Henry brief cause for concern, for if Charles's troops were no longer busy in the Mediterranean he would have scope to fight on a northern front

against the heretic King of England. But the swift move of the French
to invade Milan following the death of that city's duke in early 1536
had restarted war in Italy, and that allowed Henry some respite.
Perhaps Gregorio calculated that with renewed conflict on the way
between France and the Holy Roman Empire – the Ladies' Peace
had lasted a bare seven years – he could once again make himself
useful to the English. And perhaps the English thought so too, for
in April, Gregorio wrote to Cardinal Jean du Bellay with the news
that he had been appointed English ambassador to the emperor,
presumably for the period of Charles's visit to Rome that month.
This was Casali's opportunity to restore himself to the English favour
of times past, to re-establish himself in Henry's diplomatic service
and to prepare for a new diplomatic role in Venice.[14]

In Rome he was joined by Richard Pate, nephew of the Bishop
of Lincoln, a young cleric who had served as ambassador to the
emperor since November 1533. Pate's activities during Charles's visit
to Rome did not garner royal appreciation. He showed himself to
be enthusiastically pro-Imperial, and wrote a rather inept letter to
the king advocating reconciliation with Rome, for which he was
quickly rebuked and reined in. For Casali, Pate's friendly discussions
with the Imperial diplomats were far from good news. When Pate
told Charles's adviser Nicolas Perrenot de Granvelle that Gregorio
was to join him as ambassador, Granvelle proved decidedly hostile
to the suggestion, describing Gregorio as undeserving, malicious
and perverse. Although couched in personal terms, the hostility
probably stemmed from a perception that the Casali were irredeem-
ably tied to the anti-Habsburg camp: Gregorio had had a pension
from the French; Francesco was in the service of John Szapolyai.
Thus advised to beware of Gregorio's 'lightness', Pate requested
guidance from Henry on how best to deal with him.

Pate also recounted to the king a conversation with Casali, who
had rendered 'his most humble thanks' to Henry for his continuance
as ambassador, testimony to the king's trust in him and his own
fidelity. But Casali had also sharply questioned Pate's own commission
to the emperor, making the very reasonable point that Henry was
insincere, for he had dispatched Stephen Gardiner to France 'for a
contrary purpose'. Gregorio was quite right in his assessment: the

English were indeed playing off the contending powers, intent on staying out of the European war while they managed domestic reform, but it was probably impolitic to say so quite so bluntly.

Pate was convinced that Gregorio had told the Pope, 'with whom he often had discussions', of their commission. Gregorio frequently visited Paul III by night, wrote Pate, doing so 'by his own desire, thereby avoiding suspicion', but Pate was sure he was up to something. Pate himself, however, was freelancing, discussing, for example, a proposal to legitimise Princess Mary, in a manner that undoubtedly displeased his master. His mistrust of Gregorio was probably encouraged by the Imperial diplomats he frequented, who were highly suspicious of the Casali dealings with Szapolyai. On that front, Gregorio enquired what Henry would think of a marriage between his daughter Mary and John Szapolyai: the deal being that Mary would renounce her claims in England. It was an eccentric plan but, from the point of view of the Casali family and their multiple alliances, not entirely irrational.[15]

On 5 April 1536, Charles V made a triumphal entry into Rome, evoking the ceremonies of the ancient world and presenting himself as a new Caesar following his victories in Africa. Temporary triumphal arches were erected along his route depicting the early kings of Rome, the emperors Constantine and Titus, and Charles's own victory. The road he took was believed (wrongly) by contemporaries to be that used by the ancients on such occasions. Fifty richly apparelled Romans rode before the emperor, wrote Pate, through 'a great part of the city'. Ambassadors too followed in train. Among their companions was Casali's uncle (in fact Livia Pallavicino's), Latino Giovenale de' Manetti, a noted scholar, to show them 'the antiquities of old and new Rome'; he was, added Pate, 'most expert therein'.[16]

At such a distance from England, reliant on communication by letter and oral messages, it was always hard for Casali and his colleagues to follow the subtle manoeuvrings of Henry's courtiers. Now, there unfolded a dramatic sequence of events at court that even those close to the king and queen would not have predicted a few months before. On 2 May, Queen Anne Boleyn was arrested on charges of adultery with a series of courtiers – Henry Norris, Sir Thomas Wyatt, Francis Weston and Mark Smeaton – and accused of incest,

no less, with her own brother George. A queen's adultery constituted
treason, for it compromised the royal succession. Her trial followed
on the 15th, and on the 19th she was beheaded on Tower Green.

In the years following her death, Anne had few defenders. One of
them, though, was Étienne Dolet, former French embassy secretary
in Venice and practically minded commentator on diplomacy. In 1538,
he published an epitaph for the queen 'falsely condemned of adultery'.
The news of Anne's arrest travelled rapidly south through Europe. It
must have been a shock to the men who had toiled for six years to
achieve her marriage to Henry, but then political conspiracies and swift
executions were far from rare in Rome. Barely twenty years earlier,
Cardinal Petrucci had been secretly strangled and his servants publicly
hanged, drawn and quartered over claims they had conspired to kill
Pope Leo X. Gregorio Casali's guardian, Cardinal Riario, had been
accused of complicity in their plot. On 24 May, as yet unaware of
Anne Boleyn's execution, Gregorio wrote to Richard Pate to ask what
he knew or thought of the news of her arrest. Many in Rome who
had seen Henry's obsession with Anne as a temporary madness
thought that her fall signified a means to open discussions with the
king. Gregorio Casali was among them. On 27 May, after a meeting
with Pope Paul III, he wrote to Henry proposing that either Latino
Giovenale or Andrea Casali might come unofficially to England for
talks. His tone was one of belief that reconciliation of some sort might
yet be possible, although he probably had an inkling from Henry's
stern instructions to Pate that the king was in no mood to compromise. Henry and his ministers were set on their plans for reform.[7]

What our man in Rome did not know was that on 30 May, Henry
had married his third queen, Jane Seymour. Like Anne Boleyn, she
was the daughter of English courtiers who saw her rise as a means
to power. Unlike Anne, she lacked independence and cosmopolitan
style. But she was a means to an end: a means to a son to inherit
the English throne.

Some time in the late spring of 1536, after promises of surety
amounting to twenty thousand florins, Giambattista Casali was freed.
Szapolyai and Ferdinand had not yet made peace, but negotiations
were sufficiently advanced for Ferdinand to accept that Giambattista's
release would do no harm. He left without his valuables: his captors

kept a number of rings with precious stones. Giambattista hoped to travel to England to 'kiss the King's hand', but after a long and incommodious imprisonment, he was in poor health, suffering back problems, and went first to convalesce at the family home in Bologna.[18]

Giambattista Casali never embarked on the long journey to Henry's court. In mid-October, he died. The Venetian gannets gathered: the city's ambassador in Rome, Lorenzo Bragadin, dashed to Paul III to demand that the bishopric of Belluno be delivered to Giovanni Barozzi, Giambattista's rival of almost ten years. He received short shrift from Paul, who shrewdly granted it to Gasparo Contarini, the Venetian diplomat and now cardinal, whom his countrymen could not turn down without offending many of their own.[19]

In England, Henry and his counsellors embarked on their next step in the campaign for reform, the dissolution of the monasteries. In mid-October, there began a religious rising against Henry in the north of England. The Pilgrimage of Grace was a flare-up of rebellion, a product of social tensions colliding and coalescing. The rebels' motives were complex, but at the heart of their various risings – first in Lincoln, then York and beyond – lay hostility to religious change.[20]

News of the rebellion reached Rome, and Gregorio Casali, in the autumn of 1536. His last surviving letter, to Richard Pate, is dated 2 November. That month, he too fell seriously ill. His secretary Guido Gianetti kept an eye on diplomatic affairs. On 21 November 1536, as his master endured a fever, Gianetti wrote to Pate, who had also been ill, reporting that the rebellion in England was almost defeated. The group in Lincoln had disbanded. Casali advised Pate to go to Rome, and offered him hospitality at the family house there. Yet there was more to this offer than met the eye. Pate would later defect to the emperor, leaving Henry's service altogether. Was he considering such a move now? Casali may have known that for Pate, the defeat of the rebels was unwelcome news. Perhaps he was offering a colleague an exit to exile.[21]

Gregorio did not live to see Pate's exile, nor the later risings against Henry. On 12 December 1536, he made his will. On the 14th and the 18th, he added codicils. When he died, some time before the turn of the year, he was not yet forty.

Epilogue

When Gregorio died, the dispute over Livia's property was far from over, but their son, Michele, took over the rich inheritance acquired through his mother's line. Only decades later, after Pope Paul III had established his family as rulers of Parma and Piacenza, would the Casali consolidate their hold on Monticelli. To his daughter Ottavia Gregorio left a dowry of three thousand crowns; to his sister Giovanna he left a thousand. Six servants got legacies too. Gregorio's principal secretary, Guido Gianetti, had been naturalised as an Englishman in 1532 and granted an English benefice confiscated from Cardinal Campeggio. Gregorio took the precaution of leaving him six hundred scudi in the event that the benefice was taken away, though in fact it was not: Gianetti held it as late as 1562, four years into the reign of Queen Elizabeth, which points to some expeditious religious manoeuvring through the reigns of Edward VI and Mary. Baptista Sambuelo, the agent who did such sterling spying on the Genoese, received fifty scudi, and the right to meals in the Casali house as long as he chose to stay there. Girolamo Scaneffo, who dealt with Gregorio's legal and financial affairs, was given fifty scudi a year until the Casali children reached the age of twenty; a manservant named Terentio de Interanto got a hundred crowns. Julie de la Fontana, a maid, received sixty crowns, and Stephanea, also a maid, was granted a hundred crowns, board in the family house, and one crown a month for life. This was the core of the household that enabled Gregorio's diplomatic world to function from day to day.[1]

What of the others we have met? Girolamo Ghinucci finally got his cardinal's hat in 1535, at the same time as the ill-fated John Fisher.

Jean du Bellay and Gasparo Contarini were promoted too. Gurone Bertani, Gregorio's agent in England, had gained citizenship in Bologna at the end of 1535. He went on to have an impressive diplomatic career of his own, helped, no doubt, when his brother became a cardinal. In the four decades up until his death in 1573, he served numerous curia luminaries, and participated in a series of projects – some formal, some secret – to reconcile England with Rome. Giambernardino di Ferrara turned double agent. In the 1550s, having inveigled his way into the English service, he joined the household of Sir Richard Morison, an up-and-coming English diplomat, on whom he spied for the emperor. Benedetto Accolti, Cardinal of Ravenna, true to disreputable form, bribed his way out of trouble with Imperial backing. Had Paul III had his way, Accolti would have been condemned to death. But like Clement before him, the Pope had to give way to the emperor, though not before extracting a fine of fifty-nine thousand scudi from the unrepentant cardinal.[2]

As for the English, I am sometimes asked how many diplomats lost their heads over Henry's divorce. The answer is none. Of the ambassadors we have met in this book, only one was executed in Henry's reign. That was Sir Nicholas Carew, beheaded in 1539, alleged to have conspired with Henry Courtenay, Marquess of Exeter, to depose the king. No one, though, went to the block as a direct consequence of their foreign service. Either Henry's diplomats were disinclined to martyrdom or, perhaps more likely, potential martyrs were rapidly dropped from diplomatic service. The natural hazards of disease and the multiple dangers of early-modern travel caused far more untimely deaths.

Stephen Gardiner, who for all his efforts in the divorce was never other than conservative in his theology, was deprived of his bishopric under Edward VI, only for his career to revive when he became Mary Tudor's lord chancellor. He died, of natural causes, in 1555. His erstwhile colleague Edward Fox went the other way, religiously, dying a confirmed evangelical in 1538. In his later years, Sir Francis Bryan lost some of the influence he had enjoyed with Henry, but served the king to the end. He became Lord Marshal of Ireland in 1549 and died the following year. Pietro Vanni was the great survivor. He stayed in royal service throughout the reigns of Edward and Mary, latterly as ambassador to Venice, and in old age, under Elizabeth, kept his benefices. Richard Sampson became Bishop of Coventry and Lichfield; he died in 1554. Edward Carne was another of Henry's diplomats who thrived under the king's eldest daughter, this time as Mary's ambassador to Rome. When Elizabeth came to the throne, he connived with the Pope to stay there, and has a monument in the Venerable English College – now a seminary for English priests – near the site of the Casali house in Via Monserrato. Edmund Bonner became Bishop of London; under Mary he was known as 'bloody Bonner'. He died in prison in Elizabeth's reign. Casali's nemesis Richard Croke was at first well-rewarded for his work in Italy, but never rose to high office in either academia or royal service.[3]

But the fact that so many of Henry's diplomats ended up in the service of his Catholic daughter Mary gives one pause for thought. How far did they believe in their master's cause? Did others – like Benet – think that Henry had thrown the kingdom into chaos for a trivial amour? How many were loyal in spite of their convictions, rather than because of them? The trouble is that, with only occasional exceptions, they all told Henry what he wanted to hear. We will never know how far bravado, spin, self-delusion, cynical exaggeration or outright untruth coloured their letters. My own view is that when it came to the king's great matter, Henry was not badly served by his ambassadors. His hopes were confounded rather by Catherine of Aragon's determination and Clement VII's desire for Florence. The concern of others for their family honour, rather than diplomatic incompetence, stood in the way of Henry's design for a new wife and a male heir.

The Casali family had lost four sons in the course of Henry's quest. What Gregorio, Giambattista, Paolo and Vicenzo would have made of the king's future course is impossible to guess. Francesco Casali stayed on in Rome as John Szapolyai's ambassador until his master's death in 1540. His cousin Andrea married, and with Andrea's offspring the Bologna branch of the Casali family began. The palaces in Rome and Bologna where the Casali entertained ambassadors are both long gone, but the family villa, much rebuilt,

is still to be found in the Bolognese hills. Now an *agriturismo*, it is
a fetching destination for holidaymakers and diners.

The Casali memorials can still be seen in the family chapel in
the church of San Domenico, Bologna, just to the right of the main
altar. There, the family arms are emblazoned on the wall, and
Filippino Lippi's *Mystical Marriage of Saint Catherine* – commissioned
by Gregorio's uncles – hangs above the altar. The memorial to
Gregorio, Giambattista and Paolo, set up by their cousin Andrea
in 1537, records that Gregorio was 'Both familiar and beloved of all
Christian kings and princes; with the authority entrusted to him
under universal law he led very many embassies to the greatest
kings and the pope himself, performed with everlasting glory;
likewise in the first ranks at war he gave many and splendid proofs
of his valour.' Although Giambattista's service as Henry's ambassador to Venice is noted in his epitaph, Gregorio's service to the
excommunicate monarch is subsumed in the general. Perhaps his
role as ambassador to Rome of the schismatic King of England
was no longer something of which the Casali wished to boast.

The family's ancestral castle, the Rocca Pallavicino-Casali, still
stands strategically in the village of Monticelli d'Ongina, not far
from the River Po. An occasional bus will take you the dozen or
so miles from Piacenza. It is a little neglected now, grass creeping
up through the paving of its courtyard, but its brick walls are
imposing enough. In its own way, this is the legacy of Gregorio's
diplomatic service, for without Henry's patronage, his chances of
wedding an heiress must surely have been diminished. As the man
who, despite his best efforts, did not get Henry VIII a divorce,
Gregorio Casali might be accounted a historical failure. As the man
who left his family in possession of this castle, he might also be
accounted a historical success.

Notes

Preface

1. Erasmus, VII 335 (*LP* IV 3944). • **2.** Bedouelle and Le Gal, 12. • **3.** ASF, Fondo Accolti, b. 16, no. 17, fol. 1r.

1 *The King in Love and the Pope Besieged*

1. For the Sack and the divorce, see Scarisbrick, Hook, Parmiter, Gouwens and Reiss, Gouwens. For the May 1527 trial: Kelly, 21–37. • **2.** Gouwens, 170–1. • **3.** G. Contarini, fol. 139v. • **4.** Sanuto, XLV cols 142–3. • **5.** Arfaioli, 47. • **6.** Pawning jewels: Lebey, 426, n. 1 (*LP* IV 3090). Villa burnt: Sanuto XLIV col. 472. Stipend: Bell (1990), 161. • **7.** *CSP Sp* III.II 82. • **8.** *St P* I 189 (*LP* IV 3147). • **9.** Ives, 84–91. • **10.** End of siege: *CSP Sp* III.II 86. Thank-you letters: *LP* IV 3155–3157 and 3160–3166. • **11.** Travels through Italy: *LP* IV 3206. Giambattista in papal household: ASV, Reg. Vat. 1299, fol. 9v. His role in Venice: *CSP Ven* IV 125, 126. Alonso suspicious: *CSP Sp* III.II 96. • **12.** *LP* IV 3206. Gregorio's leaving gift: *CSP Ven* IV 131. • **13.** *St P* I 228–9 (*LP* IV 3310). English commissions to Mantua and Ferrara: ASMn, AG 45, unnumbered document of 26 August 1527; ASMo, Archivio Estense, Principi Esteri, Cardinali, b. 1435/189, unnumbered document of 27 August 1527. French credential: *Catalogue des Actes*, VI 86, no. 19331, and ASMn, AG 45, unnumbered document of 19 August 1527. • **14.** *LP* IV 3499. *St P* VII 23 (*LP* IV 3657). • **15.** On the Knight mission: Sharkey (2011), esp. 244. Henry's letter: *LP* IV 3419. Casali's first accreditation as ambassador was in 1525: *LP* IV 1649, 1650; his continuing status is confirmed in a letter of 1529, *LP* IV 5987. • **16.** Wolsey's letters: *LP* IV 3340. *St P* I 270–2 (*LP* IV 3400). Going 'on spiritual matters': BL, Cotton MSS, Vit. B IX 177 (*LP* IV 3497). Ghinucci: Creighton. • **17.** Bigamy:

Doernberg, 73–8. Knight's travels: *LP* IV 3420. • **18**. *LP* IV 3497. *St P* VII 14 (*LP* IV 3553). *St P* VII 16 (*LP* IV 3638). • **19**. *LP* IV 3571. *CSP Sp* III.II 363. For background: Hook, 229–30. • **20**. *LP* IV 3638. • **21**. ASB, Senato, Lettere VI, vol. 4, 405–6, 429–31. • **22**. *LP* IV 3680. *St P* VII 29 (*LP* IV 3687). Machiavelli, 117.

2 *How to Bribe a Cardinal (Part One)*

1. State of papal palace: Pocock, I 88–9 (*LP* IV 4090). The new 'George nobles' issued in 1526 were worth 6s. 8d: Challis, 68. Courier-sharing: ASMn, AG 877, c. 31v. • **2**. Miranda, www2.fiu.edu/~mirandas/consistories-xvi.htm. • **3**. Theiner, 549 (*LP* IV 1368). • **4**. Instructions: Burnet, IV 22 (*LP* IV 3641). Spanish spying: *CSP Sp* III.I 329. • **5**. *LP* IV 3715, 3758. Henry and the French: Richardson (2008). • **6**. *LP* IV 4120, 5152. For background: Chambers. • **7**. Bribe definition: *OED*. Friendship and favour: Burnet, IV 31 (*LP* IV 3641). *LP* IV 3715, 3751. • **8**. Bellocchi, 25. Heal, 54. Challis, 68–9, 216. Cardinals: Fragnito, 46. Henry: Gwyn (1990), 556. Bryan: *LP* IV 2972, cited in Gwyn, 562. • **9**. *LP* IV 3749, 3784. • **10**. Campeggio as cardinal-protector: Wilkie, 143. Knighthood: TNA, C82/479, unnumbered membrane (*LP* III 421). Collar: *LP* III p. 1537. Inventing ancestries: Carboni, 52. Styling as 'cavalier': Fletcher (2010b), 566–7. • **11**. Cappelletti, X 189–92. Venetian dealings: *CSP Ven* IV 161, 162, 199. Confirmation on 27 December: ASV, Arch. Concist., Acta Vicecanc., 4, fol. 10r. Letters concerning the appointment: ASV, Reg. Vat. 1299, fols 9r–12v. Further references in Williams (2009), 290, n. 649. • **12**. *LP* IV 3802. • **13**. War: *LP* IV 3827. His illness: ASMo, Cancelleria, Ambasciatori, Roma 32, c. 212i/11; *LP* IV 3949, 3995. • **14**. Gardiner: Redworth and *DNB*. Fox: *DNB*. • **15**. Post routes: Wall, 46–59 and Fedele and Gallenga, 212–13. Gregorio's London–Brescia ride: Sanuto, XXXVII col. 521 (*CSP Ven* III 918). • **16**. *St P* VII 54–56 (*LP* IV 3954). • **17**. Clough. • **18**. *St P* VII 60 and fn (*LP* IV 4077, 4078). Food and status: Grieco. Ambassadors as personifying king: Behrens, 620. • **19**. Sanuto, XLVII col. 77 (*CSP Ven* IV 251). See also *LP* IV 4090. • **20**. Their voyage: *LP* IV 3925, 3932, 3933, 3938, 3954, 4003, 4007. Herde's death: Pocock, II 88 (*LP* IV 4090). Mantuan report: ASMn, AG 877, c. 19r. • **21**. Arrival: Pocock, I 90 (*LP* IV 4119). Lack of Italian: ASMn, AG 877, c. 28r. Use of French: Brigden and Woolfson, 478; Russell, 11; (in Casali's letters) *LP* IV 2720, 2918, 3089, 3090. • **22**. Pocock, I 90 (*LP* IV 4119); *St P* VII 63fn (*LP* IV 4090). • **23**. The cardinal's hat: Cavendish, I 29. De' Grassi: BAV, MS Vat. Lat.

12270, fol. 41v. Background: Hayward, 228–30. • **24**. Casali's lodgings: Pocock, I 90–1 (*LP* IV 4119). Ten thousand ducats: Burnet, IV 22 (*LP* IV 3641). Credit and reputation: *St P* VII 64 (*LP* IV 4118). • **25**. Mantuan reports: ASMn, AG 877, cc. 38r, 47r. Other curia members: *LP* IV 3905, 3906, 3908, 3910, 3911. Pucci: Pocock, I 102 (*LP* IV 4120). Dolet (1933), 86. • **26**. *LP* IV 4167. • **27**. Ehses, 28–30. ASMn, AG 877, cc. 80v–81r.

3 A Short Tale of Kidnapping

1. Progress of war: Gleason, 45. On Francesco: G. Contarini, fol. 96v. • **2**. Raising troops in 1523: Gunn, 599, n. 5. Commission in 1524: *St P* VI 316–17 (*LP* IV 456). Changing nature of warfare during the Italian wars: Mallett. Gregorio's early commands: *LP* IV 568; Sanuto, XXXVII col. 521 (*CSP Ven* III 918); *St P* IV 121 (*LP* IV 615), cited in Bernard, 23. For background: Gwyn, 385, 552. • **3**. For an excellent account of the wars of these years, Arfaioli. Imperial worries: ASMn, AG 877 c. 290r. • **4**. TNA, SP 1/48, fol. 6v (*LP* IV 4246). Sanuto, XLVII col. 354, cited in Hook, 288. • **5**. Pocock, I 147, 149, 155 (*LP* IV 4251). • **6**. *St P* VII 68–69 (*LP* IV 4289). • **7**. Garden socialising: in general, Zimmermann and Levin and Jeanneret, 22–7; for this instance G. Contarini, fols 38v and 54v. Viterbo: Gimma, esp. 5–14. • **8**. Francesco in Riario household: see his memorial in the Chiesa di San Domenico, Bologna. Riario's career: Moroni, LVII 171–73; Shaw (1993). His connections to Casali family: Fletcher (2009). • **9**. Molini, II 37. • **10**. The Sigismondo affair is documented in BNF, MS Français 3040, fol. 58r; ASMn, AG 877, cc. 272r, 350r, 353v–354r; Molini, II 40, 42; G. Contarini, fols 17r–17v, 22r. • **11**. Napoleone's murder: Shaw (2007), 34. Background: Giry-Deloison (1987), 225. Aftermath of Sigismondo affair: ASMn, AG 877, c. 358r. ASVe, Capi del Consiglio dei Dieci, Dispacci (lettere) degli ambasciatori, b. 22, fols 166–7. • **12**. Guicciardini (1970), 40. Pontano, I 37, cited with a partial translation in Kidwell, 113. • **13**. G. Contarini, fol. 17v. ASMn, AG 877, cc. 358r, 353v–354r. • **14**. *St P* VII 70, 73–7 (*LP* IV 4338, 4361). *LP* IV 4358, 4359. • **15**. *St P* VII 81–84 (*LPIV* 4390). Clerk and Catherine: *DNB*. • **16**. Gregorio's 'lightness': TNA SP 1/48 fol. 194r (*LP* IV 4406). Confusion resolved: *LP* IV 4465. • **17**. ASMn, AG 1462, c. 185r. Gardiner dispatched: *LP* IV 4089. • **18**. Contarini's mission: Gleason, 42–59. • **19**. G. Contarini, fols 13r–13v (*CSP Ven* IV 301). *LP* IV 5038. • **20**. ASVe, Consiglio dei Dieci, Parti Secrete, filza 2, unnumbered document (*CSP Ven* IV 191). • **21**. ASV, Arch. Concist., Acta Vicecanc., 4, fol. 17. • **22**. Pocock, I 172 (*LP* IV 4380). The promise: *LP* IV 4550.

• **23**. Dolet (1933), 88, 90. Barbaro, 163. Background: Martin, 1324–5.
• **24**. BL, Cotton MSS, Vesp. F III 32r (*LP* IV App. no. 197).

4 Cardinal Campeggio has Gout

1. Paolo's mission: ASMn, AG 1461, unnumbered letter of 17 January 1527; ASMn, AG 1462, c. 145r; ASMo, Cancelleria, Ambasciatori, Venezia, 17, unnumbered letter of 27 August 1527; ASMn, AG 881, c. 463r. For background: Williams (2010). • **2**. Topkapi Palace: Necipoğlu, 96–110. Gritti: Szakály, Nemeth Papo and Papo. 'Great affection': Williams (2010), 591. • **3**. Assistance for Szapolyai: Lambeth Palace Library, MS 4434, fol. 239v. • **4**. ASMn, AG 1462, cc. 131r, 145r, 156r; AG 877, c. 379r and AG 2969, Libro 43, fols. 1v–2r. • **5**. Doria news: G. Contarini, fol. 16v (*CSP Ven* IV 308). Molini, II 36. Baptista's various roles: ASMn, AG 1153, c. 471r; ASV, Cam. Ap., Div. Cam. 101, fol. 594r. Baptista and Doria: *LP* IV 4379, 4401. Dolet (1933), 86. • **6**. Doria's defection: Gleason, 45. G. Contarini, fol. 34r (*CSP Ven* IV 321). • **7**. Campeggio's voyage: Scarisbrick, 281; Parmiter, 63. Gregorio's illness: *LP* IV 4663, 4666, 4833. ASMn, AG 877 c. 460v; ASMo, Cancelleria, Ambasciatori, Roma 32, c. 214i/6. G. Contarini, fols 46v, 59v. • **8**. Paolo: *LP* IV 4792. Vicenzo: BL, Cotton MSS, Vit. B X 158r (*LP* IV 4956). Diplomatic networks: Bell (1990); Fletcher and DeSilva; ASMn, AG 1460, c. 160r; AG 880 c. 291r. • **9**. *St P* VII 100 (*LP* IV 4813). G. Contarini, fol. 86v (*CSP Ven* IV 350). • **10**. *LP* IV 4813, 4959. Background on gifts: Fantoni, 102–5. • **11**. Arfaioli, 164. • **12**. Cited in Setton, III 311. • **13**. Rome as bride: Richardson (2009), 10. Baggage incident: *CSP Ven* IV 359. • **14**. Campeggio's arrival: ASV, Segr. Stato, Francia 1, fols 168v–69r. • **15**. Difficult journeys: *LP* IV 4918, 4959, 4960. Taddeo and Alexander: *LP* IV 5530, 5481, V pp. 311–12. Barlow: *LP* IV 3784, 4167, 4249. Anne and Rochford's letters: *LP* IV 4647, App. 197. Hercules Missolus: *LP* IV 5314. Robin the Devil and John Davy: *LP* V 454. • **16**. *LP* IV 4956, 4960. • **17**. G. Contarini, fol. 119r (*CSP Ven* IV 372). • **18**. Burnet, IV 64–73 (*LP* IV 5038). • **19**. G. Contarini, fols 140v–141r. (*CSP Ven* IV 383). Charles's letter: Lanz, 369 (*CSP Sp* IV.I 245). • **20**. *LP* IV 5037, 5073. *St P* VII 142 (*LP* IV 5149).

5 The Vicar of Hell in Rome

1. The Casali house: Fletcher (2010a). Rental properties: Lee, 98–9, 108–9. Caffarelli loans: Esposito and Piñeiro, 134–5. • **2**. Fletcher (2008),

62. • **3**. Clerk's observation: BL, Cotton MSS, Vit. B VII 67r–67v (*LP* IV 1131). Vanni's instructions: BL, Cotton MSS, Vit. B X 174v (*LP* IV 4977). • **4**. Bryan's comment: *St P* VII 144 *(LP* IV 5152). Background: Scarisbrick, 290–1; Parmiter, 80. Their instructions: *LP* IV 5050. Gregorio to Vicenzo: BL, Cotton MSS, Vit. B XI 29r (*LP* IV 5222). • **5**. The envoys' journey problems and Wolsey's response: BL, Cotton MSS, Vit. B X 179r (*LP* IV 5013); Vit. B XI fol. 184 (*LP* IV 5178). Background to voyage: *LP* IV 4661, 5027, 5151, 5213. Risk of riots: BL, Cotton MSS, Vit. BX 162r (*LP* IV 4960). • **6**. For the route: BAV, MS Vat. Lat. 12270, 19r–20v, discussed in Fletcher (2011). For their arrival date: ASMo, Cancelleria, Ambasciatori, Roma 32, c. 214ii/7, letter of 16 January 1529. Well lodged: *LP* IV 5213. • **7**. Illness: G. Contarini, fol. 155v (*CSP Ven* IV 390). Rumours of death: *LP* IV 5194, 5218, 5270, 5271, 5308. Henry preferred Farnese: *LP* VII 1255. • **8**. Bryan's praise: *St P* VII 168 (*LP* IV 5481). Dolet (1933), 86–7. Messisbugo, 71–2. • **9**. *St P* VII 406 (*LP* V 1661). Hawkins: Bell (1990), 47. Dolet (1933), 87. Machiavelli, 117. For further discussion: Fletcher (2010a). • **10**. *St P* VII 150 (*LP* IV 5213). ASMn, AG 1150, cc. 461, 463, 468; AG 1151, cc. 196, 198. Giambattista and Ercole 'cosy': ASMo, Cancelleria, Ambasciatori, Roma 32, c. 214i/33. Close friends: BNF, MS Français 3009, fol. 17r. • **11**. Accolti trial, II; 3 May 1535. ASF, Fondo Accolti, 9, no. 15, fol. 1. Rental to courtesan: Lee, 98. • **12**. Masson, 59–131; see also for background Storey, 57–66. • **13**. Bryan: Brigden, 6. *Lisle Letters*, I no. 66a. Warnings: Dolet (1933), 87. Barbaro, 166. • **14**. BL, Cotton MSS, Vit. B X 170r and *St P* VII 150 (*LP* IV 4977, 5213). The official request: ASV, Cam Ap., Div. Cam. 86, fol. 16r. Pocock, II 513 (*LP* VII 86). • **15**. Mai's arrival: ASMn, AG 878, cc. 48v–49r. G. Contarini, fol. 166r. Gregorio's description: ASF, Dieci, Responsive, 139, letter of 27 July 1529. • **16**. Gardiner's voyage: *LP* IV 5237, 5291, 5294. Salviati: Arfaioli, 49; Hurtubise. Gregorio to Vicenzo: TNA, SP 1/53 fols 20r–20v (*LP* IV 5302).

6 *Neither Fair nor Foul Will Serve*

1. *LP* IV 5329, 5529. • **2**. TNA, SP 1/52 fol. 126 (*LP* IV 5162). TNA, SP 1/52 fol. 148r (*LP* IV 5187); BL, Cotton MSS, Vit. B XI 31r (*LP* IV 5229); TNA, SP 1/52 fol. 208r (*LP* IV 5259). Rhubarb: *CSP Ven* IV 422. For background: Siraisi, 104–6. • **3**. G. Contarini, fol. 172v (*CSP Ven* IV 416). • **4**. Nesselrath and Mancinelli, 107–17. • **5**. Vicenzo: *LP* V, p. 309; Pocock, II 517 (*LP* VII 86); *LP* VII 1255. Departed 1 March: *LP* IV 5359. The

Geneva affair: *LP* IV 542. Russell's fall: *CSP Sp* III.II 35. Simon's accident: *LP* IV 6106. Background: Siraisi, 155. • **6**. G. Contarini, fols 162r, 165r, 167v (*CSP Ven* IV 401, 403, 405). • **7**. Sanuto, XLIX col. 417 (*CSP Ven* IV 408). • **8**. Mattingly (1973), 224. Bell (1998), 35. There is an extensive discussion of English diplomats' remuneration in MacMahon, 218–39. On Casali's finances: Fletcher (2010b). 'Compelled to live': BL, Cotton MSS, Vit. B XI 26r–26v (*LP* IV 5225). Bankrupt bankers and ongoing problems: *LP* IV 5235; 5313, 5375, 5476. • **9**. 'Whole house': *St P* VII 168 (*LP* IV 5481). • **10**. G. Contarini, fols 204r, 209r–v (*CSP Ven* IV 432, 436). • **11**. *St P* VII 153 (*LP* IV 5348). Burnet, IV 99 (*LP* IV 5523). The promise, dated 23 July 1528 and signed and sealed by Clement, is in Ehses, 30–1; for drafts see *LP* IV 4550, 5523. • **12**. Christmas: Ives, 97–9. Her dress: Hayward, 180–1. Letter with cramp-rings: Burnet, V 444 (*LP* IV 5422). • **13**. Bernard (2010), 37–40. Ives, 95–9. • **14**. *St P* VII 155 (*LP* IV 5401). G. Contarini, fols. 223r–v (*CSP Ven* IV 447). • **15**. Gardiner: TNA, SP 1/53 pp. 226–8 (*LP* IV 5476). Clement to Wolsey: *St P* VII 165 (*LP* IV 5475). Casali: TNA, SP 1/53, fol. 204v (*LP* IV 5478). Bryan: *St P* VII 166 (*LP* IV 5481). • **16**. Puglia: TNA, SP 1/53, fol. 232 (*LP* IV 5479). Bracciano: *CSP Ven* IV 449. France: BNF, MS Français 6636, 31–2; Gwyn, 577. • **17**. G. Contarini, fols. 233r–v (*CSP Ven* IV 452). ASMn, AG 878, cc. 147r–v, 467r. • **18**. German princes: Gardiner, 12 (*LP* IV 5476). Anonymous Florentine: ASF, Dieci di Balia, Responsive, 137 (1529), c. 271. • **19**. Bryan: *St P* VII 169–70 (*LP* IV 5519). • **20**. Gardiner, 17 (*LP* IV 5518). TNA, SP 1/54, fol. 32r (*LP* IV 5591). • **21**. *LP* IV 5523. Recall: *CSP Ven* IV 464. Less than satisfied/good cheer: G. Contarini, fol. 249v (*CSP Ven* IV 465). Departures: TNA, SP 1/54, fols 5r, 32. (*LP* IV 5553, 5591). *St P* VII 178–9 (*LP* IV 5616). Letter of introduction: ASMn, AG 878, c. 522r.

7 *Livia Pallavicino, Heiress*

1. Benet: *DNB*; for his Bologna studies, Surtz, 501. Bianchetti: *LP* VI 101, cited in MacCulloch (1996), 51, n. 32; *LP* XI 1131. • **2**. Burnet, IV 110–13 (*LP* IV 5576). • **3**. Ambassadors' concerns: *St P* VII 185 (*LP* IV 5650). Gardiner's reply: *St P* VII 190–1 (*LP* IV 5715). • **4**. *LP* IV 5638. Background: Gwyn, 464–5. • **5**. Background: Campari, 219–23; 325–34; Rocca et al., 63–5. 'None too bright': ASMo, Cancelleria, Ambasciatori, Venezia 18, unnumbered letter of 22 December 1534. Betrothal: ASC, AU, Sezione 1, vol. 594/2, fols 30r, 52v, 53v, 54r, 70r–v; vol. 776, unnumbered documents of 2 June and 13 July 1529. Clement's interest: ASV, Arm. XL 10, n. 214. Sciarra: ASV,

Segr. Stato, Venezia i, fol. 4v; ASMn, AG 1461, unnumbered letter of 27 November 1527; Molini, II 167. Manetti: *DBI*. • **6**. Campari, 326. McIver, 24 fn, 252. Litta, table 26: Pallavicino, Marchesi di Zibello. • **7**. Machiavelli, 116–17. Dolet (1933), 88. For background: Woodhouse. • **8**. *LP* IV 5641, 5650. • **9**. Accolti's letter: *LP* IV 5657. Pensions background: Potter (1995), 129; Giry-Deloison (1993). • **10**. Benet's arrival: *LP* IV 5725. Catherine's dress: Hayward, 179. • **11**. Du Bellay, I 46–7. • **12**. BL, Cotton MSS, Vit. B XI 175r–v (*LP* IV 5703). • **13**. BL, Cotton MSS, Vit. B XI 170v (*LP* IV 5721). • **14**. Gregorio 'very sincere': BL, Cotton MSS, Vit. B XI 172v (*LP* IV 5725). Campano's arrival: Parmiter, 105. • **15**. *LP* IV 5725. • **16**. Kahn, 109, 125, 150; Thompson and Padover, 256. Mattingly (1973), 238. • **17**. BL, Cotton MSS, Vit. B XI 181v (*LP* IV 5735). *LP* IV 5754. Treaty of Barcelona: Setton, III 327. Catherine's appeal: Scarisbrick, 298, citing *CSP Sp* IV.I 97. • **18**. Ruling in Giambattista's favour: ASV, Arch. Concist., Acta Vicecanc. 4, fol. 32r. Lobbying for Casali: G. Contarini, fol. 267r (*CSP Ven* IV 485).

8 *The Fall of Cardinal Wolsey*

1. Vitale, 159–60. Sanuto, LI 227. • **2**. Francesco: *DBI*. Gregorio in London: Sicca (2002), 172, 194. Catellano and Riario: Schiavo, 38–9. Riario and Caffarelli: Caffarelli, 40. • **3**. See McClung Hallman for a detailed exposition of this view. • **4**. Benet's letter: Burnet, IV 123–4 (*LP* IV 5761). Gregorio's discussion: BL, Cotton MSS, Vit. B XI 204v–205v (*LP* IV 5762). Clement's letter: BL, Cotton MSS, Vit. B XI 193 (*LP* IV 5759). Mantuan report: ASMn, AG 878, c. 258r. • **5**. Vanni's pretence: BL, Cotton MSS, Vit. B XI 189v (*LP* IV 5764); *LP* IV 5763, 5847. Local postmasters interfere: Pocock I 87 (*LP* IV 4007). Ferrara forgery: *LP* V 422. • **6**. Working night and day: BL, Cotton MSS, Vit. B XI 189v (*LP* IV 5764). Hungarian liaison: *LP* IV 5767. • **7**. G. Contarini, fols 269v–270v (*CSP Ven* IV 489). Advocation: ASV, Arch. Concist., Acta Vicecanc. 4, fol. 32r. Clement's letters: Burnet, IV 125 (*LP* IV 5785). Ehses, 118–20. Private courier: *LP* IV 5780. • **8**. ASMn, AG 1463, unnumbered letter of 2 August 1529. Imperial interception: *CSP Sp* IV.I 100. • **9**. Russell, 133–4. • **10**. Gregorio: ASF, Dieci di Balia, Responsive 139, fol. 322r. Francesco and Giambattista: ASMn, AG 1463, unnumbered letters of 4, 9 and 16 August 1529. • **11**. ASV, Arm. XL, 24, fol. 174r. Campari, 223. • **12**. *LP* IV 5878. • **13**. Casali and Florence: Sanuto, LI 462; G. Contarini, fol. 312v (*CSP Ven* IV 510). Siege begins: Arfaioli, 169. • **14**. *LP* IV 5961, 5988. • **15**. Background: Setton, III 324–7. Clement's letter: Theiner, 566 (*LP* IV 5994). • **16**. BAV, MS Vat. Lat. 12276, fol. 14v. *LP* III 1659. ASV, Arch.

Concist., Acta Misc. 31, fol. 131r. Mitchell (1971), 179–80. • **17**. G. Contarini, fol. 314v (*CSP Ven* IV 512). Giambattista's 1525 nunciature: TNA, SP 1/33 fol. 87r (*LP* IV 1002). Paolo still in Paris on 7 November: *LP* IV 6053. • **18**. Gwyn, esp. 590–4. • **19**. *LP* IV 6017, 6018. Charges: *LP* IV 6075. Shakespeare, 3166. • **20**. Chapuys: Fernández-Armesto. *CSP Sp* IV.I 224, 228. 'Young, virtuous and lovable' was the description of a Mantuan agent: ASMn, AG 880, c. 306v. Caffarelli. • **21**. Thurley, 34–6, 39, 48–50. Feast: *CSP Sp* IV.I 224. • **22**. *CSP Sp* IV.I 241.

9 A Coronation and a Wedding

1. Wall. • **2**. Grieco; for Florence 305. • **3**. *St P* VII 225–7 (*LP* IV 6092). Background on war: Hale. • **4**. *CSP Ven* IV 524. Eisenbichler, 432. • **5**. Fletcher (2011). • **6**. The house will be discussed in my future study, '"Uno palaço belissimo": town and country living in Renaissance Bologna'. • **7**. BAV, MS Vat. Lat. 12276, fol. 87r. *LP* IV 6049. • **8**. Andrea's 1514 joust: Biblioteca Universitaria di Bologna, MS 430, fol. 53v. Carew as jouster: Starkey, 79. Mantua horses: ASMn, AG 1152, c. 466r. • **9**. Wall, 89–92 (*LP* IV 6069). • **10**. Ghinucci's letter: *LP* IV 6065. Alessandro de' Medici: Brackett. • **11**. Wiltshire promotion: *LP* IV 6083. Carew and Catherine: Ives, 140, citing *CSP Sp* IV.I 182, 290. Giambattista should hinder Henry: *LP* IV 6567. • **12**. *Jeu de cannes*: Sanuto, LII, cols 352–5. Embassy entourages: Starkey, 103–4. Potter (1973), 310. • **13**. *LP* IV 6103. • **14**. Parker to Mantua: ASMn, AG 1153, c. 324r; AG 2969, Libro 44, fols 93v–94r. Reports that Henry will break with Rome: ASMn, AG 1153, c. 23v. ASMo, Cancelleria, Ambasciatori, Venezia 18, unnumbered letter of 13 January 1530. • **15**. Told Chapuys: *CSP Sp* IV.I 224. Ban on books: *LP* IV 6402. • **16**. English Parliament: Scarisbrick, 329–31; Richardson (2008), 100; Elton, esp. 516, citing Hall's *Chronicle*. • **17**. Luzio, 365. ACdM I, unnumbered document of 13 April 1531. • **18**. Gold chain: *LP* VI 339. Not the intention they should stay long: *CSP Sp* IV.I 132. • **19**. *LP* IV 6155. • **20**. Cranmer in entourage: MacCulloch (1996), 48. Chapuys' letter: Bradford, 300–1. (*LP* IV 6199). • **21**. Eisenbichler, 435. • **22**. Ambassadors expected: Molini, II 281 (*LP* IV 6268). Without honour: BAV, MS Vat. Lat. 12276, fol. 135v. *LP* IV 6284; 6285, 6290. • **23**. ASMn, AG 1153, cc. 403r, 478r. Giovanna had married Jacopo Crescenzi in May 1529, having lost her first husband, Giacomo Cenci. *LP* IV 5538; ACdM, I, no. 15.

10 *The Scholar Croke Cries Foul*

1. Ives, 132; MacCulloch (1996), 45. • **2.** On the focus of the early diplomacy I agree with Sharkey (2008), 191–3. For an alternative view, emphasising the discussion of the king's Levitical scruple, see Virginia Murphy, 'Introduction', in Surtz and Murphy, i–xliv. For full discussions of the canon law see Scarisbrick, Kelly. • **3.** For background: Grendler, 3–40; Woolfson (1998), 42–4. • **4.** Girolamo: Williams (2009), 272 n. 601. Giambattista's university: ASB, Studio Bolognese, Collegi Legali 138, fols 36v, 37r; Collegi Legali 22, fols 138r–139r. Nunciature: *LP* IV 1002. Venice: Sanuto, XL cols 555, 718–19 (*CSP Ven* III 1175, 1207, 1208). Ibid., XLI col. 84 (*CSP Ven* IV 132). Ibid., XLVIII cols 153–4 (*CSP Ven* IV 310). Ibid., XL col. 785 (*CSP Ven* III 1215). • **5.** *LP* IV 6155. *DNB*. • **6.** Pocock, I 427. (*LP* IV 6623). • **7.** Surtz and Murphy, v. Major contributors to the king's books included, as well as Stokesley, Edward Fox, Stephen Gardiner, Nicholas de Burgo, Thomas Cranmer, Edward Lee. Ibid., xxii. Ghinucci's complaint: *LP* IV 6205. • **8.** His stipend: *LP* IV 6170. On exchange rates: Challis, 68–9, 216. His cover stories: Woolfson (2000), 7, citing *LP* IV 6145, 6194, 6235. • **9.** *LP* IV 6423. • **10.** BL, Cotton MSS, Vit. B XIII 14v (*LP* IV 6149). See also *LP* IV 6159, 6165. • **11.** Diodorus: BL, Cotton MSS, Vit. B XIII 64r (*LP* IV 6280). Love for a girl: Vit. B XIII 50 (*LP* IV 6235) and Vit. B XIII 55r (*LP* IV 6236). Daily frauds: Vit. B XIII 56 (*LP* IV 6237). Poison or dagger; prostituted honour: Vit. B XIII 59v (*LP* IV 6251). • **12.** *LP* IV 6251. Privileges withdrawn: *CSP Sp* IV.I 294. Vassal of the Pope: BL, Add. MS 28580, fol. 206r (*CSP Sp* IV.I 365). • **13.** Clement's offer: Ehses 140–2; Henry agrees: *LP* IV 6324. Mandate restricting campaign: Theiner, 592 (*LP* IV 6549), 21 May 1530; an almost identical mandate was issued on 4 August 1530. • **14.** Bertani's subsequent career: Bartlett. Bryan in France: Bell (1990), 74. Letter to Montmorency: Molini, II 280–1 (*LP* IV 6268). • **15.** Rocca, et al., 65. *St P* VII 231–2 (*LP* IV 6292). • **16.** TNA SP 1/57, fol. 52 (*LP* IV 6309). Machiavelli, 118. Henry's lobbying letter: *LP* IV 6322. • **17.** To Milan: *CSP Mil* 815. Gregorio to Giambattista: TNA, SP 1/57, fol. 223 (*LP* IV 6501 (3)). • **18.** Conflict with Ghinucci: BL, Cotton MSS, Vit. B XIII, 68v (*LP* IV 6316). *LP* IV 6326, 6333. • **19.** BL, Cotton MSS, Vit. B XIII, 75v (*LP* IV 6352). • **20.** *LP* IV 6365, 6373, 6398. • **21.** ASMn, AG 1464, cc. 467–8, c. 490. Sanuto, LIII, col. 229. • **22.** Barbaro, 167. ASMn, AG 1150, c. 461; AG 1463, unnumbered letters of 4 and 16 August 1529. Sanuto, LIII cols 229, 283. Attempt to discredit: *LP* IV 6209. Blackburn, et al., 984. Unlike Blackburn et al., I do not think it absolutely certain that Giambattista knew Greek. Although in 1527 he borrowed Greek manuscripts from St Mark's Library, these

were probably to send on to Cardinal Wolsey in England. Straparola, I 9.
• **23**. Croke's Imperial faction: *LP* IV 6403. Bembo, II 432. On Argentina see
her entry in Lasagni. On Pole: Mayer (2000); for his early support of Henry
see Mayer (1988). Casali visits Pole: Sanuto, XLII col. 574 (*CSP Ven* III 1405).

11 *The Daily Frauds of the Brothers Casali*

1. BL, Cotton MSS, Vit. B XIII 82 (*LP* IV 6407, 6423). The Bishop of Vaison:
Eubel, III 327. • **2**. Niño's activities in Venice: Levin. Ascension Day: Muir,
121–2. • **3**. BL, Add. MS 28580, fols 104v–105v (*LP* IV 6422); fol. 206r (*CSP
Sp* IV.I 365); fol. 294v (*LP* IV 6528 and *CSP Sp* IV.I 384). • **4**. *St P* VII 238
(*LP* IV 6444). • **5**. Croke a 'brabeller': BL, Cotton MSS, Vit. B XIII 88r (*LP*
IV 6445). Background: Bell (1998), 31. Isom-Verhaaren, 132. Mellano, 21.
• **6**. *St P* VII 241–3 (*LP* IV 6470). Light dissimuler: BL, Cotton MSS, Vit.
B XIII 74r (*LP* IV 6328). • **7**. Ghinucci spying: *LP* IV 6470. Gurone's report:
TNA, SP 1/57 fol. 222 (*LP* IV 6501). Benet fraternising: BL, Cotton MSS,
Vit. B XIII 102r (*LP* IV 6567). • **8**. Mai's concerns: *CSP Sp* IV.I 322. Leonico:
Woolfson, 117. Such assistance as Henry eventually afforded to Florence
came too late. Roth, 193–4. • **9**. Appeal of nobility: Parmiter, 136;
Ives, 135. English subsidies: *LP* IV 6452. Bitter words: TNA, SP 1/57, fol.
219r (*LP* IV 6499). Threat of scandal: BL, Add. MS 28580, fol. 279v (*LP* IV
6521). Benet and Mai: *LP* IV 6550. Delay until November: Scarisbrick, 341.
• **10**. Panic: Nicholson, 19, and for extensive background discussion
Scarisbrick, 218–62. Andrea: ASV, Arm. XL, 10, n. 99, fol. 88; ASB, Senato,
Lettere VII, vol. 8, unnumbered letter of 14 March 1525. Previdelli:
Previdelli (1528); Previdelli (1531); Bedouelle and Le Gal, 406–9; for a more
detailed account Surtz, 514–66, esp. 525–6 for the translation of the dedi-
cation. • **11**. Gambara: Pagano, 18–34. Croke to Cranmer: Pocock, I 421
(*LP* IV 6613); to Henry, Pocock, I 423 (*LP* IV 6619). Papal interdict: Theiner,
592 (*LP* IV 6549). • **12**. *St P* VII 253–6 (*LP* IV 6633). • **13**. Niño's spying: BL,
Add. MS 28580 fol. 314r (*LP* IV 6536). Ognibene: TNA, SP 1/57 fol. 222
(*LP* IV 6501); for background, Bedouelle and Le Gal, 388–9. • **14**. Niño:
BL, Add. MS 28581, fols 56v, 122v, 125r. Croke: Pocock, II 14, 23. • **15**. The
new treatise, long thought lost, survives in the Biblioteca Marciana, Venice.
The pro-Henry and pro-Catherine treatises are Venosta (1530a) and
(1530b). 'Intellectual exercise': Venosta (1530b), fol. C.3r. Pocock, I 588 (*LP*
IV 6607). • **16**. Croke to Venosta: Pocock, II 23 (*LP* IV 6684). Surtz, 368–72.
• **17**. BL, Cotton MSS, Vit. B XIII, 133r (*LP* IV 6728). • **18**. Surtz, 379–82.
LP IV 6695. • **19**. Pocock, II 477–8 (*LP* IV App. 264). • **20**. *DNB*.

12 *The Custom of England*

1. Molini, II 322–3. G. Contarini, fol. 336r (*CSP Ven* IV 523). • 2. ASMn, AG 1464, cc. 59r, 84v, 103r. *CSP Sp* IV.I 428. Shaw (2007), unpaginated geneaological tables. • 3. Roth, 193–4. • 4. Lobbying Grammont: Le Grand, III 544 (*LP* IV 6593). Bigamy: *LP* IV 6627; Doernberg, 75. • 5. BL, Add. MS 28,581 fol. 207r (*CSP Sp* IV.I 446). • 6. Praemunire: Gwyn, 621–3; Scarisbrick, 358–9. Pius II: Richardson (2009), 63–4. • 7. Ambassadors' concerns: *LP* IV app. 262. Henry's reply: *St P* VII 261 (*LP* IV 6667). Background: Gwyn, 49–50. Scarisbrick, 342–5. Greenfeld, 27–88. • 8. ASMn, AG 879, c. 175v. Gombrich, 104–8. Campitelli, 28–33. • 9. Gregorio to Bologna: *LP* IV 6700. Flooding: BL, Add. MS 25114, fol. 37r (*LP* IV 6705). • 10. Gwyn, 599–639; Scarisbrick, 315–16. • 11. Break of relations: Ives, 146. Gift: *LP* IV 6738. • 12. Giambattista and Niño: *LP* IV 6742. Mantuan report: ASMn, AG 879, c. 342r. • 13. ASMn, AG 879, c. 356r-v. • 14. Henry to Clement: Theiner, 594 (*LP* IV 6759). To Benet and Carne: *St P* VII 270–1 (*LP* IV 6760). • 15. ASV, Arch. Concist., Acta Vicecanc. 4, fol. 59; for the letters see the copy in ASMn, AG 578, c. 41r. *LP* IV 6765. Fray Garcia Laoysa, Cardinal of Osma, to the Emperor: BL, Add. MS 28582, fols. 158r–159r (*LP* IV 6766). Henry's reply: *LP* V 28. • 16. *CSP Sp* IV.I 548. • 17. Borasca investigation: ASV, Arm. XL, 31, n. 557. Giambernardino's accusation: ASF, Fondo Accolti, b. 9, doc. 15 fol. 1. On the practice of pillory: Edgerton Jr., 65–6. • 18. Trust: ASV, Cam. Ap., Div. Cam. 81, fols 202v–203r. July 1531 brief: Campari, 327. Rimini governorship: ASMn, AG 1464, c. 278r. • 19. *St P* VII 272 (*LP* IV 6769). • 20. Secret consistory: BL, Add. MS 28582, fol. 181 (*LP* IV 6772). Brief: *LP* V 27. Publication dates: Bedouelle and Le Gal, 340–1, 360–1. Imperial report: BL, Add. MS 28582 fol. 286 (*LP* V 39).

13 *Murder in Naples*

1. BAV, MS Vat. Lat. 12276, fol. 153r. Processional route: Fernández, 148–50. Candlemas: *Catholic Encyclopaedia* at www.newadvent.org/cathen/03245b. htm. • 2. Ives, 139. • 3. Bostick, 185. Carne's arrival: Scarisbrick, 369. • 4. ASMn, AG 880, c. 376r. ASV, Arch. Concist., Acta Vicecanc., 4, fol. 63r. Joint meeting with French: Le Grand, III 519 (*LP* V 104). • 5. Two-month suspension: ASMn, AG 880 c. 404v. Feint to buy time: *LP* V 93. Mai's laments: BL, Add. MS. 28,583, fols 102r, 123v (*LP* V 137, 158). • 6. French lobbying: Molini, II 363, 366. BNF, MS Italien 1131, fol. 59r. Jewellery:

ACdM I, unnumbered document of 13 April 1531. • **7**. Rumours: Molini, II 366–7. The rider: Scarisbrick, 361. • **8**. BNF, MS Français 3040, fols 41r, 44r, 47r. • **9**. Raince: BNF, MS Français 3040, fol. 47r. Casali: Molini, II 369 (*LP* V 229). • **10**. *St P* VII 297–9 (*LP* V 206). • **11**. *St P* VII 300–1 (*LP* V 245). • **12**. Consistory: ASV, Arch. Concist., Acta Vicecanc, 4, fol. 67r. Cambrai moves: BNF, MS Italien 1131, fol. 58r; ASV, A. A., Arm. I–XVIII, 6523, fols 66, 72–74v. *LP* V 255. Catherine refuses: Ives, 146. Bernard (2010), 60. *LP* V 287. Campeggio: Wilkie, 207. Blamed Casali: *LP* V 283. 'Much hated': Du Bellay, I 431. • **13**. Previdelli authorisation: ASB, Senato, Lettere VII vol. 11. Henry's instructions: *LP* V 326, 327. 'Fine game': *LP* V 351. • **14**. ASB, Senato, Lettere VII, vol. 11, letters of 14 and 27 August 1531. ASMn, AG 880, c. 171v. Cranmer: Pocock, II 318 (*LP* V 1449). • **15**. Imperial suspicions: *LP* V 421. Henry's requests for promotions: *LP* V 418, 419. Chapuys: *LP* V 432. Provisions: ASV, Arch. Concist., Acta Vicecanc. 4, fol. 76r. • **16**. *St P* VII 251 (*LP* IV 6626). • **17**. Clement to Campeggio: ASV, A. A., Arm. I–XVIII, 6523, fol. 87r. Catherine excluded: Bedouelle and Le Gal, 451. Insulting letter: BL, Add. MS 28,584, fol. 25. (*CSP Sp* IV.II 821). • **18**. Very obstinate: TNA SP 1/68, fol. 13r (*LP* V 467). King's offer: Pocock, II 144 (*LP* V 611). The date is given by Pocock as 3 December 1531. This is unlikely: on that date Benet was en route to England, having received his notice of recall. It is more likely that Benet received these instructions while in England. Private business: Theiner, 598 (*LP* V 511). Arrival: Sanuto, LV col. 445 (*CSP Ven* IV 714). Mai's report: BL, Add. MS 28,584, fols 53v–54r (*LP* V 557). • **19**. Authorisation: *LP* V 691. Chapuys' reports: HHStA, England, Kart. 5, Korr., Ber. 1531–4, unnumbered folios (*LP* V 614, 696). Mai's report: BL, Add. MS 28584, fol. 206v (*CSP Sp* IV.II 909). • **20**. Clement's request for aid: *LP* IV 5994. Henry's reply: *St P* VII 325 (*LP* V 464). Cold words: BL, Add. MS 28584, fol. 129 (*LP* V 616). Szapolyai's excommunication: Setton, III 335. His letter to Paolo: *LP* V 471. • **21**. ASMn, AG 880 c. 249. • **22**. ASV, Arch. Concist., Acta Vicecanc. 4, fol. 79r–v. Property sales: ACdM, I, nos. 85–90. Carne's letter: *St P* VII 330 (*LP* V 586). House purchase: ACdM, I, no. 84. Value of Bolognese money: Bellocchi, 28–9. Henry's thanks: Pocock, II 153 (*LP* V 691). Protecting Livia's land: ASMo, Cancelleria, Ambasciatori, Roma 33, unnumbered letters of 28 November and 5 December 1531. • **23**. Giambattista's letters: *LP* IV 6309, 6310; *LP* V 115, 923; *LP* VI 991. Oysters: ASMn, AG 1465, c. 633r. Andrea in Bologna: ASB, Studio Bolognese, Collegi Legali 127, fol. 52v. • **24**. ASMo, Cancelleria, Ambasciatori, Roma 33, unnumbered letter of 5 December 1531. ASMn, AG 880, cc. 251v, 306; AG 1465, c. 378v; AG 1466, c. 413r. • **25**. Pocock, II 516 (*LP* VII 86).

14 *How to Bribe a Cardinal (Part Two)*

1. Casali's claim: *LP* V 695. Henry's letter: *St P* VII 345 (*LP* V 792).
• 2. Accolti trial, II; 3 May 1535. • 3. ASF, Fondo Accolti, 9, no. 15, fol.
1v, and 16, no. 17, fol. 1v. Accolti trial II; 3 May 1535. • 4. Accolti trial,
II; articles against the cardinal. • 5. For background: *DBI* and Costantini.
Corruption: Accolti trial, II; articles against the cardinal. Note to
lawyer: ASF, Fondo Accolti, 9, no. 30, fol. 2r. • 6. No adjournment:
LP V 692. Consistory: ASV, Arch. Concist., Acta Vicecanc. 4, fols 80v,
82r. Bonner: *DNB*. • 7. Clement's letter: *LP* V 750. New Year in England: ✓
Ives, 148; *LP* V 696. • 8. Benet's offers: *LP* V 778. ASF, Fondo Accolti,
9, no. 30, fol. 2. Ely revenues: Heal, 54. Cardinal's demands: Pocock,
II 213–16 *(LP* V 777). France pretence: *LP* V 891. Norfolk's letter: *St P*
VII 350 (*LP* V 831) Henry: *LP* V 887. • 9. Dondolus and Conradus:
Bedouelle and Le Gal, 341. 'Chiding and scolding': Burnet, IV 179 (*LP*
v 892). Consistory dates: BAV, MS Vat. Lat. 12276, fols 169r–170v.
Henry's letter: *LP* V 833. • 10. Background: Biblioteca Universitaria di
Bologna, MS 2137, fols 18v–19r. Benet/Casali letter: *LP* V 889. Bandino.
Lobbying of Guicciardini: Guicciardini (1927), 205. Gregorio's 'injuries':
St P VII 371 (*LP* V 1025). Henry's letter: *LP* V 1032. Giambattista lobbying:
LP V 770; ASMn, AG 1466, c. 35v. • 11. Guicciardini (1927), 112. Murphy,
286. • 12. For background: Williams (2010). ASMo, Cancelleria,
Ambasciatori, Roma 33, unnumbered letter of 14 January 1532. ASMn,
AG 881 c. 463r. HHStA, Rom, Korrespondenz, 6, fols 18r, 30r. HHStA,
UA 20a contains a series of intercepted letters from these months.
• 13. Easter celebrations: BAV, MS Vat. Lat. 12276, fols 171r–173r. ASV,
Arch. Concist., Acta Vicecanc. 4, fols 87–8. Previdelli: ASBo, Senato,
Lettere VII, vol. 11, unnumbered letter of 20 April 1532. Bedouelle and
Le Gal, 408. • 14. Pocock, II 252–3 (*LP* V 974). • 15. Elton; Scarisbrick.
• 16. Horses: ASMn, AG 881, c. 627r; also c. 653r. Further adjournment:
Parmiter, 180. Campeggio letter: ASV, A. A., Arm. I–XVIII, 6523, fol.
154v. • 17. Rex. • 18. Pocock, II 288 (*LP* V 1173). *St P* VII 379 (*LP* V 1321).
ASF, Fondo Accolti, 16, no. 17, fol. 1. • 19. Reports of his mission:
Sanuto, LVII col. 25 (*CSP Ven* IV 809); *LP* V 1364. Mai's letters: BL,
Add. MS 28585, fol. 133r (*LP* V 1401); fol. 174 (*LP* V 1448; *CSP Sp* IV.II
1028). • 20. Celebrations: 'The Manner of the Triumph', 3–8. Anne:
Ives, 158, 160, 166; Scarisbrick, 399. Anne lambasts Casali: *LP* V 1538.
• 21. Bribery continues: *LP* V 1493, 1507. Mai's report: *LP* V 1353.
• 22. ASF, Fondo Accolti, 16, no. 17, fol. 1. Accolti trial I, fol. 64; II, 3
May 1535, evidence of Giambernardino; II; 6 May 1535, evidence of

Flavio Crisolino; ASF, Fondo Accolti, 9, no. 30, fols 2–3. Dolet (1933), 86. • **23**. Clement's warning: *LP* V 1545. Giustinian's report: Sanuto, LVII col. 336 (*CSP Ven* IV 829). Niño forwards: *LP* V 1634. • **24**. Benet and Henry: *LP* V 1659, 1662; Henry's reply: *St P* VII 416 (*LP* VI 194). Agents' evidence: Accolti trial I, fol. 71r; and II, 10 May 1535. Costantini, 309. • **25**. Sanuto, LVIII col. 77 (*CSP Ven* IV 877). ASF, Fondo Accolti, 9, no. 30, fol. 3v.

15 *The Break with Rome*

1. Clement: *LP* V 1659. Henry and Anne marry: Ives, 162, says 'probably' on 25 January; Bernard (2010), 66, is less willing to commit to a date: his citations of Chapuys' letters point to a mid-February marriage. Charles and Clement: *LP* VI 23, cited by Bostick, 245. • **2**. Capello: Sanuto, LVII cols 535–6 (*CSP Ven* IV 846). Clement: *LP* VI 11. • **3**. Sanuto, LVII col. 536 (*CSP Ven* IV 846). • **4**. Chapuys: *LP* VI 89. Capello: Sanuto, LVII cols 538–9, 579 (*CSP Ven* IV 847, 850). Scotland rumour: ASV, Segr. Stato, Venezia, 1, fol. 99v. • **5**. Pocock, II 434–41 (*LP* VI 102). • **6**. *St P* VII 417–18 (*LP* VI 194), cited in Bostick, 252. • **7**. Camusat, 122r–v (*LP* VI 110). • **8**. Granvelle, II 7–19 (*LP* VI 182). • **9**. *LP* VI 177. ASV, Arch. Concist., Acta Vicecanc., 4, fol. 103v. Scarisbrick, 404. Ives, 164. • **10**. *St P* VII 440–1 (*LP* VI 222). • **11**. *St P* VII 448–9 (*LP* VI 225). • **12**. Ives, 164. *LP* VI 324. *DNB*. • **13**. Mood in Rome: *LP* VI 445, 506. Gregorio to Norfolk: *St P* VII 455 (*LP* VI 456). Five hundred crowns: TNA, SP 1/77, fol. 102r (*LP* VI 736). • **14**. *LP* VI 543, 584, 585. • **15**. TNA SP 1/76, fols 231–2 (*LP* VI 635). ASMn, AG 882, cc. 64r, 70r, 75v, 80v. • **16**. *St P* VII 472–3 (*LP* VI 643). *LP* VI 670. • **17**. Feast of Saints Peter and Paul: BAV, MS Barb. Lat. 2799, fol. 257. Henry's appeal: *LP* VI 721. • **18**. BAV, MS Barb. Lat 2799, fols 257v–258r. *LP* VI App. 3, 810, 953. • **19**. Orders to leave: *LP* VI 980. Peregrino's report: ASMn, AG 882, c. 105v. Cardinal Merino: BL, Add. MS. 28,585, fols 337v–338r (*LP* VI 980). • **20**. *St P* VII 512–14 (*LP* VI 1300). • **21**. Elizabeth's birth: Ives, 184–6. Bernard (2010), 74. Clement's departure: Parmiter, 264. Marseilles wedding: Scarisbrick, 402, 415. Wanegffelen, 79–81; Knecht, 15–17; Richardson (2008), 106. • **22**. Accreditation: ASV, A. A., Arm. I–XVIII, 2503, and Williams (2010), 595. Imperial suspicion: HHStA, Rom, Korrespondenz, 7/1, fol. 56r. Gregorio's involvement: *LP* VI 1509. • **23**. Gianetti: *LP* V 1693. *Fasti*, III 2 and 60. Francesco's meetings: HHStA, UA 23b, fol 81; 23c, fols 21r, 23r, 28r–30v. • **24**. *LP* VI 1392, 1425. • **25**. HHStA, UA 23c, fols 49r, 51r,

53r, 60r. 23c, fols. 69r–70r. • **26**. Sanuto, LVIII cols 406, 687 (*CSP Ven* IV 925, 980). Cappelletti, 191.

16 *The Ingratitude of Princes*

1. *CSP Ven* V 3. • **2**. Sicca (2002), 172, 194. • **3**. Ives, 246–59. Suspicion: HHStA, UA 27a, fol. 63r. • **4**. Pocock, II 511–22 (*LP* VII 86). • **5**. Scarisbrick, 419–20. Parmiter, 287. Catherine's accommodation: Mattingly (1950), 269, 281. Mary's accommodation: *LP* VI 1296, fn. • **6**. Final sentence: ASV, Arch. Concist., Acta Vicecanc. 4, fol. 111v. Giambernardino: *LP* VII 144. Chapuys' report: *LP* VII 83. Giambattista: *CSP Ven* V 2 and 3. • **7**. Ghinucci loses Worcester: Wilkie, 216. Campeggio lost Salisbury at the same time. Corsini: HHStA, UA 24a, fol. 87r; 24b, fols 53r–54v. Chapuys' report: HHStA, England, Kart. 5, Korr., Ber. 1531–34, letter of 29 May 1534 (*LP* VII 726). • **8**. Setton, III 383–4, 391. HHStA, UA 24c, fols 12r, 45r. • **9**. Credential: HHStA, UA, 24c, fol. 56r. Anne's pregnancy: Ives, 191; Bernard (2010), 75. • **10**. Gregorio and conclave: *LP* VII 1057, 1095, 1181, 1228. Rejoicing of populace: *St P* VII 574–5 (*LP* VII 1262, 1263). Chapuys on Cromwell: *LP* VII 1257. • **11**. Du Bellay, I 430. *CSP Ven* V 22. • **12**. See Gregorio's letters to Cromwell: *LP* VII 1185, 1255; to Norfolk: *LP* VII 1262; and to Lord Rochford: *LP* VII 1263. On blanks see Queller, 130. Enquiries via Manetti: *St P* VII 576 (*LP* VII 1298). Correspondence from Gregorio in Rome: *LP* VII 1405, 1406; *LP* VIII 17, 251 • **13**. *LP* VII 1397. For background, Ives, 192–5. • **14**. On the infrequency of the correspondence: *LP* VIII 712. • **15**. Crusics' servant: HHStA, UA 25c, fols 118–125. Informing French: BNF, MS Français 19751, fols 121v–122r (abstract at Du Bellay, I 450–51). Hopes for French favour: *LP* VIII 399. Attempt to dissuade: HHStA, UA 27a, fol. 63v, cited in Williams (2010), 602. • **16**. Gregorio ill: *LP* VIII 713. Financial troubles: HHStA, UA 27a, fols 62v, 73v (Giambattista), 73r (Corsini). Leaving gift: *CSP Ven* V 38, 40. Disguise: Williams (2010), 603. • **17**. HHStA, UA 27a, fol. 71r. Du Bellay, I 483–5.

17 *A Mother's Tears*

1. Description of room: Friedensburg, I 560. Gregorio's fears: *St P* VII 600 (*LP* VIII 713). Giambattista: HHStA, UA 27a, fol. 63r. • **2**. HHStA, UA 27a, fols 71–2. It seems likely that this was an early confession, for

it is written in Italian and includes none of the interrogators' questions.
• **3**. Her approximate age is established by her parents' marriage in
1475 and her own in 1492: Caffarelli, 36–7; BAV, MS Vat. Lat. 11980, fols
121r, 131v. City connections: Amayden, 226. • **4**. Sanchez: HHStA, Rom,
Korrespondenz, 9, fols 72v–73v. Ricalcati: Setton, III 418, note 82. Task
of nuncio harder: *CSP Ven* VI Misc. 1535, 114. • **5**. Nomination will 'ruin
him': Du Bellay, I 490 (*LP* VIII 747). Remonstrates with cardinals: *LP*
VIII 777. Further letters to Cromwell: *LP* VIII 807, 808. Hopes of escape
dashed: *LP* VIII 874. • **6**. *LP* VIII 1144. • **7**. *LP* VIII 948 and 1018; *CSP Sp*
V.I 178, 181. • **8**. Letters to Cromwell: *LP* VIII 972, 1052, 1121. Cardinal
of Trent lobbies for Giambattista's release: ASV, Arm. XL, 53, fol. 134r.
• **9**. Retreats to Bologna: TNA SP 1/96 fol. 2v (*LP* IX 202). Gurone:
BL, Add. MS 8715, fol. 124r (*LP* IX 492). Letter to Gardiner: *LP* IX 999.
• **10**. Pocock, II 355–6 (*LP* V 1648, but the *LP* editors' date of 1532 is
wrong: the letter refers to a letter of Henry to Ferdinand concerning
Giambattista's liberation, clearly dating it to 1535). • **11**. *LP* VIII 713. F.
Contarini, fols 81r, 82v (*CSP Ven* V 50, 51). This particular phrase does
not appear in the numerous poems on Accolti's imprisonment given
in Marci, Marzo and Romano. • **12**. F. Contarini, fols 116r, 123r (*CSP
Ven* V 87). Pledges: Williams (2010), 608–9, citing HHStA, UA27e, fols.
63–64. • **13**. Catherine's death: Mattingly (1950), 304–11. Chapuys' report:
HHStA, England, Kart. 5, Korr., Ber. an Karl V. u. Granvelle 1535–6 (*LP*
X 200). Jane Seymour: Ives, 292–312. • **14**. Gregorio's reports: *LP* X
297, 546, 620, 682, 683, 687, 796, 814, 906, 955, 977, XI 70, 179, 181,
182, 744, 963. Invasion of Milan: Ives, 294–6. Appointment to Emperor:
Du Bellay, II 313. • **15**. BL, Cotton MSS, Vesp. C. XIII 251 (*LP* X 683).
• **16**. *LP* X 670 (the decipher of the text is given in the Calendar). The
triumph: Stinger, 117. • **17**. Anne: Ives, 350; Dolet (1538), 162. Petrucci
conspiracy: Hyde, 141. Letter to Pate: *LP* X 955. Letter to Henry: *LP* X
977. • **18**. Williams (2010), 609. Lost rings: *LP* XI 963. Illness: *LP* XI 182.
• **19**. ASVe, Archivio Propria Roma 5, fol. 141r. ASV, Arch. Concist.,
Acta Vicecanc., 4, fol. 153r. • **20**. Hoyle. • **21**. Last letter: *LP* XI 963.
Gianetti's letter: *LP* XI 1131.

Epilogue

1. Michele and Ottavia: ACdM, I, no. 14. Guidicini, II 134. Molossi,
229. Gianetti: *LP* V 1693; *Fasti*, III 2 and 60. Codicil to Gregorio
Casali's will, 14 December 1536. ACdM, I, no. 15. • **2**. Cardinals: Miranda,

http://www2.fiu.edu/~mirandas/consistories-xvi.htm. Bertani's citizen-ship: Angelozzi and Casanova, 228; subsequent career: Bartlett. Giambernardino: Sowerby, 201. Accolti: *DBI*. • **3**. For their subsequent careers: *DNB*.

Bibliography

There is a huge bibliography concerned with both English and Italian history for this period, and it has proved impossible to be exhaustive here. In the notes I point readers to the original sources for Casali's story, and to a selection of key background literature. The monumental Victorian guides to English state papers (*Letters and Papers, Foreign and Domestic* and so on) are the starting points for any research on Tudor diplomacy, although they should be used with caution. They leave out many details, and in various cases after consulting the original manuscript or printed transcription I have amended the calendar translation for accuracy or style. When I quote directly from a manuscript I have given its archive reference; otherwise I refer to a calendar number (when one exists). Readers who would like to consult the original documents can find the full references by checking the calendar number at www.british-history.ac.uk.

The spelling of names has, as far as possible, been standardised in line with the *Dictionary of National Biography* for English names and the *Dizionario Biografico degli Italiani* for Italian names. Except in the case of monarchs for whom standard English names exist (Charles V, Francis I) I have avoided anglicising foreign names, so, for example, Gregorio Casali and Pietro Vanni are used in preference to Gregory Casale and Peter Vannes. More generally, I have modernised spellings of original documents throughout. When referring to the *Letters and Papers* and *Calendars of State Papers*, I have given document numbers, except in the case of unnumbered items, where a page reference is given. When citing Sanuto's diaries,

I have given column numbers. The following abbreviations have been used in the notes:

Accolti trial	Archivio di Stato di Roma, Tribunale del Governatore di Roma, Processi, vol. 3, trial number 2
ACdM	Archivio dei Casali di Monticelli d'Ongina
ASB	Archivio di Stato di Bologna
ASC, AU	Archivio Storico Capitolino, Archivio Urbano
ASF	Archivio di Stato di Firenze
ASMn, AG	Archivio di Stato di Mantova, Archivio Gonzaga
ASMo	Archivio di Stato di Modena
ASR	Archivio di Stato di Roma
ASV	Archivio Segreto Vaticano
ASVe	Archivio di Stato di Venezia
BAV	Biblioteca Apostolica Vaticana
BNF	Bibliothèque Nationale de France
BL	British Library
F. Contarini	Biblioteca Nazionale Marciana, Codices Italiani VII 802 (=8219)
G. Contarini	Biblioteca Nazionale Marciana, Codices Italiani VII 1043 (=7616)
CSP Mil	*Calendar of State Papers and Manuscripts, existing in the archives and collections of Milan*
CSP Sp	*Calendar of Letters, Despatches and State Papers relating to the negotiations between England and Spain*
CSP Ven	*Calendar of State Papers and Manuscripts relating to English affairs existing in the archives and collections of Venice*
DBI	*Dizionario Biografico degli Italiani*
DNB	*Oxford Dictionary of National Biography*
HHStA	*Österreichisches Staatsarchiv, Haus–, Hof– und Staatsarchiv*
LP	*Letters and Papers, Foreign and Domestic, of the Reign of Henry VIII*
St P	*State Papers Published under the Authority of Her Majesty's Commission: King Henry the Eighth*
TNA	The National Archives
b.	busta
c.	carta (leaf)
fol.	folio.

Full publication details of the works listed above are given below.

Manuscript sources

Archivio dei Casali di Monticelli d'Ongina
    Cassetta I (1420–1547)

Archivio di Stato di Bologna
    Senato
        Lettere VI di Principi e Prelati 4
        Lettere VII dell'ambasciatore 8, 11
    Studio Bolognese
        Collegi Legali 22, 127, 138

Archivio di Stato di Firenze
    Fondo Accolti bb. 9, 16
    Dieci di Balia, Responsive, 137, 139

Archivio di Stato di Mantova
    Archivio Gonzaga 45, 578, 877–82, 1150–3, 1460–6, 2969

Archivio di Stato di Modena
    Archivio Estense
        Cancelleria, Ambasciatori, Roma, bb. 32, 33
        Cancelleria, Ambasciatori, Venezia, bb. 17, 18
        Principi Esteri, Cardinali, b. 1435/189

Archivio di Stato di Roma
    Tribunale del Governatore di Roma, Processi 3

Archivio di Stato di Venezia
    Consiglio dei Dieci – Capi
        Lettere di Ambasciatori, b. 22
        Parti Secrete, filza 2
    Senato
        Archivio Propria Roma 5

Archivio Storico Capitolino
    Archivio Urbano, Sezione 1, vols 594/2, 76

Archivio Segreto Vaticano
    Archivio Concistoriale

Acta Vicecancellarii, 4
Acta Miscellanea, 31
Archivum Arcis, Arm. I–XVIII, 2503, 6523
Armadio XL, vols 10, 24, 31, 53
Camera Apostolica
    Diversa Cameralia, 81, 86, 101
Registri Vaticani 1299
Segretaria di Stato
    Francia, vol. 1
    Venezia, vol. 1

Biblioteca Apostolica Vaticana
    MSS Barberini Latini
        2799: Biagio Martinelli da Cesena, *Diario 1518–1540*
    MSS Vaticani Latini
        11980: *Notizie delle famiglie romane dal 1000 al 1500*
        12270: Paride Grassi, *De Oratoribus Curiae Romanae*
        12276: Biagio Martinelli da Cesena, *Diario 1518–1532*

Biblioteca Nazionale Marciana, Venice
    Codices Italiani VII 1043 (=7616) Lettere di Gasparo Contarini
    (1528–9)
    Codices Italiani VII 802 (=8219) Lettere di Francesco Contarini

Biblioteca Universitaria di Bologna
    MS 430, *Cronaca di Friano dell'Ubaldini Bolognese*
    MS 2137, Valerio Rinieri, *Diario, overo Descrittione delle cose più notabili seguite in Bologna dall'Anno 1520 in sino à tutto l'anno 1586*

Bibliothèque Nationale de France
    MSS Français 3009, 3040, 3096, 6636, 19751
    MS Italien 1131

British Library
    Additional MSS 8715, 25114, 28580-28585
    Cotton MSS, Vitellius B VII, IX, X, XI, XIII; Vespasian C XIII

Österreichisches Staatsarchiv
    Haus–, Hof– und Staatsarchiv
        England, Kart. 5, Korr., Ber. 1531–4

England, Kart. 5, Korr., Ber. An Karl V u. Granvelle 1535–6
Rom, Korrespondenz 6, 7, 9
Ungarische Akten 20, 23–5, 27

Lambeth Palace Library
    MS 4434, Letter book of the papal mission to England, 1526–7

National Archives
    State Papers series 1: 1/33, 1/48, 1/52, 1/53, 1/54, 1/68, 1/77
    Signed Bill C82/479

Printed works

Adamson, John, ed. (1998). *The Princely Courts of Europe: Ritual, Politics and Culture under the* Ancien Régime *1500–1750*. London: Weidenfeld & Nicolson.

Amayden, Teodoro (1967). *La Storia delle Famiglie Romane*, ed. Carlo Augusto Bertini. Bologna: Forni.

Angelozzi, Giancarlo, and Cesarina Casanova (2000). *Diventare Cittadini. La Cittadinanza ex Privilegio a Bologna (Secoli XVI–XVIII)*. Bologna: Comune di Bologna.

Arfaioli, Maurizio (2005). *The Black Bands of Giovanni: Infantry and Diplomacy during the Italian Wars (1526–1528)*. Pisa: Edizioni Plus.

Bandino, Giacomo Zenobi (1992). 'Feudalità e patriziati cittadini nel governo della "periferia" pontificia del Cinque-Seicento'. In Visceglia, 94–107.

Barbaro, Ermolao (1969). 'De Officio Legati', ed. Vittore Branca. In *Nuova collezione di testi umanistici inediti o rari* XIV, 157–67. Florence: Olschki.

Bartlett, Kenneth (1992). 'Papal policy and the English crown, 1563–1565: the Bertano correspondence'. *Sixteenth Century Journal* 23: 643–59.

Bedouelle, Guy and Patrick Le Gal (1987). *Le 'divorce' du roi Henry VIII: études et documents*. Geneva: Droz.

Behrens, Betty (1936). 'Treatises on the ambassador written in the fifteenth and early sixteenth centuries'. *English Historical Review* 51: 616–27.

Bell, Gary M. (1998). 'Tudor–Stuart diplomatic history and the Henrician experience'. In Woods et al. (1998), 25–43.

—— (1990). *A Handlist of British Diplomatic Representatives, 1509–1688*. London: Royal Historical Society.

Bellocchi, Lisa (1987). *Le monete di Bologna*. Bologna: Cassa di Risparmio di Bologna.

Bembo, Pietro (1987–). *Lettere*, ed. Ernesto Travi, 4 vols. Bologna: Commissione per i testi di lingua.

Bernard, G. W. (1986). *War, Taxation and Rebellion in Early Tudor England: Henry VIII, Wolsey and the Amicable Grant of 1525*. Brighton: Harvester Press.

—— (2010). *Anne Boleyn: Fatal Attractions*. New Haven and London: Yale University Press.

Bietenholz, Peter G., ed. (1985–7). *Contemporaries of Erasmus: A Biographical Register of the Renaissance and Reformation*. 3 vols. Toronto: University of Toronto Press.

Blackburn, Bonnie J., Edward E. Lowinsky and Clement A. Miller, eds (1991). *A Correspondence of Renaissance Musicians*. Oxford: Clarendon Press.

Bostick, Theodora (1967). 'English foreign policy, 1528–1534: the diplomacy of the divorce'. Unpublished doctoral dissertation, University of Illinois.

Brackett, John (2005). 'Race and rulership: Alessandro de' Medici, first Medici duke of Florence, 1529–1537'. In Earle and Lowe, 303–25.

Bradford, William (1850). *Correspondence of the Emperor Charles V and his Ambassadors at the Courts of England and France*. London: Bentley.

Brigden, Susan (1996). '"The shadow that you know": Sir Francis Bryan and Sir Thomas Wyatt at court and in embassy'. *Historical Journal* 39: 1–31.

—— and Jonathan Woolfson (2005). 'Thomas Wyatt in Italy'. *Renaissance Quarterly* 58: 464–511.

Burnet, Gilbert (1865). *History of the Reformation of the Church of England*, ed. Nicholas Pocock. 7 vols. Oxford: Clarendon Press.

Caffarelli, Filippo (1959). *I Caffarelli*. Le Grandi Famiglie Romane XVIII. Rome.

Calendar of State Papers and Manuscripts, existing in the archives and collections of Milan (1912). London: HMSO.

Calendar of Letters, Despatches and State Papers relating to the negotiations between England and Spain (1862–1916). 13 vols. London: Longman.

Calendar of State Papers and Manuscripts relating to English affairs existing in the archives and collections of Venice (1864–1967). 38 vols. London: HMSO.

Campari, Francesco Luigi (1910). *Un Castello del Parmigiano attraverso i secoli*. Parma: Battei.

Campitelli, Alberta (2009). *Gli horti dei papi: I giardini vaticani dal Medioevo al Novecento*. Vatican City/Milan: Jaca Book.

Camusat, Nicolas (1619). *Meslanges historiques*. Troyes: Moreau.

Cappelletti, Giuseppe (1844–70). *Le chiese d'Italia*. 21 vols. Venice: Giuseppe Antonelli.

Carboni, Mauro (1995). *Il debito della città: Mercato del credito, fisco e società a Bologna fra Cinque e Seicento*. Bologna: Il Mulino.

Catalogue des Actes de François I^{er}(1887–1908). 10 vols. Paris: Imprimerie Nationale.

The Catholic Encyclopedia: an international work of reference on the constitution, doctrine, discipline, and history of the Catholic Church (1907–18), ed. Charles G. Herbermann et al. Online at www.newadvent.org/cathen.

Cavendish, George (1825). *The Life of Cardinal Wolsey*, ed. Samuel Weller Singer. 2 vols. London: Harding, Triphook and Lepard.

Challis, C. E. (1978). *The Tudor Coinage*. Manchester: Manchester University Press.

Chambers, D. S. (1966). 'The economic predicament of Renaissance cardinals'. *Studies in Medieval and Renaissance History* 3: 289–313.

Clough, Cecil H. (2003). 'Three Gigli of Lucca in England during the fifteenth and early sixteenth centuries: diversification in a family of mercery merchants'. *The Ricardian* 13: 121–747.

Costantini, Enea (1891). *Il Cardinal di Ravenna al governo d'Ancona e il suo processo sotto Paolo III*. Pesaro: Federici.

Creighton, Mandell (1911). 'The Italian bishops of Worcester'. *Historical Essays and Reviews*. London: Longmans, Green, 202–34.

Cross, Claire, David Loades and J. J. Scarisbrick, eds (1998). *Law and Government under the Tudors*. Cambridge: Cambridge University Press.

Dizionario Biografico degli Italiani (1960–). Rome: Enciclopedia Italiana.

Doernberg, Erwin (1961). *Henry VIII and Luther: An Account of their Personal Relations*. London: Barrie and Rockliff.

Dolet, Étienne (1538). *Carminum libri quatuor*. Lyons.

—— (1933). 'Étienne Dolet on the functions of the ambassador, 1541', ed. Jesse S. Reeves, *American Journal of International Law* 27: 80–95.

Du Bellay, Jean (1969–). *Correspondance du Cardinal Jean du Bellay*, ed. Rémy Scheurer. 3 vols. Paris: Klincksieck.

Earle, T. F., and K. J. P. Lowe, eds (2005). *Black Africans in Renaissance Europe*. Cambridge: Cambridge University Press.

Edgerton Jr., Samuel Y. (1985). *Pictures and Punishment: Art and Criminal Prosecution during the Fiorentine Renaissance*. Ithaca: Cornell University Press.

Ehses, S., ed. (1893). *Römische Dokumente zur Geschichte der Ehescheidung Heinreichs VIII von England, 1527–1534*. Paderborn: Schöningh.

Eisenbichler, Konrad (1999). 'Charles V in Bologna: the self-fashioning of a man and a city'. *Renaissance Studies* 13: 430–9.

Elton, G. R. (1951). 'The Commons' supplication of 1532: Parliamentary manoeuvres in the reign of Henry VIII'. *English Historical Review* 66: 507–34.

Erasmus, Desiderius (1905–58). *Opus Epistolarum Des. Erasmi Roterodami*, ed. Allen & Allen. Oxford: Clarendon Press.

Esposito, Anna, and Manuel Vaquero Piñeiro (2005). 'Rome during the Sack: chronicles and testimonies from an occupied city'. In Gouwens and Reiss, 125–42.

Eubel, Conrad (1910–). *Hierarchia Catholica Medii Aevi*. Regensburg.

Fantoni, Marcello (1994). *La Corte del Granduca: Forma e simboli del potere mediceo fra Cinque e Seicento*. Rome: Bulzoni.

Fasti Ecclesiae Anglicanae 1300–1541 (1962–65), compiled by Joyce M. Horn, et al. 11 vols. London: IHR, Athlone Press.

Fedele, Clement, and Mario Gallenga (1998). *Per servizio di Nostro Signore: Strade, corrieri e poste dei papi dal Medioevo al 1870 (= Quaderni di Storia Postale* 10).

Fernández, Henry Dietrich (1999). 'The patrimony of St Peter: the papal court at Rome c.1450–1700'. In Adamson, 141–63.

Fernández-Armesto, Felipe (1985). 'Eustace Chapuys'. In Bietenholz, 293–5.

Flandrin, Jean-Louis, and Massimo Montanari, eds (1999). *Food: A Culinary History from Antiquity to the Present*. New York: Columbia University Press.

Fletcher, Catherine (2008). 'Renaissance diplomacy in practice: the case of Gregorio Casali, England's ambassador to the papal court, 1527–33'. Unpublished doctoral thesis, University of London.

—— (2009). 'Notes on Catellano Casali'. *The Medal* 54 (Spring): 35–6.

—— (2010a). '"Furnished with gentlemen": the ambassador's house in sixteenth-century Italy'. *Renaissance Studies* 24: 518–35.

—— (2010b). 'War, diplomacy and social mobility: the Casali family in the service of Henry VIII'. *Journal of Early Modern History* 14: 559–68.

—— (2011). 'The city of Rome as a space for diplomacy'. *Atti del convegno Early Modern Rome 1341–1667*, ed. Julia L. Hairston and Portia Prebys. Rome: forthcoming.

—— and Jennifer M. DeSilva (2010). 'Italian ambassadorial networks in early modern Europe: an introduction'. *Journal of Early Modern History* 14: 505–12.

Fragnito, Gigliola (1993). 'Cardinals' courts in sixteenth-century Rome'. *Journal of Modern History* 65: 26–56.

Friedensburg, Walter, ed. (1892). *Nuntiaturen des Vergerio 1533– 1536*. Gotha: Perthes.

Gardiner, Stephen (1933). *The Letters of Stephen Gardiner*, ed. James Arthur Muller. Cambridge: Cambridge University Press.

Gimma, Maria Giuseppina, ed. (2001). *Il centro storico di Viterbo*. Viterbo: BetaGamma.

Giry-Deloison, Charles (1987). 'Le personnel diplomatique au début du XVIe siècle. L'exemple des relations franco-anglaises de l'avènement de Henry VII au Camp du Drap d'Or'. *Journal des Savants* (1987): 205–53.

—— (1993). 'Money and early Tudor diplomacy: the English pensioners of the French king (1475–1547)'. *Medieval History* 3: 128–46.

Gleason, E. G. (1993). *Gasparo Contarini: Venice, Rome and Reform*. Berkeley and Los Angeles: University of California Press.

Gombrich, E. H. (1972). *Symbolic Images: Studies in the Art of the Renaissance*. London: Phaidon.

Gouwens, Kenneth (1998). *Remembering the Renaissance: Humanist Narratives of the Sack of Rome*. Leiden: Brill.

—— and Sheryl E. Reiss, eds (2005). *The Pontificate of Clement VII: History, Politics, Culture*. Aldershot: Ashgate.

Granvelle, Antoine Perrenot de (1841–52). *Papiers d'état du Cardinal de Granvelle*. 9 vols. Paris: Imprimerie Royale.

Greenfeld, Liah (1992). *Nationalism: Five Roads to Modernity*. Cambridge, MA: Harvard University Press.

Grendler, Paul F. (2002). *The Universities of the Italian Renaissance*. Baltimore and London: Johns Hopkins University Press.

Grieco, Allen J. (1999). 'Food and social classes in late medieval and Renaissance Italy'. In Flandrin and Montanari, 302–12.

Guicciardini, Francesco (1927). *Dall'assedio di Firenze al secondo convegno di Clemente VII e Carlo V (28 giugno 1530 – 2 dicembre 1532). Lettere inedite a Bartolomeo Lanfredini*. ed. André Otetea. Aquila: Vecchioni.

—— (1970). *Maxims and Reflections of a Renaissance Statesman (Ricordi)*, trans. Mario Domandi. Gloucester, MA: Smith.

Guidicini, Giuseppe di Gio. Battista (1876–7). *I Riformatori dello Stato di Libertà della Città di Bologna dal 1394 al 1797*. Bologna: Guidicini.

Gunn, S. J. (1986). 'The duke of Suffolk's march on Paris in 1523'. *English Historical Review* 101: 596–634.

Gwyn, Peter (1990). *The King's Cardinal: The Rise and Fall of Thomas Wolsey*. London: Barrie & Jenkins.

Hale, J. R. (1985). *War and Society in Renaissance Europe 1450–1620*. Leicester: Leicester University Press.

Hayward, Maria (2007). *Dress at the Court of King Henry VIII*. Leeds: Maney.

Heal, Felicity (1980). *Of Prelates and Princes: A Study of the Economic and Social Position of the Tudor Episcopate*. Cambridge: Cambridge University Press.

Hook, Judith (2004). *The Sack of Rome, 1527*. Second edition. Basingstoke: Palgrave Macmillan.

Hoyle, R. W. (2001). *The Pilgrimage of Grace and the Politics of the 1530s*. Oxford: Oxford University Press.

Hurtubise, Pierre (1985). *Une Famille-Témoin: Les Salviati*. Vatican City: Biblioteca Apostolica Vaticana.

Hyde, Helen (2009). *Cardinal Bendinello Sauli and Church Patronage in Sixteenth-Century Italy*. Woodbridge: Boydell.

Isom-Verhaaren, Christine (2004). 'Shifting identities: foreign state servants in France and the Ottoman empire'. *Journal of Early Modern History* 8: 109–34.

Ives, Eric (2004). *The Life and Death of Anne Boleyn: 'The Most Happy'*. Oxford: Blackwell.

Jeanneret, Michel (1991). *A Feast of Words: Banquets and Table Talk in the Renaissance*. Cambridge: Polity Press.

Kahn, David (1996). *The Codebreakers: The Story of Secret Writing*. New York: Scribner.

Kelly, H. A. (1976). *The Matrimonial Trials of Henry VIII*. Stanford: Stanford University Press.

Kidwell, Carol (1991). *Pontano: Poet and Prime Minister*. London: Duckworth.

Knecht, R. J. (1998). *Catherine de' Medici*. London: Longman.

Lanz, Karl (1844). *Correspondenz des Kaisers Karl V*. Leipzig: Brockhaus.

Lasagni, Roberto (1999). *Dizionario Biografico dei Parmigiani*. Parma: PPS.

Lebey, André (1904). *Le Connétable de Bourbon, 1490–1527*. Paris: Perrin.

Lee, Egmont, ed. (2006). *Habitatores in Urbe: The Population of Renaissance Rome*. Rome: La Sapienza.

Le Grand, Joachim (1688). *Histoire du Divorce de Henry VIII*. 3 vols. Paris: Martin.

Letters and Papers, Foreign and Domestic, of the Reign of Henry VIII (1862–1932), ed. J. S. Brewer, J. Gairdner and R. H. Brodie. 22 vols. London: HMSO. Online at www.british-history.ac.uk.

Levin, Michael J. (2005). *Agents of Empire: Spanish Ambassadors in Sixteenth-Century Italy*. Ithaca and London: Cornell University Press.

The Lisle Letters (1981), ed. Muriel St Clare Byrne. 6 vols. Chicago: University of Chicago Press.

Litta, Pompeo (1819–99). *Celebri Famiglie Italiane.* II vols. Milan: Giusti.

Luzio, A. (1908). 'Isabella d'Este e il sacco di Roma'. *Archivio Storico Lombardo* series 4, vol. 10: 5–107 and 361–425.

MacCulloch, Diarmaid, ed. (1995). *The Reign of Henry VIII: Politics, Policy and Piety.* Basingstoke: Macmillan.

—— (1996). *Thomas Cranmer: A Life.* New Haven and London: Yale University Press.

McIver, Katherine A. (2006). *Women, Art and Architecture in Northern Italy, 1520–1580: Negotiating Power.* Aldershot: Ashgate.

McClung Hallman, Barbara (2005). 'The "disastrous" pontificate of Clement VII: disastrous for Giulio de' Medici?'. In Gouwens and Reiss, 29–40.

MacMahon, Luke (1999). 'The ambassadors of Henry VIII: the personnel of English diplomacy, c.1500–c.1550'. Unpublished doctoral thesis, University of Kent.

Machiavelli, Niccolò (1965). *The Chief Works and others*, trans. Allan Gilbert. 3 vols. Durham, NC: Duke University Press.

Mallett, Michael (2006). 'The transformation of war, 1494–1530'. In Shaw (2006), 3–21.

'The Manner of the Triumph at Calais and Boulogne' (1903). In *Tudor Tracts 1532–88*, ed. Thomas Seacombe, 1–8. Edinburgh: Constable.

Marci, Valerio, Antonio Marzo and Angelo Romano, eds (1983). *Pasquinate Romane del Cinquecento.* 2 vols. Rome: Salerno.

Martin, John (1997). 'Inventing sincerity, refashioning prudence: the discovery of the individual in Renaissance Europe'. *American Historical Review* 102: 1309–42.

Masson, Georgina (1975). *Courtesans of the Italian Renaissance.* London: Secker & Warburg.

Mattingly, Garrett (1950). *Catherine of Aragon.* London: Jonathan Cape.

—— (1973). *Renaissance Diplomacy.* Harmondsworth: Penguin.

Mayer, Thomas (1988). 'A mission worse than death: Reginald Pole and the Parisian theologians'. *English Historical Review* 103: 870–91.

—— (2000). *Reginald Pole: Prince and Prophet.* Cambridge: Cambridge University Press.

Mellano, Maria Franca (1970). *Rappresentanti italiani della corona inglese a Roma ai primi del Cinquecento.* [Rome]: Istituto di Studi Romani.

Messisbugo, Cristoforo da (1992). *Banchetti, composizioni di vivande e apparecchio generale*, ed. Fernando Bandini. Vicenza: Neri Pozza.

Millon, Henry A., ed. (1980). *Studies in Italian Art and Architecture 15th through 18th Centuries.* Rome: Edizioni dell'Elefante.

Miranda, Salvador (1998–). *The Cardinals of the Holy Roman Church*. Online at www2.fiu.edu/~mirandas/cardinals.htm.

Mitchell, Margaret (1971). 'Works of art from Rome for Henry VIII: a study of Anglo-Papal relations as reflected in papal gifts to the English king'. *Journal of the Warburg and Courtauld Institutes* 34: 178–203.

Molini, Giuseppe, ed. (1836–7). *Documenti di storia Italiana*. 2 vols. Florence: Tipografia all'Insegna di Dante.

Molossi, Lorenzo (1832–4). *Vocabolario topografico dei ducati di Parma, Piacenza e Guastalla*. Parma: Tipografia Ducale.

Moroni, Gaetano (1840–61). *Dizionario di erudizione storico-ecclesiastica*. 103 vols. Venice: Tipografia Emiliana.

Muir, Edward (1981). *Civic Ritual in Renaissance Venice*. Princeton: Princeton University Press.

Murphy, Caroline P. (2006). *The Pope's Daughter*. London: Faber & Faber.

Necipoglu, Gülru (1991). *Architecture, Ceremonial and Power: The Topkapi Palace in the Fifteenth and Sixteenth Centuries*. New York: The Architectural History Foundation.

Nemeth Papo, Gizella, and Adriano Papo (2002). *Ludovico Gritti: Un principe-mercante del Rinascimento tra Venezia, i Turchi e la corona d'Ungheria*. Venice: Edizioni della Laguna.

Nesselrath, Arnold, and Fabrizio Mancinelli (1992). 'Gli appartamenti del Palazzo Apostolico Vaticano da Giulio II a Leone X'. In Pietrangeli, 107–17.

Nicholson, Graham (1998). 'The Act of Appeals and the English reformation'. In Cross et al., 19–30.

Oxford Dictionary of National Biography. Online at www.oxforddnb.com.

Oxford English Dictionary. Online at www.oed.com.

Pagano, Sergio (1995). *Il Cardinale Uberto Gambara Vescovo di Tortona (1489–1549)*. Florence: Olschki.

Parmiter, Geoffrey de C. (1967). *The King's Great Matter: A Study of Anglo-Papal Relations 1527–34*. London: Longmans, Green.

Pietrangeli, Carlo, ed. (1992). *Il Palazzo Apostolico Vaticano*. Florence: Cardini.

Pocock, Nicholas, ed. (1870). *Records of the Reformation: The Divorce 1527–1533*. 2 vols. Oxford: Clarendon Press.

Pontano, Giovanni (1518). *Ioannis Ioviani Pontani Opera Omnia Soluta Oratione Composita*. Venice: Aldo Manuzio.

Potter, David (1995). 'Foreign policy'. In MacCulloch (1995), 101–33.

—— (1973). 'Diplomacy in the mid-sixteenth century: England and France, 1536–1550'. Unpublished doctoral thesis, University of Cambridge.

Previdelli, Girolamo (1528). *Tractatus Legalis de Peste*. Bologna: Ioanne Baptista Phaello.

—— (1531). *Consilium D. Hieronymi Previdelli, pro Invictiss. Rege Angliae, una cum responsione eiusdem ad consilium Domini Bernardi Reatini pro Illustrissima Regina editum*. Bologna: Ioannes Baptista Phaellus.

Queller, Donald E. (1967). *The Office of Ambassador in the Middle Ages*. Princeton, NJ: Princeton University Press.

Ramsey, P. A., ed. (1982). *Rome in the Renaissance: The City and the Myth*. Binghamton, NY: Center for Medieval and Renaissance Studies.

Redworth, Glyn (1990). *In Defence of the Church Catholic: The Life of Stephen Gardiner*. Oxford: Blackwell.

Rex, Richard (2003). 'Redating Henry VIII's *A Glasse of the Truthe*'. *The Library* 4: 16–27.

Richardson, Carol (2009). *Reclaiming Rome: Cardinals in the Fifteenth Century*. Leiden: Brill.

Richardson, Glenn (2008). 'The French connection: Francis I and England's break with Rome'. In his *'The Contending Kingdoms': France and England 1420–1700*. Aldershot: Ashgate.

Rocca, Emilio Nasalli, Vincenzo Pancotti and Emilio Ottolenghi (1933). *Monticelli d'Ongina: Memorie storiche e artistiche*. Piacenza: Società Tipografica Editoriale Porta.

Roth, Cecil (1925). 'England and the last Florentine Republic'. *English Historical Review* 40: 174–95.

Russell, Joycelyne G. (1992). *Diplomats at Work: Three Renaissance Studies*. Stroud: Sutton.

Sanuto, Marin (1969). *I diarii*, ed. Rinaldo Fulin, Federico Stefani, Nicolò Barozzi, Guglielmo Berchet and Marco Allegri. 59 vols. Bologna: Forni.

Scarisbrick, J. J. (1971). *Henry VIII*. Harmondsworth: Pelican.

Schiavo, Armando (1963). *Il Palazzo della Cancelleria*. Rome: Staderini.

Setton, Kenneth M. (1976). *The Papacy and the Levant (1204–1571)*. 4 vols. Philadelphia: American Philosophical Society.

Shakespeare, William (1997). *The Norton Shakespeare*, ed. Stephen Greenblatt, et al. New York: Norton.

Sharkey, Jessica (2008). 'The politics of Wolsey's cardinalate, 1515–1530'. Unpublished doctoral thesis, University of Cambridge.

—— (2011). 'Between king and pope: Thomas Wolsey and the Knight mission'. *Historical Research* 84: 236–48.

Shaw, Christine (1993). *Julius II: The Warrior Pope*. Oxford: Blackwell.

—— (2006). *Italy and the European Powers: The Impact of War, 1500–1530*. Leiden: Brill.

—— (2007). *The Political Role of the Orsini Family from Sixtus IV to Clement VII. Barons and Factions in the Papal States*. Rome: Istituto Storico Italiano per il Medio Evo.

Sicca, Cinzia M. (2002). 'Consumption and trade of art between Italy and England in the first half of the sixteenth century: the London house of the Bardi and Cavalcanti company'. *Renaissance Studies* 16: 163–201.

—— (2006). 'Pawns of international finance and politics: Florentine sculptors at the court of Henry VIII'. *Renaissance Studies* 20: 1–34.

Siraisi, Nancy G. (1990). *Medieval and Early Renaissance Medicine: An Introduction to Knowledge and Practice*. Chicago: University of Chicago Press.

Sowerby, Tracey A. (2010). *Renaissance and Reform in Tudor England: The Careers of Sir Richard Morison c. 1513–1556*. Oxford: Oxford University Press.

Starkey, David (1987). 'Intimacy and innovation: the rise of the Privy Chamber, 1485–1547'. In Starkey (ed.), *The English Court from the Wars of the Roses to the Civil War*, pp. 71–118. London: Longman.

State Papers Published under the Authority of Her Majesty's Commission: King Henry the Eighth (1832–50). 11 vols. London: Record Commission.

Stinger, Charles L. (1985). *The Renaissance in Rome*. Bloomington: Indiana University Press.

Storey, Tessa (2008). *Carnal Commerce in Counter-Reformation Rome*. Cambridge: Cambridge University Press.

Straparola, Giovan Francesco (2000). *Le piacevoli notti*, ed. Donato Pirovano. 2 vols. Rome: Salerno.

Surtz, Edward (1974). *Henry VIII's Great Matter in Italy: An Introduction to Representative Italians in the King's Divorce, mainly 1527–1535*. Ann Arbor, Michigan: University Microfilms.

—— and Virginia Murphy, eds (1988). *The Divorce Tracts of Henry VIII*. Angers: Moreana.

Szakály, Ference (1995). *Lodovico Gritti in Hungary, 1529–1534: A Historical Insight into the Beginnings of Turco-Habsburgian Rivalry*. Budapest: Akadémiai Kiadó.

Theiner, Augustinis, ed. (1864). *Vetera Monumenta Hibernorum et Scotorum: Historiam Illustrantia*. Rome: Typis Vaticanis.

Thompson, James Westfall, and Saul K. Padover (1963). *Secret Diplomacy: Espionage and Cryptography 1500–1815*. New York: Frederick Ungar.

Thurley, Simon (1993). *The Royal Palaces of Tudor England*. New Haven and London: Yale University Press.

Venosta, Raffaele (1530a). *Determinatio D. Raphaelis Comensis Canonici Regularis, facta super contractu matrimoniali Clementiss. Henrici Anglorum Regis Octavi, Qui contraxit cum Fratrissa, de mente Theologorum*. [Venice.]

—— (1530b). *Raphaelis Comensis Canonici Regularis Quaestiones duae de potestate Foeliciss. memoriae Iulii. II. Pont. Max. in dispensatione Matrimonii Christianiss. Henrici Octavi Anglorum Regis, & Christianiss. D. Catherinae Olim Arthuri fratris sui Uxoris.* Venice.

Visceglia, Maria A., ed. (1992). *Signori, patrizi, cavalieri in Italia centro-meridionale nell'età moderna.* Rome-Bari: Laterza.

Vitale, Vito (1907). 'L'impresa di Puglia degli anni 1528–1529'. In *Nuovo Archivio Veneto* 13.ii: 6–68 and 14.i: 120–92.

Wall, Thomas (1959). *The Voyage of Sir Nicholas Carewe to the Emperor Charles V in the year 1529*, ed. R. J. Knecht. Cambridge: Cambridge University Press.

Wanegffelen, Thierry (2005). *Catherine de Médicis: Le pouvoir au feminin.* Paris: Payot.

Wilkie, William E. (1974). *The Cardinal Protectors of England: Rome and the Tudors before the Reformation.* Cambridge: Cambridge University Press.

Williams, Megan K. (2010). '"Dui Fratelli . . . Con Dui Principi": family and fidelity on a failed diplomatic mission'. *Journal of Early Modern History* 14: 579–611.

—— (2009). 'Dangerous diplomacy and dependable kin: transformations in central European statecraft, 1526–40'. Unpublished doctoral dissertation, Columbia University.

Woodhouse, J. R. (1994). 'Honourable dissimulation: some Italian advice for the Renaissance diplomat'. *Proceedings of the British Academy* 84: 25–50.

Woods, Robert L., et al., eds (1998). *State, Sovereigns and Society in Early Modern England: Essays in honour of A. J. Slavin.* Stroud: Sutton.

Woolfson, Jonathan (1998). *Padua and the Tudors: English Students in Italy, 1485–1603.* Toronto: University of Toronto Press.

—— (2000) 'A "remote and ineffectual Don"? Richard Croke in the Biblioteca Marciana'. *Bulletin of the Society for Renaissance Studies* 17: 1–11.

Zimmermann, T. C. Price and Saul Levin (1982). 'Fabio Vigile's *Poem of the Pheasant*: humanist conviviality in Renaissance Rome'. In Ramsey, 265–78.

Acknowledgements

Very many people have offered advice, comments and support in the course of my research for this book. It is impossible to thank them all here. A Rome Fellowship at the British School at Rome and a Max Weber Fellowship at the European University Institute enabled me to complete the writing; earlier research was funded by the Arts and Humanities Research Council, the Department of History at Royal Holloway, University of London, a Scouloudi Fellowship at the Institute for Historical Research, a Society for Renaissance Studies study fellowship and the Gladys Krieble Delmas Foundation Venetian Research Program. I am particularly grateful to the Casali family of Piacenza and the Isolani-Lupari family of Bologna for allowing me to visit their private archives and to Megan Williams for sharing with me her references to the Casali documents in Vienna. Thanks too to Sandra Cavallo, Kate Lowe, Susan Brigden, to all my colleagues at the British School at Rome, to Tracey Sowerby, Sarah Cockram, Jenn DeSilva, Angela Quattrocchi, Deborah Lerech, Sarah Easterby-Smith, Rebecca Zahn, Rosemary Fletcher, Peter Murdoch, Catherine Clarke, Will Sulkin and Kay Peddle for their indispensable input, support and encouragement. Any errors that remain are, of course my own. Mark Sandell lived with my Casali research for several years, and was a wonderful friend throughout. This book is for him.

Index